Gorseinon College

Learning Resource Centre

Belgrave Road : Gorseinon : Swansea : SA4 6RD   Tel: (01792) 890731
This book is **YOUR RESPONSIBILITY** and is due for return/renewal
on or before the last date shown.

RETURN OR RENEW - DON'T PAY FINES

Key Concepts in Philosophy
Series Editors: John Mullarkey (University of Dundee) and
Caroline Williams (Queen Mary, University of London)

Mind: Key Concepts in Philosophy, Eric Matthews
Language: Key Concepts in Philosophy, José Medina
Logic: Key Concepts in Philosophy, Laurence Goldstein,
Andrew Brennan, Max Deutsch, Joe Y.F. Lau
Ethics: Key Concepts in Philosophy, Dwight Furrow

Epistemology

Key Concepts in Philosophy

Christopher Norris

continuum
LONDON • NEW YORK

Continuum
The Tower Building
11 York Road
London SE1 7NX

15 East 26th Street
New York
NY 10010

www.continuumbooks.com

British Library Cataloguing-in-Publication Data
A catalogue record for this book is available from the British Library.

ISBN: 0–8264–7731–3 (hardback)
0–8264–7732–1 (paperback)

Library of Congress Cataloging-in-Publication Data
A catalog record for this book is available from the Library of Congress.

Typeset by Servis Filmsetting Ltd, Manchester
Printed and bound in Great Britain by
MPG Books Ltd, Bodmin, Cornwall

CONTENTS

For Rob Stradling

ACKNOWLEDGEMENTS

This book more than most enjoyed the benefit of regular feedback from my colleagues and students in the Philosophy Section at Cardiff University. When the series editors first approached me I put off deciding for a long while, not least because I doubted the possibility of covering so vast and complex a subject area within the tight restrictions of length laid down for the 'Key Concepts' series. This seemed to present a flat choice between offering a whistle-stop tour of what struck me as the most live and prominent topics of debate or else taking a definite 'line' – a defence of epistemological realism in its various forms – which would be more rewarding to write (and most likely to read) but wouldn't fit in so well with the series guidelines. However these doubts were largely dispelled by talking things over and reflecting on the kinds of experience gained from teaching courses on epistemology and related topics at various levels over the past few years. I should therefore like to thank my students – postgraduates mainly, but also a good few keen and independent-minded undergraduates – for keeping me on track with regard to the interests, needs and priorities of a (relatively) non-specialist readership. Of my colleagues in the Section I have said it before but will say it again: that they provided just the kind of friendly, supportive and intellectually sustaining community that relieved the solitude of authorship and restored an (again relative) sense of proportion when the work wasn't going so well.

I have had to keep the series length-limit very much in mind so I won't include a great list of names that would seek to repay all the manifold debts of friendship, practical support and philosophical guidance accrued in the course of its writing. Still I should like to give special mention for various reasons to Robin Attfield, Manuel

Barbeito, Andrew Belsey, Gideon Calder, Pat Clark, Reg Coates, Andrew Edgar, Richard Gray, Terence Hawkes, Dave Hume, Keith McDonald, Stephen Moller, Scott Newton, Alison Scott-Baumann, Pete Sedgwick, Rob Stradling, Alessandra Tanesini, Alison Venables, Debbie Way, Barry Wilkins and Robin Wood; also to the members of my PhD discussion-group at Cardiff – among them Paul Gorton, Theo Grammenos, Keith McDonald, Lawrence Peddle, Robert Reay-Jones, Julian Ryall and Rea Walldén – who offered no end of stimulating talk on their (and my own) work-in-progress. I am grateful to the series editors for commissioning this book and to Hywel Evans and Anya Wilson at Continuum Publishers for providing much useful guidance and advice as the project shaped up.

Some portions have appeared previously in journals and edited volumes. For permission to reprint that material here in revised or expanded form I am grateful to the publishers E. J. Brill, Peter Lang, Routledge and Sage; also to the editors of *Facta Philosophica*, *Journal of Critical Realism*, *Philosophy and Social Criticism*, and *Richmond Journal of Philosophy*.

Cardiff   January 2005

INTRODUCTION

I

There is no shortage of books currently in print about epistemology
– or the theory of knowledge – so I had better start out by attempting to justify this further addition to the groaning library shelves.
First is the fact that I have here made a point (in keeping with the
series guidelines) of ensuring that my arguments and style of presentation are accessible to undergraduate students and to readers
with a genuine but non-specialist interest in the field. Second – and
closely related to that – is my aim to bring out the relevance of these
often rather complex and technical debates to the sorts of concern
that engage many people when confronted with issues of truth,
knowledge or justified (rationally warranted) belief. Putting it like
this makes the whole thing sound very abstract and remote from
everyday questions of what we should think or believe about this or
that real-world topic of dispute. And indeed – to be honest – any
reader who falls into either of the above-mentioned categories and
who runs a quick Google check or trawls through an academic
library catalogue under the search-term 'epistemology' will most
likely come away with a strong sense that the subject has been
hijacked by ultra-specialist types with absolutely no interest in such
matters. Hence my third aim: to convince said reader that this is
a topic which can and should speak to some of her most pressing
concerns as one who is daily confronted with a whole barrage of
statements, truth-claims, opinions, moral and political viewpoints,
etc., and required to decide – 'on the balance of evidence' – just what
or whom to believe. Such was at least one motive for the inaugural
Greek distinction between *doxa* and *epistēmē*, or 'opinion' on the

one hand (with strong connotations of 'mere taken-for-granted belief') and on the other hand 'knowledge' that passes the test of good evidential warrant or rational accountability.

As we shall see, that distinction – first developed clearly in Plato's dialogue *Theaetetus* – is by no means unproblematic and has since given rise to a vast amount of often quite complex and technical debate. Still it is one that bears importantly on matters of real-life thought, judgement and conduct and which ought to be of interest to anyone concerned to sort out issues of media (mis)representation or to sift truth from falsehood in the statements of politicians and others. Besides, it is a crucial question for philosophy of science and the current, much-publicized war of words between those who uphold the realist values of scientific truth, objectivity and scientific progress and those who regard such claims as the merest of smoke-screens designed to conceal and preserve the socio-cultural status quo. Thus the very idea that there might be some other than partisan or ideologically motivated grounds for maintaining Plato's cardinal distinction is nowadays a matter of fierce dispute on numerous academic fronts. These are some of the reasons why 'truth' has itself become a kind of ideological shuttlecock, batted back and forth as a term of abuse on the one (postmodernist, cultural-relativist, or social-constructivist) side and on the other as a strident rallying-call by – among others – spokespersons for the Public Understanding of Science. What is all too often lacking in these high-profile, media-propagated squabbles is a grasp of the finer philosophical points that separate realists from anti-realists, or those who argue for an objectivist ('recognition-transcendent') concept of truth from those who would deny on principled grounds that truth can possibly be thought to exceed the scope and limits of human knowledge. At the same time philosophers who discuss these issues do so for the most part in a highly technical language and – with just a few striking exceptions – mainly for the benefit of others with a likewise specialist take on the topic.

This is not to deny that specialization has a proper and legitimate place in philosophy, or that a certain level of technicality is perfectly in order when debating such questions. On the contrary: with just a bit of good-willed effort on the reader's part there is much to be gained from the careful defining of terms and even from the introduction, where needed, of new items of vocabulary that capture some salient epistemological distinction or reveal some latent ambiguity in our everyday, 'pre-philosophical' modes of expression. This has long been the trademark of so-called 'analytic' philosophy, that is to say, the kind of work that had its chief source in the logical analysis of language pioneered by thinkers like Gottlob Frege and Bertrand Russell, and which acquired a predominant status among (mainly) Anglophone philosophers throughout much of the twentieth century. Its virtues are those of conceptual precision, clearly focused address to a range of well-defined problems, and a dogged refusal to be drawn off into other, more speculative realms of enquiry. Nowhere are these features more strongly evident than in the kinds of epistemological debate that have set the agenda and the standards of legitimate, analytically acceptable discourse over the past half-century and more. One positive result has been to clarify certain previously somewhat blurred or disputed boundaries, as for instance between the topic-domains of epistemology, ontology and metaphysics. I shall have more to say in this regard later on and will, I hope, manage to convince those readers who start out with a healthy resistance to technical jargon and the proliferation of abstract-sounding categories that these are distinctions well worth making and not, after all, so remote from the business of getting straight about issues of wider human concern.

All the same, to repeat, they have very often been treated by philosophers – especially by those in the analytic mainstream – in such a way as to discourage any sense of that connection among non-specialist readers. So I hope that this book will do something to bring epistemology back down to earth by occasionally taking time off from the sorts of question that typically preoccupy academic philosophers and asking what relevance all this might have to matters in the wider public domain. For if there is one point that needs stressing here it is the fact that issues of epistemology – of truth, knowledge and evidential warrant – are closely bound up with the shared human interest in arriving at informed and considered judgements across a whole range of subject areas from mathematics and the natural sciences to ethics, politics, psychology, sociology and (not least) the interpretation of historical events. Indeed it has been a curious, though welcome, feature of recent epistemological debate that increasing levels of specialization in certain respects have nonetheless gone along with a growing sense that issues like that between realists and anti-realists, or objectivists and verificationists about truth, have a crucial bearing on every such area of discourse. What has tended to characterize current work on these topics is a readiness to ask the same sorts of question with regard to whether or just how far statements of a certain type – mathematical, scientific, ethical, historical, etc. – should be thought of as possessing an objective truth-value (perhaps unbeknown to us) or rather as subject to varying kinds or degrees of 'warranted assertibility'. This has come about largely through the widespread 'linguistic turn' in many branches of philosophy – epistemology included – where issues of language, meaning and representation have displaced the older (presumptively discredited since scepticism-inducing) concern with supposed goings-on 'in the mind' of this or that individual subject. Hence the claim – often advanced with reference to Wittgenstein's later work – that philosophy has at long last emerged from the travails of sceptical doubt bequeathed by thinkers such as Descartes, Locke, Berkeley, Hume and other subscribers to the 'way of ideas' in its rationalist or empiricist guise.

Whether this much-vaunted revolution in modern philosophy has perhaps brought along certain problems of its own – among them other kinds of sceptical impasse – is a question I shall raise in subsequent chapters. Meanwhile my point is that it has had the effect, more beneficially, of focusing philosophers' attention on the different kinds of statement (together with their different orders of truth-aptness or assertoric warrant) that typify our various linguistic dealings with the world and each other. One way of putting it – a useful piece of jargon – is that statements can be thought of either as possessing *alethic* (that is, objective) truth-values quite apart from the extent of our knowledge or evidence concerning them, or else as *epistemically constrained* in so far as their warrant is precisely a matter of our having (or being able to obtain, perhaps under ideal epistemic conditions) such knowledge or evidence. Some philosophers espouse a strong – in effect, an ontological or metaphysical – version of alethic realism which insists that truth can always come apart from our present-best or even best-possible state of knowledge, and hence that there exist any number of statements (mathematical, scientific, historical and so forth) whose truth-value is to us unknown or unknowable but which are nonetheless objectively true or false. Others take an equally strong anti-realist line and deny that it could ever make sense to assert of any given statement *x* that '*x* is either true or false – objectively so – despite our not being epistemically placed to prove, ascertain, or establish its truth-value'. However there has also emerged a range of more nuanced or discriminate positions according to which different discourses occupy different points on a scale that runs from objective truth, via truth-aptness 'in the ideal epistemic limit', to warranted assertibility in keeping with certain communal norms or shared evaluative standards.

Quite often – I shall argue – this overtly pluralist or even-handed approach conceals a marked bias toward anti-realism, or at least toward a scaled-down compromise version of 'realism' that admits various kinds and degrees of epistemic constraint. Such is most strikingly the case with response-dispositional (or response-dependence) theories which seek something like a 'third-way' solution to all these epistemological dilemmas. In brief, that solution picks up on Locke's idea of 'secondary qualities' – such as colour, taste or smell – which cannot be thought of (like the 'primary qualities' of shape and size) as intrinsically pertaining to the object itself but must rather be conceived as involving some mode of perceptual or cognitive response on the perceiver's part. The task then becomes that of specifying – without the resort to tautologous or merely circular forms of definition – just what should count as a normal, proper or optimal response under likewise suitably specified physical or ambient conditions. I shall not pursue this topic any further now since it receives a fairly detailed treatment in Chapter 4. My point for the moment is that here again – and despite these theorists' overt desire to counter the more extreme forms of anti-realist thinking – there is an inbuilt tendency to privilege epistemic conceptions of truth (or assertoric warrant) even in cases, such as those of mathematics and the physical sciences, where an alethic approach seems better able to accommodate our normal range of working intuitions. Nor is this at all surprising, given the natural bias of response-dispositional accounts toward a treatment of these issues that finds some room for the knower's or perceiver's active role in determining what is actually 'there' to be known or perceived. Indeed a large part of the recent literature has been devoted to just this difficult – maybe impossible – project of meeting the anti-realist's challenge on terms that they might be brought to accept while conserving a sufficiently robust conception of truth to satisfy the realist with respect to this or that particular topic-domain. Hence such proposals as those put forward by Crispin Wright for 'superassertibility' and 'cognitive command' as criteria applying to certain kinds of statement that stop just short of specifying knowledge in full-fledged objectivist, truth-based terms but which should – so he thinks – go a long way toward resolving the realist/anti-realist dispute.

Whatever the problems with this sort of middle-ground approach it does at least have the virtue of attempting to break the gridlocked pattern of argument and counter-argument that has typified a good deal of work in the field. Thus anti-realists argue that if truth is conceived as verification-transcendent – that is to say, as always potentially standing apart from our best methods of proof or ascertainment – then *ex hypothesi* it lies beyond our utmost scope of knowledge, in which case there can be no defence against radical scepticism. This argument is supposed to go through with maximum force in the instance of abstract 'objects' such as mathematical numbers, classes or sets. With regard to these latter – so sceptics maintain – we can *either* have knowledge within the scope and limits of formal provability *or* the idea of objective mathematical truths that again ex hypothesi cannot be known since we possess no remotely conceivable means of epistemic access to them. On the other hand, realists argue that *unless* the truth-value of statements is specified in alethic (objectivist) terms, and *unless* knowledge is conceived as a matter of justified true belief, then clearly the way is wide open for sceptics or cultural relativists to press their case for the non-existence of any 'truths' beyond those that happen to enjoy credence among this or that community of like-minded believers. Such – at any rate on one (and in my view the most plausible) reading – is the message to be gleaned from Wittgenstein's idea that truth-claims of whatever kind, from those of mathematics, logic and the natural sciences to those of ethics, aesthetics and religion, are all bound up with our manifold 'language-games', cultural practices, or 'forms of life' and are therefore to be judged each by its own *sui generis* criteria of valid or meaningful utterance.

II

Let me say straight off – lest the reader be in any doubt – that I am fully in agreement with the realist in thinking that one cannot give an adequate characterization of truth or knowledge in such communitarian, language-game-relative, or consensual belief-based terms. The anti-realists' position is in many ways more challenging since it comes equipped with a complex battery of logical and metaphysical arguments which offer a full-scale and, by their own lights, a forcefully articulated set of counter-theses to the realist position. Nevertheless I shall put the case here that those theses cannot be transposed into an epistemological context – that is, required to give some detailed account of truth, knowledge and (crucially) our grasp of the relationship between them – without showing up as grossly inadequate in that regard. Nor is the prospect much improved by those various refinements and modifications proposed by philosophers – like Wright and the response-dependence theorists – who take the point of such objections to anti-realism in its full-strength doctrinal form but who still fight shy of adopting an alethic realist position on account of its supposed vulnerability to sceptical attack. Still, as I said above, epistemology has been challenged in many ways and taken on a much wider range of interests and concerns as a result of these recent developments.

Thus we have moved a long way from the old top-down 'unity of science' programme (championed by the 1930s logical positivists) wherein the various disciplines or branches of enquiry were ranked on a single, hard-to-soft scale of descending scientific warrant. On this view physics took pride of place, followed by chemistry, biology, and certain empirically based approaches to economics, sociology and psychology. Then – very much at the bottom end of the scale – came ethics, aesthetics, literary criticism and other such quasi- (or pseudo-) disciplines. The demise of logical positivism is a story that has often been told, with the main credit (if such it be) going to W.V. Quine's famous 1951 essay 'Two Dogmas of Empiricism'. Here Quine mounted a brilliantly argued, though by no means conclusive, attack on the twin chief pillars of that doctrine, namely the distinction between analytic and synthetic statements (or 'truths of reason' and 'matters of fact'), and the idea that scientific claims, predictions or hypotheses could be tested one-by-one against observational findings or items of empirical evidence. In their place he put a thoroughly holistic approach according to which theories were always 'underdetermined' by the empirical evidence, such evidence was itself always in some degree 'theory-laden', and the 'unit of empirical significance' was not the single observation or statement concerning it but rather the entire 'web' or 'fabric' of accepted belief at any given time. In which case – according to Quine – there was no such thing as the kind of 'crucial experiment' envisaged by many philosophers of science from Bacon down that would serve to adjudicate decisively between rival theories or hypotheses on the basis of empirical evidence produced under carefully controlled conditions. Rather, if the empirical results turned out to conflict with some deeply entrenched item of belief, then one always had the option of putting them down to a defect in one's measuring apparatus or to a limit on the powers of precise observation allowed by existing technology. Or again, one could always save some cherished theory *despite and together with* certain seemingly discrepant empirical results by adducing one or more 'auxiliary hypotheses' (or background presuppositions) which might be abandoned without too much disruption to the system as a whole. In the limiting case of empirical anomaly one might be reduced to pleading 'perceptual hallucination', while in the limiting case of well-established theories under strong empirical pressure one might even choose – for reasons of 'pragmatic convenience' as well as good scientific warrant – to revise or suspend certain putative 'laws' of logic, such as bivalence or excluded middle. For instance, Quine suggests, this could yet turn out to be the best, most effective, or at any rate least problematical way of dealing with the kinds of apparent contradiction thrown up by statements concerning quantum phenomena like superposition or wave/particle dualism.

It would be hard to exaggerate the depth and extent of Quine's influence on subsequent debates in epistemology, whether among those who have continued and developed or those who have rejected his radically revisionist approach to issues of truth, knowledge and scientific method. What has complicated matters, on both sides, is the fact that Quine maintains a resolutely physicalist or science-led conception of epistemology – one that rejects all its normative claims and treats it as mere sub-branch of behavioural psychology – while on the other hand advancing his holistic account of knowledge wherein the various 'posits' of the physical sciences occupy a strictly non-privileged role. Thus, famously, there is no ultimate difference in point of ontological status between such diverse entities as numbers, sets, classes, centaurs, the gods of Homer and brick houses on Elm Street. They are all just as 'real' as each other though belonging to different ontological schemes – or conceptual frames of reference – which make it strictly impossible to assess them (or evaluate the truth of statements concerning them) by reference to a single, superordinate or all-encompassing adjudicative scheme. Yet this doctrine sits oddly askew with Quine's insistence that the physical sciences are by far our best guide in philosophic matters and hence that epistemology should forthwith 'fall into place' as a thoroughly naturalized study of the processes by which the 'meagre input' of sensory stimuli somehow gives rise to the 'torrential output' of conjectures, hypotheses, theoretically informed observation statements, and so forth. Indeed it could be argued that the problem of squaring these two (on the face of it) flatly conflicting commitments is one that has exerted a powerful hold on the course of epistemological discussion over the past half-century and more. That is to say, it has fed into the wider debate between realism and anti-realism, and again – more directly – into those particular branches of that debate (as described above) which focus on the question whether truth should be thought of in objectivist or epistemic terms.

One lesson to be drawn from Quine is the way that his notion of 'ontological relativity' started out as a highly controversial thesis in philosophy of language, logic and metaphysics but then acquired the status of a wholesale framework-relativist creed with far-reaching – some would say dire – implications for the project of epistemology. All the more so since Quine's espousal of a thoroughly naturalized, i.e., physicalist and science-based approach to such issues is one that leaves philosophy wholly bereft of normative standards or values. What then drops out – or would if this programme were carried right through – is any prospect of explaining the growth of knowledge (or our knowledge of the growth of knowledge) in terms that provide a basis for informed and rational theory-choice, as distinct from Quine's somewhat ad hoc appeal to a process of negotiated trade-off between the interests of economy, conservatism and sheer pragmatic convenience. This normativity-deficit has been noted by various critics, along with the conceptual problems induced by a narrowly empiricist (behaviourist) account of belief-acquisition – albeit shorn of the 'two dogmas' – which likewise conspicuously fails to explain how and why certain theories are superior to others in point of rational and causal-explanatory power.

I shall have much to say in the course of this book about the various directions taken by post-Quinean epistemology and philosophy of science. Some have sought to make good the normativity-deficit by rejecting Quine's holistic thesis, that is to say, by offering more precise and detailed accounts of what constitutes a genuine advance in knowledge or a way of bringing empirical data under certain theories that can be shown to improve upon others with respect to their scope and depth of conceptual grasp. This approach basically accepts Quine's point about about the theory-laden character of empirical observations – and the 'underdetermination' of theory by evidence – but sees no reason to deny, on such grounds, that theories can be more or less strongly supported by the best evidence to hand and such evidence more or less convincingly explained by the best available theory. Others have focused more on the problems with Quine's radical empiricism and its failure to provide an adequate account of the various kinds of causal interaction that operate both in the physical object-domain and through the effects of applied, e.g., technologically enhanced investigation. Thus the past few decades have seen a striking revival in the fortunes of causal realism, due in part to certain closely related developments in philosophical semantics – such as the Kripke/Putnam causal theory of reference-fixing – and in part to a widespread rejection of the sceptical outlook with regard to causal explanations that had loomed large in Anglophone debate from Hume to the heyday of logical empiricism. However, as I have said, this period has also witnessed the rise of a countervailing movement of thought which takes anti-realism as something like a default position, and which aims not so much to refute that position as to come up with a range of alternative middle-ground proposals whereby truth is conceived in epistemic rather than alethic terms.

Just recently some philosophers have put the case that this whole debate has run into a dead-end through its chronic fixation on certain issues – like those between realism and anti-realism or objectivist truth versus warranted assertibility – which have more to do with metaphysical disputes or with problems in philosophy of logic and language than with epistemology, properly conceived. One idea that has gained ground as a result is the claim that any adequate theory of knowledge must include some account of the *epistemic virtues* or the various kinds of knowledge-conducive attitude, mindset, intellectual character, and so forth, that enable virtuous (well-motivated) enquirers to pursue their task with best prospect of success. Only thus – so it is thought – can we break the hold of those sterile antinomies that have come down from philosophers like Descartes, Berkeley, Hume and Kant, not to mention their latter-day 'analytic' progeny who are still (despite Quine's animadversions) hooked on the same kinds of strictly insoluble dilemma. What is required is an approach that, more in the spirit of Aristotle, allows for a distinctively ethical conception of knowledge, one that gives pride of place to the epistemic virtues and sets out to reconceive the relationship between knower and known in terms that avoid such stark dualisms as those that have so far hobbled the debate at every turn. It would then be a matter of specifying just how and why their exercise in certain particular contexts of enquiry – whether in the natural or the social and human sciences – should have proved especially sound, reliable or apt to maximize the truth-content of those theories and hypotheses arrived at under their guidance. In which we should surely have to conclude that epistemology got off to a false start when it allowed its agenda to be set by the 'problem of knowledge' as conceived by philosophers in the old Cartesian-Humean line of descent. On their account the sole alternative to all-out scepticism was some kind of bedrock 'foundational' appeal, whether to the rationalist (Cartesian) chimera of 'clear and distinct ideas' or to Hume's empiricist notion of sense-data as a last-ditch defence against otherwise all-consuming epistemological doubt. Given the extent – as outlined above – to which similar problems have continued to resurface in a variety of shapes and forms it is understandable that some philosophers should cast around for an alternative theory which shifts the very grounds of debate.

In Chapter 5 I raise a number of questions with regard to these proposals for a virtue-based epistemology that purports to avoid all the well-known objections (among them the normativity-deficit) brought against Quine and other advocates of a thoroughly naturalized approach. I trace the problems back to Kant – more specifically, to certain obscure passages in the First *Critique* concerning the role of judgement as a mediating term between sensuous intuitions and concepts of understanding – and then forward to John McDowell's revisionist (but still deeply problematical) reading of Kant. What the virtue-theorists claim to provide is an account of those particular qualities – of caution, attentiveness, non-dogmatism, respect for the evidence, openness to rational persuasion, etc. – which enable us to specify just what it takes for epistemic agents to pursue their enquiries with a due regard for the interests of knowledge and truth. However (I argue) those criteria apply only in the epistemic context of discovery, i.e., as concerns the motivating interests or character attributes that may or may not be knowledge-conducive in some given investigative setting. Where the virtue-theorists overstep the mark is in taking those attributes to bear directly on the context of justification, that is to say, when it comes to issues of objective knowledge and truth. I proceed to locate their argument in relation to other – e.g., reliabilist and deontological – approaches, and to show how the virtue-based theory falls into the same kinds of dilemma that afflict those alternative accounts. That is to say, it conspicuously fails to close the gap between a normative conception that relativizes truth to 'best opinion' in the manner of response-dependence theorists and a realist (or objectivist) conception that takes truth to be always in principle verification-transcendent. Moreover this brings it out on the side of an anti-realist approach according to which truth cannot possibly elude or surpass the limits of present-best, virtuously formed belief. Thus the virtues no doubt have their legitimate place in any theory that seeks to explain how enquirers can best cultivate a mind-set that puts them on a reliably knowledge-conducive path. What they cannot provide – any more than McDowell's or the response-dependence approach – is a means of reconciling truth (or veridical knowledge) with the deliverance of optimized epistemic warrant or accredited best judgement. Hence – I suggest – the various unresolved problems and tensions that continue to surface in recent proposals for a virtue-*based* as distinct from a more modest, i.e., virtue-*oriented* epistemology.

III

Such are at any rate the currently most active topics of debate in this field, and I have therefore chosen to take them as a focus for much of my discussion here. On the other hand, I should not wish readers to come away with the impression that epistemology is exclusively an 'analytic' preserve, or that all the main developments have been going on in the Anglophone rather than the so-called 'continental', i.e., mainland-European context. Since much of my own work during the past two decades has been devoted to challenging the attitudes of reciprocal mistrust and (very often) of downright mutual incomprehension that have marked the relationship between these 'two traditions' it seemed best to take a similar line and explain their various points of convergence and divergence. This approach also has the merit – I hope – of giving my book a distinctive slant as compared with most other introductory volumes on epistemology that present these issues from a wholly (or predominantly) 'analytic' viewpoint. More than that, it seeks to emphasize the various ways in which a better understanding of developments in that 'other' tradition might help not only to widen horizons amongst the analytic fraternity, but also to point some possible ways beyond the kinds of problem that have often resulted from a certain overspecialized narrowing of conceptual as well as of cultural-historical focus. After all, there has to be something decidedly selective, not to say grossly skewed, about any treatment of modern epistemology that omits consideration of major figures such as Edmund Husserl, Pierre Duhem, Alexandre Koyré and Gaston Bachelard. Besides, in each case there are useful comparisons to be drawn between the arguments advanced by these thinkers and developments nearer home.

Thus, for instance, it is becoming steadily more apparent through recent studies that Husserl's contributions to philosophy of logic, mathematics and language are by no means so utterly remote from those of Frege as to justify the hitherto prevalent idea (among most analytic philosophers) that such comparisons were wildly off-the-point. As concerns Duhem it has long been recognized – not least by Quine himself – that the underdetermination of theory by evidence and the theory-laden character of observation-statements were theses that Duhem was the first to advance and that Quine later arrived at by a somewhat different route of thought. Then again, there is a strong case to be made that Bachelard's studies in the history and philosophy of science – especially his work on the nature, structure and dynamics of scientific theory-change – exhibit a certain similarity to those of Thomas Kuhn but also some significant differences of emphasis. Indeed it can be argued that in many ways Bachelard's approach to these issues is one that confounds the received idea of 'continental' philosophy as deplorably prone to excesses of cultural relativism while 'analytic' philosophy cleaves to the virtues of disciplined truth-seeking rigour.

For all of these reasons – and others besides – I have included some fairly detailed discussion of 'continental' epistemology and used the broader perspective thus gained to provide (where appropriate) a distinctive slant on other, more typically 'analytic' themes and concerns. Meanwhile I should perhaps offer my reader some idea of the motivating interests behind this book, since despite being pitched at a fairly introductory level and attempting to provide an even-handed coverage of the various arguments and counter-arguments it does – as will perhaps be evident by now – have a certain philosophical case to advance. The approach throughout is strongly inclined toward a realist standpoint, and (more specifically) toward a form of critical realism that rests on the following principal theses. (1) There exists a 'real-world', objective, mind-independent physical domain wherein various items on every scale – from electrons, atoms and molecules to chairs, continents and galaxies – exhibit certain likewise objective structures, properties and causal powers which they possess or exert quite apart from our present-best or even our future-best-attainable knowledge of them. This is basically an *ontological* thesis, that is to say, one having to do with matters that by very definition (as sceptics are always quick to remark) cannot be known in the sense 'established beyond any possible doubt by our powers of cognitive or epistemic grasp'. Hence (2) the *epistemological* claim that we can nonetheless acquire increased knowledge of those objects, properties and powers through our various kinds of physical interaction with them, ranging all the way from everyday experience to the most refined and sophisticated methods of applied scientific research. Hence also (3) what critical realists describe as the complexly 'stratified' nature of that interaction, some of it transpiring at a level where objectivity is at a premium and where the knower (e.g., the observer or experimental scientist) has least involvement in setting things up with a view to finding things out, while some transpires through a far more active, interventionist mode of enquiry. Even so (4), in the latter sorts of case, what is actually *discovered* through those various investigative methods and techniques is a range of (maybe hitherto latent or physically uninstantiated) properties and powers that are nonetheless real – there to be discovered – by just such newly devised or technologically enhanced means. Thus, for instance, there are now certain kinds of entity – such as synthetic DNA proteins or transuranic elements produced in particle supercolliders – which are products of human scientific know-how but whose potential existence is now and always was a matter of real (objectively valid) microstructural attributes, capacities and laws of nature.

This approach also has the great advantage of extending to the social-science disciplines where it makes allowance for the highest degree of practical, reflective and self-critical involvement on the part of human agents while explaining how the scope of that agency is both enabled and constrained by the various physical and social realities with which it has to deal. Not least, it helps to show where cultural relativists and 'strong' sociologists go wrong by exaggerating the extent to which scientific knowledge (and the objects of such knowledge) should be thought of as socially or culturally 'constructed', while failing to take due account of just those crucial factors. At the same time it offers a useful corrective to the kinds of sharply polarized debate – as described above – in which objectivist (alethic) realists about truth are ranged against anyone who takes the view that truth must be subject to certain forms of epistemic or cognitive constraint. What critical realism chiefly brings out is the frequent confusion here between matters metaphysical and issues epistemological. That is to say, on the one hand it highlights the mistake of supposing that truth can be thought of as in any sense epistemically constrained, while on the other rejecting that reactive tendency which pays insufficient heed to the various well-tried methods, procedures and modes of reasoning that have proved reliably knowledge-conducive. In which case we can best make rational-explanatory sense of the natural and the social sciences alike by maintaining that crucial distinction between ontology and epistemology, or – in critical-realist terms – between the 'intransitive' domain of objects, structures, properties, causal dispositions, etc., and the 'transitive' domain where human agency plays a more-or-less decisive interventionist role. This in turn marks a notable shift away from the top-down, physics-led, strongly reductionist programme espoused by the early logical positivists and also – in somewhat less aggressive form – by their logical-empiricist successors. It allows the social sciences a fair claim to methodological and epistemological rigour while critiquing those other, 'strong'-sociological schools of thought that would simply invert that order of priorities and give themselves the master-key to every disciplinary domain.

IV

So this book does have a certain palpable design on the reader, namely that of making the case for realism both as a matter of generalised ontological commitment and – more specifically – as a means of accounting for the growth of scientific knowledge by way of inference to the best (most rational) explanation. To be sure, there have been some powerful arguments raised against this whole approach and I shall try to give them a decent airing so as not to leave readers in doubt that my book has presented the issues with adequate regard for opposing views. Among them (to repeat) is that of response-dependence, i.e., the issue as to whether an approach that makes due allowance for normalized (or optimized) modes of human perceptual or cognitive response might satisfy the realist as providing 'objectivity' enough while meeting all the standard forms of anti-realist or sceptical challenge. Despite drawing a negative conclusion – that it cannot make good on that promise – I shall emphasize the range, ingenuity and resourcefulness of various arguments advanced in this vein, especially by Crispin Wright. My discussion here picks up on the issue between the internalist and externalist theories of knowledge, the latter currently enjoying greater success as a means of overcoming the problems thrown up by more traditional, first-person oriented modes of epistemological enquiry. A main concern at this stage will be with the variety of semantic externalism ('meanings just ain't in the head!') advanced on modal-logical grounds by thinkers like Hilary Putnam and Saul Kripke. Likewise highly promising are the kinds of naturalized epistemology – chiefly that developed by Alvin Goldman – which seek to conjoin a causal account of knowledge-acquisition with an adequately normative, reason-based rather than reductively physicalist (e.g., Quinean) approach.

Chapter 2 is centrally concerned with these debates between realism and anti-realism. I begin by discussing Kripke's arguments for the existence of a posteriori necessary truths, or those that have to be discovered through some process of scientific enquiry but which nonetheless hold as a matter of necessity in any world physically congruent with our own. This claim is backed up by Hilary Putnam's famous series of 'Twin-Earth' thought-experiments designed to make the case for modal realism, that is, the idea that certain names (prototypically natural-kind terms like *gold*, *water*, *acid*, *lemon* or *tiger*) have their reference fixed across all 'possible worlds' by what it is to be an entity of just that kind. Thus the reference-fixing may be in virtue of its molecular constitution (*water* = H_2O) or its subatomic structure (*gold* = 'metallic element with atomic number 79'). Likewise *acids* have the property 'proton-donor' which defines their reference more precisely than earlier descriptions like 'corrosive' or 'apt to turn litmus-paper red'. In the same way *tigers* and *lemons* are distinguished by reason of their possessing certain distinctive genetic or chromosomal features, rather than through descriptive attributes such as 'striped, carnivorous, and fleet-footed' or 'yellow of skin, with a white rind, and bitter in taste'. Those features belong to them essentially and did so even at a time when nobody possessed the relevant scientific knowledge. Their usage was therefore 'truth-tracking' or 'sensitive to future discovery', rather than failing to refer altogether or – as the rival (descriptivist) account would seem to entail – involving so disparate a range of imputed properties that we cannot think of early users as referring to the same kind of thing. This approach also claims to resolve the problem with anomalous items such as unripe (green) and sugar-saturated lemons or fleet-footed, striped and carnivorous creatures that just happen *not* to be tigers. What the Kripke/Putnam approach thus provides is a means of conserving fixity of reference across large (even radical) episodes of scientific theory-change.

I hope that this preliminary run around the field will have given some idea of how my book is designed to fit in with the 'Key Concepts' rubric. The aim is not so much to work on a straightforward coverage principle with the various concepts – that is to say, the various schools and movements of epistemological enquiry – laid out for inspection in a style of judiciously neutral or non-partisan treatment. Rather it is to flag the salient issues as and when they arise in the course of an argument that engages those issues from a definite and clearly articulated critical viewpoint. Thus the book proceeds mainly through a series of interlinked debates – realism versus anti-realism, alethic versus epistemic conceptions of truth, externalism versus internalism, objectivist versus response-dispositional or otherwise specified middle-ground positions – which aim to give a fairly comprehensive view of the field while offering a sense of sustained argumentative involvement with complex and important questions. 'Important', I should add, not only in so far as they have engaged the minds of some exceptionally bright and well-qualified thinkers whose conclusions we should be unwise to ignore, but also in so far as they bear directly on matters of ethical and social (as well as more 'narrowly' epistemological) concern.

(*NB*: I have not provided references for works and authors cited in this Introduction since they are all discussed more extensively elsewhere in the book and the details can be tracked readily enough via the Index and endnotes to subsequent chapters.)

CHAPTER 1

STAYING FOR AN ANSWER: TRUTH, KNOWLEDGE AND THE RUMSFELD CREED

I

On 12 February 2003 the US Secretary of Defense Donald Rumsfeld gave voice to some distinctly philosophical thoughts during a press conference about issues surrounding the planned 'liberation'/'occupation'/'invasion' of Iraq, one's choice of term depending very much on one's particular view of the matter.[1] More specifically, the issue was whether or not the war could be justified on the grounds first advanced by its US and British protagonists, i.e., Iraq's much-hyped development of 'weapons of mass destruction'. At the time of this conference there were signs that the US administration was anticipating certain problems on that score and preparing a range of alternative justificatory arguments. Still Rumsfeld's statement contrived to keep up appearances while leaving sufficient room for retreat should the invasion go ahead, the search be carried out, and those weapons fail to materialize.

So it was – in response to this challenging predicament – that Rumsfeld came up with his compact rumination on truth, knowledge and the limits thereof. 'Reports that say that something hasn't happened are always interesting to me, because as we know, there are known knowns; there are things we know we know. We also know there are known unknowns; that is to say we know there are some things we do not know. But there are also unknown unknowns – the ones we don't know we don't know.' This delphic pronouncement was widely debated at the time, not least among subscribers to various philosophy-oriented Internet sites who again tended to divide along politically motivated lines. The debate became highly charged for several reasons, among them the fact that Rumsfeld was well known for his habit of indulging in oddly homespun yet tortuous pronouncements on any topic that took his fancy. Also his utterance on this occasion had been awarded first prize in the Foot in Mouth competition for gobbledegook – that is, for impressive-sounding but confused and obfuscatory language – by the (British) Society for Plain English.[2] This award drew the ire of pro-war commentators, such as a writer for the (British) *Daily Telegraph* who ran his piece under the title 'Rumsfeld Talks Sense, not Gobbledegook' and lambasted the judges for passing off politically biased opinions under cover of a simple concern for standards of straightforward rational-communicative sense.[3]

So there were all sorts of interests bound up with the discussion as to whether Rumsfeld was indeed just rambling in his usual, linguistically challenged way, or cutting right through the political issues to enunciate some basic philosophic truths that urgently needed stating quite apart from such differences of view. I shall not here enter into further debate (although the impulse is almost irresistible) as to which of these hypotheses was nearer the mark. Nor shall I elaborate on the question concerning those weapons of mass destruction whose singular elusiveness – date of writing: 23 December 2004 – despite the US–British claim to have had proof of their existence through a number of detailed intelligence reports gives, to say the least, some reason for scepticism in that regard. (Hence the suggestion by one cynic that the initials 'WMD' might better be taken as standing for 'Words of Mass Deception'.) Rather my point is that Rumsfeld's remarks, whether wittingly or not, lead us straight into some central issues of epistemological debate. Also they serve to emphasize that such questions are not the exclusive domain of philosophers with a specialized interest in various, often highly technical debates about truth, knowledge and belief. For, as Rumsfeld's little homily makes clear, they are issues that can often have a close bearing on the conduct, not only of our intellectual lives as students of philosophy, but also of our moral and political lives as persons whose considered judgement in matters such as the supposed justification for invading Iraq must always involve the attempt to sift truth from falsehood, or knowledge from ignorance.

Thus his first proposition – that there are 'known knowns', or 'things that we know we know' – is a claim that most people would probably accept even though some of them (philosophers especially) might wish to enter a caveat or two. After all, the history of science provides many examples of beliefs that once enjoyed widespread credence among those considered best qualified to judge yet which subsequently turned out false, or at any rate to hold only for a limited (e.g., spatio-temporally restricted) range of applications. Moreover, this holds not only for empirical, i.e., observation-based beliefs that are always open to future (likewise empirical) disconfirmation but also for supposedly a priori truths – like those of Euclidean geometry according to most philosophers up to and including Kant – which were thought to obtain as a matter of jointly intuitive and logical necessity quite apart from any such putative evidence for or against. These were once thought to be 'known knowns' or 'things that we knew we knew' but later proved either false or true only relative to a certain (e.g., Euclidean) frame of reference. That is, there were other geometries which departed from Euclid's with regard to one crucial axiom – simply put, the impossibility that parallel lines should ever meet or diverge – yet which turned out first to be logically conceivable and then (with the advent of Einsteinian relativity-theory and the concept of space-time curvature) to be candidates for the best alternative description of physical reality.[4] Hence the widespread debate as to whether there exist *any* statements that can rightly be considered 'synthetic a priori' in Kant's sense of the term, i.e., statements which are self-evident to reason yet which also articulate an item of knowledge concerning the physical world or our experience of it. Some would even extend this doubt to a priori truth-claims of whatever sort, or whittle them down to a point of purely logical (and trivial) self-confirmation where only one candidate survives, namely the sentence 'Not every statement is both true and false'.[5] However, such extreme forms of scepticism aside, it is clearly the case that a great deal of what once passed for 'knowledge' no longer enjoys any right to that description, just as – we can safely infer – a great deal of what we presently *think* or *believe* we know will at length prove false or groundless.

So this particular item of the Rumsfeld creed needs amending so as to accommodate the distinction between 'know' = 'believe without question to the best of our knowledge or powers of rational comprehension' and 'know' = 'correctly and justifiably believe on the best, most reliable or truth-conducive grounds'. In other words it is the crucial difference between knowledge as a self-imputed, first-person, 'psychological' state of mind ('I simply *know* this or that to be the case'), and knowledge as a term that properly applies only to that subset of beliefs which meet the twofold require-ment of truth and epistemic or justificatory warrant. Otherwise there would be nothing odd – semantically as well as philosophically dubious – about saying that 'Ptolemy *knew* the Sun went around the Earth', or 'Priestley *knew* that combustion involved the emission of phlogiston', or 'Kant *knew* that Euclidean geometry and Newtonian space-time physics were a priori valid for all mathematical and sci-entific purposes'. Or again, it would raise no question about proper usage if one said 'Tony Blair *knew* that Iraq possessed WMDs at the time of his taking the country to war', even though – as now seems clear – there was no hard evidence and his statements to that effect were either mendacious, misinformed, or the result of willing self-deception. Yet in each of these instances there is something wrong – epistemologically confused – about the failure to distinguish cases where someone can properly be said to know this or that from cases where their 'knowledge' amounts to no more than unquestioning assurance, passionate conviction, or deeply held belief.

Thus disciplines such as history and philosophy of science could scarcely make a start in the business of explaining how scientific progress comes about except on the basis of that cardinal distinc-tion. For unless they take it that veridical knowledge can always come apart from *what counts* as such at any given time they will be unable to offer any adequate, i.e., rational and normative account of how science has achieved genuine advances by giving up various hitherto entrenched beliefs under pressure from discrepant empiri-cal results or perceived theoretical shortcomings.[6] Moreover, the debate about WMDs would have little point – and scarcely stir such vigorous differences of view – were it not for the implicit acceptance by all parties (even those least anxious that the truth be known) that any claim to knowledge in this regard has its truth-value fixed by the fact of their existence or non-existence, rather than by the strength of conviction (genuine or otherwise) expressed by partisans of either view. That is to say, Rumsfeld's first axiom – 'as we know, there are known knowns' – is one that the epistemologist may want to endorse though not without raising certain pertinent questions with respect to what properly counts as knowledge and what might more aptly be ascribed to the capacity for self-deception, manufactured consent, or the will-to-believe. This latter phrase was famously the topic of a now century-old exchange between the American pragmatist philos-opher William James (who espoused the view that 'truth' could indeed be cashed out as what's 'good in the way of belief') and his realist opponent Bertrand Russell (who thought it a philosophically confused as well as morally reprehensible doctrine).[7] Their quarrel has often been repeated since then in a range of alternative philosophic guises or variant technical vocabularies. Sufficient to say – in this context – that it works out as the difference between a viewpoint from which 'truth' can appear only under this or that currently accepted or preferred description and a viewpoint from which truth must be conceived (in realist terms) as always potentially transcending the limits of present-best, communally warranted, or socially desirable belief.[8]

Of course there are important, philosophically salient distinctions to be drawn between these last three ways of construing the claim that truth-values cannot (or should not) be thought of as exceeding the bounds of warranted assertibility. James's view – like Richard Rorty's after him – is that justification is principally a matter of 'what works' in the sense of promoting our best psychological, social and ethico-political interests.[9] Russell's case against this, simply put, is that it 'works' only in so far as it encourages an attitude of placid and unthinking acquiescence in taken-for-granted (hence reassuring) habits of thought and belief. Still there is a valid distinction to be drawn between 'present-best' (i.e., expert) opinion and 'communal warrant' as a matter of consensus amongst all those whose opinions might be polled in some culture-wide survey of beliefs on the topic. Even then their opinions might go against the Jamesian-Rortian idea that truth *just is* whatever has gained credence – or should most 'desirably' do so – according to the pragmatist criterion of that which promotes the psychological and social well-being of those concerned. For it is taken for granted in most debates on this topic – not only philosophical debates but also in controversies around issues like that concerning the Iraqi weapons of mass destruction – that there *do* exist objective truth-values for statements which cannot as yet be verified (or falsified) and that these may yet controvert 'best opinion' as certified by the notionally highest, best-placed authorities. Russell's classic rejoinder to James comes down to the realist and truth-based argument that 'wishing cannot make it so', or that no amount of social-psychological utility can offset the normative deficit involved in reducing truth to a matter of communal or psycho-therapeutic benefit.[10]

However there remains the challenge to be faced from epistemological theories – more in line with the current anti-realist trend – that would never endorse so overtly pragmatist or psychologistic a view yet would still hold out against any realist or objectivist conception that placed truth beyond the scope and limits of best-attainable belief.[11] Whence we may proceed to Rumsfeld's more gnomic second pronouncement, namely that 'we also know there are known unknowns . . . we know there are some things we do not know'. At face value this is just the kind of statement that any realist about truth – that is to say, any defender of objective truth-values as opposed to notions of 'truth' as epistemically or evidentially constrained – could perfectly well accept as meeting their most rigorous requirements. What it seems to say (*does* in fact say, realistically construed) is that truth cannot ever in principle be reduced to the limits of present-best belief or officially authorized opinion. Thus the question as to whether or not those damned elusive weapons existed might very well be a 'known unknown', which we are nonetheless able to pose since we know that they either did or did not exist quite aside from our present lack of evidence either way. Still one may suspect that this cannot have been Rumsfeld's motive in advancing his thesis of the 'known unknowns'. Rather that thesis had to do with the absence of so-far discovered WMDs and the prospect that such weapons might never be discovered despite the best efforts of highly motivated teams on the ground. That is to say, Rumsfeld took 'known unknowns' as synonymous with 'some things that we do not know', thereby suggesting that the issue would remain forever moot *even if* no weapons had been found by the time the inspectors left off their search and *even if* – though one could hardly expect him to spell this out – there was plentiful evidence (such as the 'dodgy dossier' concocted by British government and intelligence sources) of a large-scale campaign of disinformation during the months leading up to the war.[12]

Thus the axiom of 'known unknowns' has its place in Rumsfeld's philosophic credo as a means of inducing scepticism with regard to any prospect that the issue might finally be resolved, or that there might be some objective truth of the matter aside from these epistemological quandaries. So far from making the realist point – that the fact of our not knowing either way has absolutely no bearing on the question as to whether or not those weapons actually existed – Rumsfeld's dictum works rather to suggest that the question is pointless or misconceived since we are simply in no position to raise it.

Indeed his intended gist is much closer to the anti-realist position, namely that truth is 'epistemically constrained', i.e., that it cannot make sense to suppose the existence of objective truth-values for statements – such as 'Iraq did/did not possess WMDs' – whose truth or falsehood is beyond our best means of proof or verification.[13] This impression is further borne out by the last item in Rumsfeld's litany, his statement that 'there are also unknown unknowns – the ones we don't know we don't know'. Here again there is a possible interpretation which would bring him out on the side of those realists who maintain, like Hamlet, that 'there are more things in heaven and earth than are dreamt of in [our] philosophy', that is, more objective truths about (e.g.) physics, mathematics and history than we could ever come to know or even get around to framing in the form of truth-apt (though unverifiable) propositions. For the attempt to draw up any comprehensive list of such items would of course exceed the utmost capacity of human knowledge, investigative powers, or time available to compile it.

However – once again – this realist conception of truth seems not to be the message that Rumsfeld is keen to get across when he speaks of 'unknown unknowns' or of things 'we don't know we don't know'. Rather his point is to persuade us that the reality of those WMDs (or the truth of statements proclaiming their existence) cannot be disproved or legitimately called into question since mere lack of evidence – the fact of their not having turned up – will always be inadequate grounds for asserting a negative verdict. After all, among the range of 'unknown unknowns' might be all sorts of items – such as (for instance) a definitive proof of the existence of God or a conclusive yet so far unguessed-at source of evidence for Iraq's possession of WMDs – which would overturn such a verdict. What Rumsfeld thus contrives to suggest with this final variation on his theme is that we had best adopt an attitude of due epistemic humility and not presume to raise doubts – still less make accusations of fraudulence, mendacity, faked 'evidence' and so forth – concerning matters the truth of which lies beyond our present-best and maybe (who knows?) even our future-best-attainable knowledge.

II

I have pressed rather hard – absurdly so, some might think – on these choice specimens of Rumsfeldspeak because they serve to bring out both the complex nature of epistemological questions and their relevance to issues outside the philosophy seminar-room. For it is clear that one's considered position on matters such as the existence or non-existence of WMDs and the relationship between knowledge, evidence and truth in the controversy surrounding them will be affected at least in some degree by one's particular philosophic view. Moreover, this applies even to relatively 'technical' debates in epistemology which appear to be conducted at a far remove from such topics of wider concern but which in fact have large implications for our working grasp of those matters. Take for instance the issue currently raised between realists and anti-realists concerning whether sentences of the so-called 'disputed class' – hypotheses, conjectures, speculative statements, unproven theorems and so forth – can be thought of as possessing an objective truth-value even though we cannot find it out by any means at our disposal.[14] On the realist's submission they can and do possess such a value just so long as the sentence in question is well-formed and truth-apt, that is, just so long as it makes some definite claim with respect to some objectively existent state of affairs. What renders it true (or false) is the way things stand in reality, quite apart from any issue concerning the scope and limits of our knowledge in that regard. 'Reality' here would extend all the way from physical objects, structures and properties on whatever scale to historical events in the remote past and also to abstract entities like those which have their place in mathematics, logic and the formal sciences. So there are 'truth-bearers' (statements) and 'truth-makers' (the portions of reality to which those statements refer) and the statements in question are true just so long as they are borne out – objectively speaking – by some knowledge-independent, verification-transcendent or 'epistemically unconstrained' fact of the matter.[15]

To an anti-realist such as Michael Dummett this position seems highly problematic and even (in some contexts) utterly implausible. Thus Dummett takes the view that talk of truth should be replaced by talk of 'warranted assertibility', and this latter restricted to just those statements for which we possess some bona fide means of proof or verification.[16] For we shall otherwise be making a self-contradictory claim to the effect that we know statement x to be true or false – i.e., to possess an objective truth-value subject to the logical law of bivalence – even though we cannot determine its truth or falsehood to the best of our knowledge or investigative powers.

Dummett has three main arguments in support of this anti-realist position. First is the 'acquisition-argument' according to which we could not possibly acquire a working knowledge of language except via a grasp of the truth-conditions (more precisely: the conditions for warranted assertibility) which apply to the various sentences endorsed by members of our speech-community. Second is the 'manifestation-argument' which holds that such knowledge must be manifestable in our own speech-behaviour and thereby exhibit that working grasp – our understanding of the relevant conditions – in a way that enables other people to correctly interpret our meanings and beliefs. Third is the 'recognition-argument' whose premise, in brief, is that no sentence can legitimately count as true or false unless we are able to recognize those same conditions and hence interpret it as falling within the scope of our best available knowledge concerning what would qualify as adequate grounds for asserting or denying its validity. Thus, quite simply, it cannot make sense – so Dummett maintains – to assert the existence of objective truth-values for statements belonging to the 'disputed class', that is, statements for which we lack any means of formal proof (in mathematics or logic) or empirical verification (in history or the natural sciences). For this would amount to the self-refuting claim that we know something to be the case despite our not having acquired the capacity to recognize the conditions under which such a statement is warranted or to manifest our knowledge of those same conditions in a manner acceptable to others in possession of the relevant standards and criteria.

Taken together these arguments amount to a more sophisticated, logico-semantic version of the Verification Principle advanced by 'old-style' (1930s) logical positivists and later subject to refinement under pressure of various well-known objections.[17] The chief problem with that principle was that it met neither of its own criteria for meaningful statements, i.e., that such statements should be either empirically verifiable or self-evidently valid in virtue of their logical form. Despite the best efforts of rearguard defenders like A.J. Ayer, it proved impossible to come up with any alternative formulation that met one or other of these stringent demands. Hence Dummett's claim to have shifted the debate onto different and more fertile ground by recasting the argument in terms that are subject to no such charge of patent inconsistency or self-refutation. On his account the issue is much better raised as a topic within the philosophy of language and one that has to do with our warrant (or lack of it) for adopting a realist view of some particular area of discourse. What this involves, to repeat, is a programme for testing various kinds of statement – mathematical, scientific, historical, etc. – with a view to determining whether or not they are candidates for ascription of objective truth-values even in cases (those of the 'disputed class') where their truth or falsehood is beyond our utmost means of proof or verification. Thus a realist with respect to mathematics would hold that a well-formed, extensively tested, and intuitively plausible claim such as Goldbach's Conjecture – that every even number greater than two is the sum of two primes – must be either true or false (objectively so) despite our possessing no formal proof and our not being able to test it thoroughly, i.e., against the entire (infinite) range of such numbers even by use of the most powerful computational techniques. The principle of bivalence holds for such cases irrespective of whether we are now or might ever be so placed – epistemically speaking – as to prove or disprove the conjecture. For the Dummettian anti-realist, conversely, there is no making sense of such claims since they involve the appeal to an order of verification-transcendent truth which *ex hypothesi* exceeds the furthest bounds of assertoric or epistemic warrant. Mathematical truth extends only so far as the scope of mathematical knowledge and that knowledge no further than the range of those statements that we are able to prove, demonstrate or compute to the best of our ability.

In his later writings Dummett accepts that this stricture needs relaxing somewhat to allow that mathematical statements may properly count as truth-apt – or as candidates for warranted assertibility – just so long as we can form an adequate conception of how they might yet be removed from the 'disputed class' through the advent of more powerful or sophisticated proof-procedures.[18] Still he makes it clear that this is no major concession to the realist on the main point at issue, but rather a way of accepting the possibility of progress in such matters while maintaining his position with regard to the impossibility that truth could be conceived as recognition-transcendent or 'epistemically unconstrained'. Thus despite his occasional professions of even-handedness – of attempting simply to adjudicate the issue between realism and anti-realism – Dummett's approach is strongly partisan and in effect works out as a full-scale rehearsal of the anti-realist case across various topic-domains. Among them, as I have said, is the domain of historical discourse where he likewise takes the view that there is nothing – no objective truth of the matter – that could somehow, albeit unbeknown to us, decide the truth-value of any conjecture or speculative statement that went beyond the best available evidence. Here again, such utterances may be well-formed and may therefore strike us (at any rate, strike the realist) as making some perfectly specific claim with regard to matters – in this case historical persons, events or states of affairs – that merely happen to have passed without notice, or for which the evidence has since gone missing. Perhaps they were just too trivial for anyone to register at the time (like the fact, if such it is, of Napoleon's having scratched his left ear as he disembarked on St Helena), or occurred without witnesses (like the fact, if such it is, of Tony Blair's having muttered a *sotto voce* prayer for forgiveness just before officially declaring war on Iraq). Or perhaps they were actions, events or decisions of great historical import which – through some unfortunate fluke – have not come down to us by any reliable, truth-preserving means of transmission. Still we can frame conjectures or hypotheses about them which give every appearance of raising some definite, truth-apt claim even though they cannot be verified or falsified by any means at our disposal.

Then again, there is the whole vast tract of pre-history for which, by definition, we possess no archival or documentary sources and where historians therefore have to rely on various kinds of material, e.g., archaeological evidence, itself frustratingly gappy or incomplete. Still the realist will say that any well-formed statement with respect to each of the above sorts of case – e.g., 'archaeopteryx [the reptile-bird hybrid] actually existed in region x at prehistoric time y' – will have its truth-value fixed by the way things once stood in reality quite aside from our lack of certainty regarding (in this case) the disputed fossil record. To which the anti-realist will respond that such statements *cannot* have a truth-value since it is strictly inconceivable that truth should exceed the limits of assertoric warrant. Thus the realist is deluded – logically as well as epistemologically confused – if she claims to *know* that there exist certain truths that are recognition- or verification-transcendent. For what could such knowledge consist in (Dummett demands) if not in her capacity to recognize those truths as borne out by some proven and reliable method of verification? Moreover, what could that capacity amount to were it not manifestable in terms of her linguistic (i.e., logico-semantic) grasp of just which sentences fell within the bounds of

warranted assertibility and which others failed to meet that requirement and should therefore be excluded as candidates for truth or
falsehood? In which case – to put it plainly – there are no historical
truths that we are not capable of finding out by some means within
our available range of investigative methods or procedures. To
suppose otherwise (like the realist) is to court the charge of patent
self-contradiction since it entails our claiming to know that which
lies beyond our utmost epistemic reach.

To the realist this is just another cautionary instance of how badly
philosophers are prone to go wrong when they require that our most
basic working convictions about the relationship between truth,
knowledge and belief – not to mention the entire body of evidence
from scientific progress to date – should be set aside in the interests
of pursuing some speculative thesis in philosophy of language.[19]
That is to say, we have far better reason to trust the deliverances of
scientific method (or of disciplined, well-researched historiography)
than for going along with a linguistically oriented anti-realist programme which makes it such a mystery how truth could ever have
eluded the best efforts of previous expert enquirers. Secretary
Rumsfeld was not so far off the mark – philosophically speaking –
when he opined that 'there are known unknowns', or that 'we know
there are things we do not know'. The first statement is somewhat
unfortunate since its phrasing invites the standard anti-realist charge
of downright self-contradiction. But the second is exactly right in
maintaining that there have been, still are, and no doubt will always
be, truths beyond our cognizance. Where anti-realism constantly
skews the issue is in mixing up two different senses of the verb 'to
know'. On the one hand is the epistemic sense in which 'knowledge'
is defined – Dummett-style – as coextensive with our utmost capacities of proof, ascertainment, verification, falsification and so forth.
On the other is the realist/objectivist sense in which 'knowledge' may
be taken to extend beyond that to whatever we are rationally justified
in claiming to know by inference from the fact that truth has so often
turned out to elude or transcend the best efforts of previous enquiry.
Thus there is something absurd – so the realist will argue – about a
theory that so doggedly refuses to extrapolate from our present
understanding of where past thinkers came up against the limits of
their knowledge to the conclusion that we ourselves must be simi-
larly placed (i.e., in a state of ignorance) with respect to any number
of mathematical, scientific, historical or other such truths.[20] Besides,

one may doubt that Dummett makes good his case for the non-bivalent (neither-true-nor-false) character of statements belonging to the 'disputed class', or those that we are unable to assign a truth-value for reasons having to do with the limits of our cognitive or epistemic powers. For we can produce any number of well-formed, truth-apt, yet unverifable statements – e.g., concerning the existence (or non-existence) of remote astrophysical bodies of a specified type beyond the furthest reach of radio-telescope detection – which we can indeed *know* to be either true or false (that is, to possess an objective truth-value) despite their eluding not only our present-best but also our best possible means of ascertainment.[21] To deny this claim in pursuit of an anti-realist philosophic agenda is very much to put the logico-semantic cart before the scientific (as well as the historical and everyday-commonsense) horse.

As concerns history Dummett presses a long way in this direction and can indeed be found endorsing some pretty extreme anti-realist conclusions. Thus he claims that any 'gaps in our knowledge' with regard to certain historical periods, persons or events must also be construed as 'gaps in reality' since, should we frame a statement concerning them, then that statement will be epistemically void (i.e., fall foul of the acquisition, recognition and manifestation arguments) and hence lack both a truth-value and genuine referential content.[22] So, by Dummett's strange logic, it is not just a matter of the occurrence or non-occurrence of some event *x* being indeterminate 'to the best of our knowledge' but rather of that event's inhabiting a kind of historical limbo, a region of the past where truth-values simply have no hold. Indeed, there is a curiously self-revealing passage where Dummett contrasts the realist's willingness to accept that 'the effects of a past event may simply dissipate' – though of course without affecting the truth-value of any statement concerning it – with the anti-realist's inability to tolerate 'unknowability in principle', and hence his inclination 'to view our evidence for and memory of the past as constitutive of it'.[23] And again, whereas 'realism about the past entails that there are numerous propositions forever in principle unknowable', for the anti-realist 'there cannot be a past fact no evidence of which exists to be discovered, because it is the existence of such evidence that would make it a fact, if it were one'.[24]

This seems to me a quite extraordinary passage, not least for its frankly psycho-motivational (even confessional) tenor, that is, its suggestion that anti-realism in this refined logico-semantic form is a kind of defence-mechanism thrown up against the otherwise 'intolerable' knowledge of our ignorance regarding past events. Equally strange – from any but a hard-line anti-realist viewpoint – is the claim that our evidence (or lack of it) is 'constitutive' not only of our state of knowledge with respect to those events at any given time but also of their very reality, i.e., their having actually occurred or not. In which case, quite simply, the historical past must be thought of as a highly selective backward projection from whatever we are currently able to find out and hence as including lacunae – 'gaps in reality', as Dummett says – corresponding to our areas of ignorance.

III

There are readings of Dummett – and occasional passages in his own work – that would appear to stop short of this extreme anti-realist position and allow that historical truth might conceivably surpass the scope and limits of knowledge. Still they are offset by those other, more typical, passages which deny the possibility of objective (i.e., recognition-transcendent) truths, and which come out firmly against the realist claim that historical reality fixes the truth-conditions of our various statements about it, rather than itself being somehow 'fixed' by those statements or our epistemic warrant for them.

This impression is reinforced by Dummett's willingness at least to entertain the idea that past events may be 'brought about' by some change in our present state of knowledge, or some newly acquired piece of evidence that throws a fresh light on the antecedent course of events.[25] One example he gives is that of a man who prays that his son might not have been killed in battle despite his knowledge that the battle has already taken place and its outcome (presumably) decided before the prayer is offered up.[26] On a realist view this would count as perfectly understandable in psychological or motivational terms but as making no sense – running into all kinds of well-known 'back-to-the-future' paradoxes – if seriously taken to involve the idea of retroactive causation or the 'bringing about' of past events through some change in our present (supposed) justification for believing one way or the other. A careful reading of the three essays where Dummett engages most closely with this issue will I think leave the reader convinced that he takes due stock of the considerations that count so strongly against it, but that he nevertheless holds out for its intelligibility as a matter of philosophic principle.[27] That is to say, Dummett sees nothing inherently absurd about the notion that 'wishing (or praying) might make it so', or that the outcome of some past event for which, as yet, we possess no definite evidence might somehow be decided by our coming into possession of just the desired piece of information that had hitherto eluded our grasp.

It is not (I think) crucial to the issue here that Dummett's convictions in this regard – and his choice of the above-mentioned example to make his point – may seem to indicate a strong theological leaning toward the idea that even the upshot of bygone ('realistically' determinate) events is within God's power to affect through some kind of *après-coup* intervention. Rather it is my point that Dummettian anti-realism carries along with it a strong commitment to the thesis that any truths concerning the historical past are always revisable – open to confirmation or disconfirmation – with the advent of new evidence which may retroactively decide the issue with respect to this or that hitherto disputed or unverified item of belief. What is simply inadmissible, on Dummett's account, is the existence of truths – or of truth-values pertaining to certain well-formed historical statements – which possess that character just in virtue of their corresponding to the way things stood in reality rather than the way they happen to stand according to our best current knowledge or means of verification. This is basically what Dummett means when he contrasts the realist's willingness to accept that 'the effects of a past event may simply dissipate' with the anti-realist's resistance to the notion of 'unknowability in principle', and hence his desire 'to view our evidence for and memory of the past as constitutive of it'.[28]

That desire may have a lot going for it in terms of motivational psychology, that is, as a matter of what's 'good in the way of belief' or likely to produce maximum benefit for anyone disposed to believe (for instance) that praying for the favourable outcome of some past event can somehow retroactively decide the issue. However, it is open to the same kind of argument that Russell brought against James – briefly put, that wishing cannot make it so – and also to the more basic objection that what distinguishes past and future temporal domains is precisely the fixity, i.e., the unalterable character of that which has already occurred *however much or little we may know concerning it* as distinct from the contingency of future events, or the yet-to-be-decided truth-value of any predictions we may offer. Such was Aristotle's view of the matter and such, pace Dummett, the only

way of thinking that doesn't create all manner of well-known temporal problems and paradoxes. Also there is the point that anti-
realism of this sort plays straight into hands of those who would
deny (perhaps for propagandist, historical-revisionist or mass-
deceptive purposes) that truths about the past can be thought of as
epistemically unconstrained, that is, as always potentially transcending our present-best knowledge or evidence.[29] For it is then a short
step to the sceptical position – much touted by US and British
government sources – that since nobody could *prove* the non-
existence of those weapons of mass destruction (since absence of
proof is after all not proof of absence), therefore the question concerning their reality must remain now and perhaps forever moot.

What tends to create confusion here is the way that such scepticism can come out sounding very much like a strong endorsement of
the realist/objectivist case. Thus it is hard to imagine any realist
taking issue with articles 2 and 3 of the Rumsfeld creed, i.e., that
there are 'known unknowns' (hypothetical statements concerning
which we knowingly lack any means to determine their truth-value)
and also 'unknown unknowns' (possible or maybe for us impossible
statements which so far exceed our conceptual grasp as not to figure
even in the realm of hypothetical conjecture). After all, it is precisely
the realist's claim that truth can always in principle transcend not
only our best current sources of evidence or epistemic warrant but
also our ability to frame any statement that would qualify as truth-
apt in the relevant respect. This is where anti-realism gets a hold, that
is, by pointing out that the realist (or objectivist) conception of truth
yields a crucial hostage to sceptical fortune in so far as it concedes
that truth can come apart from our present-best state of knowledge
or means of verification.[30] For in making this claim it drives a wedge
between truth – objectively conceived – and whatever we are able to
know of it according to our own limited powers of comprehension.
Hence the line of thought – especially prominent in recent philosophy of mathematics – that one can *either* have truth as a matter of
objective, recognition-transcendent warrant *or* knowledge that falls
within the scope of our best epistemic, probative or investigative
powers and thus de facto meets the conditions for knowing this or
that to be the case.[31] From which its proponents often conclude that
this is a strictly insoluble dilemma but one which had better be
defused in favour of an anti-realist approach that reformulates
'truth' in terms of epistemic warrant and thereby brings it safely

back within the bounds of human knowability. Such is Dummett's intuitionist conception of truth in mathematics as whatever we are able to prove or ascertain by the best formal methods at our present or perhaps (on his more liberal account) our rationally optimized or future-best disposal.[32] However this leaves it a mystery how mathematical discoveries could ever have occurred unless through the proven capacity of thought to find out truths that went against currently accepted standards of proof or verification. What counts as epistemic, probative or assertoric warrant in such matters is always and in principle subject to disconfirmation by that which lies beyond our present-best powers of proof or epistemic warrant.

Scepticism in such matters very often trades on a false double-bind or, more exactly, an unjustified appeal to the principle of *tertium non datur*. Thus it takes for granted that one can *either* have the notion of objective, verification-transcendent truths (in which case, by very definition, they cannot be known), *or* a scaled-down epistemic conception that redefines 'truth' in keeping with the scope and limits of knowability, but surely not both unless by some disreputable fudging of the issue. However there is no good reason for the realist or objectivist about truth to accept her impalement on the former horn of this artfully contrived dilemma. As I have argued elsewhere, there are viable realist alternatives in philosophy of mathematics, logic and the formal sciences which fully retain the commitment to objective truth while denying that this leads to the sceptical impasse – the unbridgeable gulf between truth and knowledge – that anti-realists routinely impute to it.[33] These include, for instance, the standpoint of Gödelian realism about abstract entities like numbers, sets or classes which maintains that we can indeed acquire knowledge of those entities though not through some quasi-perceptual means of epistemic 'contact' which the sceptic is easily able to show up as a figment of Platonist imagining. Indeed, the chief philosophical lesson of Gödel's incompleteness-theorem is that certain objective truths in mathematics and logic – among them, that of the theorem itself – can be known (i.e., first discovered and then repeatedly tested and proved) despite their having to do with the limits of any computational or purely formal proof-procedure. Thus the fact that any system complex enough to generate the axioms of elementary arithmetic will contain one or more theorems unprovable within that system is a result that we are able to grasp or recognize only on condition that we do (contra Dummett) have access to such strictly verification-transcendent truths.[34]

Of course there are important distinctions to be drawn between issues of truth, knowledge and evidence in the domain of the formal sciences and the kinds of broadly analogous question that arise with regard to matters of empirical (e.g., historical) fact. Nevertheless it is a chief merit of Dummett's work to have shown, across both areas of discourse, how the realist/anti-realist debate ultimately turns on this basic disagreement as to whether the truth-value of statements should be thought as epistemically constrained or as determined by objective factors quite apart from the scope of our best knowledge, evidence or powers of conceptual grasp. That Rumsfeld's credo so adroitly managed to obfuscate the issue and promote an outlook of generalized scepticism while overtly adopting a realist view of the question concerning Iraq's possession or non-possession of WMDs is one example of how important it is to get straight about these seemingly arcane epistemological issues. For although it is the case – as suggested by his talk of 'unknown unknowns' – that absence of proof is not proof of absence, still we are entitled (on probabilistic but nonetheless rational grounds) to draw a negative conclusion in that regard. Among the reasonings that would count toward that conclusion are (1) the various conflicting claims put forward by the US and British governments, intelligence agencies, etc.; (2) the mounting evidence of public disinformation, doctored reports, propaganda spin, misleading statements to Congress and Parliament; and (3) – crucially – the fact that those weapons have not yet materialized despite the most sustained and intensive efforts to seek them out. In other words the strong likelihood of their non-existence can justifiably be maintained as a matter of inference to the best, most rational, or least credibility-stretching explanation.

This kind of argument clearly takes us onto different philosophical ground from that occupied by parties to the Dummett-inspired dispute about realism and anti-realism. What it shows, I suggest, is that while such debates are important for clarifying fundamental issues about knowledge and truth, they are apt to confuse matters – to have just the opposite effect – when we need to form a judgement on complex and case-specific questions like that raised by the claim about WMDs. For in this context it is a necessary presupposition (one to which Rumsfeld seemingly subscribes in his remarks on the topic) that there are truths which may or may not be discovered in the course of diligent enquiry and, moreover, that their standing is in no way affected by the extent of our knowledge, ignorance or uncertainty about them. Such is the starting-point or default assumption of any dispute – outside the realms of metaphysics or philosophy of language – which involves some contention over well-defined issues of scientific, historical or factual truth. Beyond that, it is a matter of rationally weighing the evidence and attempting to reach an informed estimate which takes in as much of that evidence as possible, along with due allowance for the motivating interests of those whose judgements (or overt professions of belief) may always be subject in varying degrees to the pressure of ideological commitment or political self-interest.

At this stage the realism/anti-realism debate in its Dummettian form can look very much like a distraction – in some contexts a convenient distraction – from other, more pressing, concerns. That Rumsfeld managed to hit unerringly on just this current philosophical hot topic is perhaps an indication that all is not well with the kinds of debate that preoccupy many thinkers in the mainstream analytic tradition. That is to say, it points toward something distinctly askew with an agenda that could take as its central concern the question as to whether there are truths that elude our present-best or maybe our utmost powers of proof or verification. That there *must* be such truths – a whole vast range of them in every domain from mathematics to physics, history and even the dispute regarding Iraq's possession of WMDs – is itself a truth which (again *pace* Dummett) cannot be denied without falling into manifest absurdity. This is why Rumsfeld got it right, from a realist standpoint, with his talk of 'known unknowns' (those things 'we know we do not know') and the yet more elusive category of 'unknown unknowns' ('the ones we don't know we don't know'). All the same there is no good reason to conclude – in standard sceptical fashion – that objectivism about truth leads straight to the pyrrhic upshot whereby truth comes *completely apart* from knowledge and knowledge is thus deprived of any claim to veridical, i.e., objective warrant. For this is just a version of the false anti-realist dilemma that results from confusing ontological with epistemological issues, or questions regarding what is/is not objectively the case quite aside from the scope and limits of our present-best knowledge with questions of the sort: what can we justifiably claim to know on the basis of rational inference from the best information to hand?

It is the latter rather than the former type of question that offers most help in arriving a properly informed, reasoned and judicious assessment of claims and counter-claims such as those advanced with respect to the existence or non-existence of Iraqi WMDs. On the other hand, the likeliest rhetorical effect of Rumsfeld's remarks – despite their vaguely metaphysical-realist tone – was to put people off enquiring any further into this tricky issue since, after all, any statement on the matter (his own previous, more confident claims included) could never be conclusively falsified by any amount of fruitless searching on the ground. However, as I have said, this ignores a whole range of pertinent considerations that would count strongly against adopting such a sceptical view. Among them are the now well-documented facts of a concerted US–British intelligence and government-sponsored disinformation campaign which was instrumental in gaining public and congressional/parliamentary support at a critical stage just before the invasion went ahead. Besides, there is the steady erosion of trust in a great number of once 'reliable' claims with regard to specific details of Iraqi weaponry – its scale, nature, stage of development, capacity for being deployed at short notice over large distances, etc. – which have since turned out to be either false or grossly exaggerated. As the evidence stacks up in favour of rejecting those claims so it becomes – on any rational assessment – increasingly a matter of hard-put doctrinal or ideological adherence to maintain that the issue is still (perhaps forever) moot since absence of proof is not proof of absence.

Indeed as I write (24 December 2004) Tony Blair's continued professions of faith in the existence of those weapons despite the apostasy of just about everyone else – weapons inspectors and well-placed US government sources included – resembles nothing so much as 'arguments' for the existence of God that invoke the impossibility of proving that God doesn't exist. He has not yet been reduced to Tertullian's last-ditch argument 'credo quia absurdum' ('I believe because it is absurd') but his fideist standpoint against all the odds is rapidly approaching that desperate conclusion. However this is just the kind of epistemic fallacy – the misplaced burden of proof – that theologians typically exploit by demanding that their atheist opponents offer demonstrative grounds for God's non-existence when the same sort of argument would require (for example) that one *prove* the non-existence of kangaroos on Alpha Centauri or of a Disneyland replica somewhere in the outer reaches of the expanding universe. Of course it is just conceivable that WMDs might yet turn up in Iraq or perhaps – as one current fallback scenario would have it – in Syria,

Iran or some other proximate location to which they were transported before the invasion. No realist would wish to deny this possibility since, after all, it is a cardinal point in any realist ontology worthy of the name that truth might always in principle transcend the limits of our present-best knowledge or evidence. Still she will maintain that our assessment of such evidence can justifiably proceed and lay claim to a capacity for sorting truth from falsehood through various kinds of applied documentary and critical-investigative work.

This also raises the currently very live issue of *testimony* and its role in what we know, or in what we can justifiably (with adequate reason or warrant) take ourselves to know. Philosophers – rationalists and empiricists alike – have sought to explicate the 'grounds' or 'foundations' of knowledge, often with reference to goings-on in the minds of solitary, first-person thinkers. Yet surely most of what we claim to know is derived from various, more or less reliable 'second-hand' sources. Consider for instance the following cases: asking for directions in an unfamiliar town; believing (or knowing?) that water has the molecular structure H_2O; asserting as a matter of fact – of 'justified true belief' – that Caesar crossed the Rubicon or that Napoleon was defeated at the Battle of Waterloo. With few exceptions philosophers have treated testimony as an inferior (less reliable) source of knowledge when compared with first-hand knowledge-by-acquaintance or truths arrived at through independent reasoning from first (self-evident) principles. If we must rely on testimony – so the argument runs – then we should always bear in mind that it loses credibility or becomes ever more dubious with the passage from one informant to the next. (This argument is to be found in Locke and Hume, among others.) However, might there not be cases when an expert in the field – e.g., a specialist historian – is able to compare and criticize various sources and thereby produce a more accurate account than anything produced by earlier historians or even by first-hand witnesses who may have had a very confused or partial impression of what went on?

Take again the case of mathematics, where some philosophers would argue that we cannot rightly claim to know any item of mathematical truth unless we can work through the proof-procedure for ourselves and understand just how the result was obtained.[35] Yet there are certain theorems whose proof lies beyond the powers of unaided human mathematical reckoning and can only be achieved through the use of powerful computer programs that far exceed our

capacity to run a stage-by-stage mental check on their various operations. And again: even where a mathematician has worked out some
complex proof for herself, nevertheless she will most likely want to
check the results against those obtained by other workers in the field.
Maybe she got something wrong, in which case the weight of conflicting testimony might be sufficient to shake her confidence in the
original (first-hand) result. Or maybe she got the whole thing right
but still wants independent confirmation before going public at the
next big maths conference. Whichever way – right or wrong – the
proof needs support from 'outside' corrobative testimony. Consider
also the case of personal experiences (perceptions, memories, self-
attributed states of mind, etc.) where it might seem obvious that the
individuals concerned are by far the best (most reliable) source of
evidence. Yet this ignores various counter-instances, among them
perceptual distortion, false (or artificially induced) memory syn-
drome, and cases where people can sometimes be convinced –
perhaps through psychoanalysis – that they had misinterpreted their
own feelings or repressed the real source of their fears, anxieties,
periods of emotional uplift, etc.

In each of the above cases there is good reason to think that beliefs
arrived at on the strength of eye-witness 'knowledge' or first-person
epistemic authority are not, or not always, the best source of truth
as compared with other (more detached or impersonal) accounts. So
it is clear that testimony of various sorts plays a large and philosophically underestimated role in a great many aspects of human knowledge and experience. One notable advocate of this view was the
eighteenth-century Scottish Enlightenment philosopher Thomas
Reid who espoused an outlook of 'commonsense' realism with
regard to our knowledge of the (so-called) 'external world' and also
to our ways of finding things out by various indirect means, e.g.,
through the witness of sound documentary sources or good testimonial warrant.[36] Although Reid's epistemology had a good deal in
common with the empiricist principles of his compatriot David
Hume, he rejected Hume's sceptical conclusions and argued for a
much more robust conception of the mind's capacity to arrive at
truth on the basis of just such evidence. One of his chief arguments
in this regard – and currently a topic of revived interest – was the
claim not only that we *do* very often rely on testimony for much of
our presumed knowledge but also that we *can and should* place trust
in its various sources and means of transmission just so long as they

stand up well to critical and methodological scrutiny.[37] All the more so when – as with those fugitive WMDs – it is matter of compensating for the lack of 'hard' evidence either way by a process of reasoning that has to weigh up a great mass of more-or-less reliable, expert or trustworthy information.

It is just this prospect that is obscured from view if one accepts the sceptical dilemma posed by advocates of anti-realism in its present-day Dummettian (logico-semantic) form. However – as I have argued – it is a false dilemma and one that ignores the wide range of reliably knowledge-conducive procedures which no doubt fall short of absolute, indubitable truth yet which nonetheless offer sufficient grounds for rejecting the kind of anti-realist 'solution' currently on offer. That is to say, statements of the so-called 'disputed class' cannot be consigned to some limbo of ultimate undecidability beyond the furthest reach of rational adjudication. To endorse such a view is in effect to declare that anything less than proof as established by the best methods of the formal sciences or truth as vouchsafed by the surest methods of empirical verification must *ipso facto* be counted beyond the pale in point of its rational assertibility or its claim to represent our best, most considered and carefully arrived-at judgement in the matter. Thus verificationism of this new, sophisticated sort is after all not so different from the old-style, logical-positivist approach that famously ran into just such problems when it tried to account for scientific progress or our knowledge of the growth of knowledge.[38] Quite simply there is no such account to be had if one adopts an approach (like Dummett's) which starts out from the supposed short-comings of realism in philosophy of mathematics, logic and the formal sciences and goes on to impute the same problematical status to our purported knowledge of facts or events in the empirical domain. Yet this is just another version of the fallacy that John Stuart Mill detected in Humean and other sceptical arguments against the validity of induction, that is to say, the mistake of imposing inappropriate (deductive) standards of truth on modes of reasoning – such as inference to the best explanation – that involved much wider, more practically accountable, sources of knowledge and evidence.[39] It is my contention that Mill got it right and that anti-realism of the Dummett variety (which derives in large part from his case against objectivist philosophies of mathematics) gets it wrong on just those grounds.[40] For there is a great deal more to our knowledge of such matters – as likewise to our grasp of disputes about historical episodes much further back – than found room in Mr Rumsfeld's metaphysically intriguing ruminations on the topic. In Chapter 2 I shall unpack some of the arguments and concepts that philosophers have lately developed by way of providing those additional resources.

REALISM, REFERENCE AND POSSIBLE WORLDS

I

This chapter resumes my discussion of current debates between epistemological realism and anti-realism. However it also marks a shift of emphasis from the Dummett-inspired way of posing these issues in primarily logico-semantic (and metaphysical) terms to an approach more focused on the question of just how knowledge accrues in various scientific and other fields of enquiry. There is still, I should add, a distinctly metaphysical aspect to the types of argument involved since they have to do not only with the ways and means of knowledge-acquisition, but also with matters concerning the ultimate nature of physical reality, the capacity of human intelligence to grasp it, and the scope and limits of rational conjecture in these speculative regions of thought. To this extent philosophy is still working through the problems bequeathed by Kant's great attempt – in the *Critique of Pure Reason* – to delimit the sphere of cognitive understanding (where sensuous intuitions must be 'brought under' adequate concepts) from that of metaphysics where reason has a licence to raise such speculative issues but only on condition that it not lay claim to any kind of determinate knowledge. All the same there have been some striking new developments in post-1970 philosophy of language, logic and science that hold out the promise not only of offering a fresh perspective on the realism/anti-realism debate but also of substantially redrawing the Kantian line between questions of an epistemological nature and those of a strictly metaphysical import. What's more, they have the distinct merit (for my own purpose) of treating such questions from a standpoint that takes full stock of the 'linguistic turn' yet which puts the case –

unusually in that context – for a strong causal-realist and objectivist approach to epistemological issues.

Saul Kripke and Hilary Putnam are the two thinkers who have done most to advance this case. Kripke is known chiefly for the arguments developed in his book *Naming and Necessity* where he proposes a causal theory of reference as against the once prevalent descriptivist theory descending from Frege and Russell.[1] According to the latter we pick out referents (objects or persons) through a cluster of descriptive attributes which serve to specify and hence to individuate just those uniquely designated objects or persons. Thus people once referred to *gold* under some such description as 'yellow, ductile metal that dissolves in weak nitric acid', whereas now it is defined (for scientific purposes) as 'metallic element with atomic number 79'. Or again: when we refer to a historical individual such as *Aristotle* we do so by applying certain salient descriptions such as 'pupil of Plato', 'tutor of Alexander', 'author of *The Poetics*, the *Prior Analytics*', etc.

Hence Frege's cardinal dictum that 'sense determines reference', i.e., that in so far as such proper names refer it must be in virtue of our grasping the relevant descriptive criteria. On the contrary, Kripke maintains: the reference of *gold* was fixed by an inaugural 'baptism' or act of naming, and has since held firm despite and across all subsequent changes in our knowledge concerning its nature, identifying features, physical properties, microstructural constitution, or whatever. Otherwise – on the descriptivist theory – every time that we made a new discovery about gold we should have to say (absurdly) that 'gold is not gold', since our previous beliefs had turned out false or inadequate, and it was just those beliefs that had fixed its reference. Or again: if we discovered that Aristotle had *not* in fact been a student of Plato, tutored Alexander, authored the *Poetics*, etc., then we should have to say 'Aristotle wasn't Aristotle'. Rather, what allows us to avoid this absurd consequence is the Kripkean causal theory of naming and necessity whereby 'Aristotle' refers to just that historical individual who was so named and whose identity was fixed – necessarily so – at his moment of conception. Likewise: had George W. Bush not become US President as a result of the controversial 2001 election – had there been a recount of the Florida vote, let us say, and the Supreme Court not decided against it by upholding the official outcome – then he would still have been the self-same George W. Bush despite this significant change of descriptive attribute. In the case of natural-kind terms like *gold* the argument works in a similar way: what the term picks out is just that substance (i.e., the element with atomic number 79) which received its name through an initial act of baptism and has always since then been designated 'gold'. Thus the term referred to the identical stuff even when nobody knew about atomic numbers and when people had to make do with rough-and-ready descriptive attributes. From which it follows that they were always wrong in mistaking fool's gold (iron pyrites) for the genuine item despite its superficial resemblance. What made them wrong was (1) the necessity that 'gold' should refer to *gold* in any conceivable world where the substance thus named possessed just that kind of uniquely distinctive microstructure; and (2) the linguistic 'chain' of transmission whereby its reference had been preserved through every shift in its associated range of descriptive criteria.[2]

On the strength of this argument Kripke advances some far-reaching proposals with regard to modal logic, that is, the branch of logic having to do with matters of possibility and necessity. In brief, he makes a case for the existence of a posteriori necessary truths – like those about the atomic constitution of *gold* or the genetic-chromosomal identity of *Aristotle* – which are neither analytic, i.e., true-by-definition, nor a priori, that is to say, self-evident to reason, but which nonetheless hold necessarily in any world where their referents exist or once existed.[3] Thus gold *cannot but* be that kind of stuff in all worlds physically compatible with ours in respect of their constituent natural kinds while Aristotle *cannot but* have been just that individual in all worlds where his identity was fixed by the self-same act of conception. And of course one could multiply similar examples, such as *water* having the molecular structure H_2O just in virtue of its being water, or acids being proton-donors just in virtue of their being acids, or tigers possessing a certain chromosomal make-up since that is what constitutes the membership-condition for any creature that belongs to the species 'tiger'.[4] Of course these criteria haven't always applied since 'water' was once defined vaguely as the kind of stuff that fell as rain, filled up lakes, was liquid under normal ambient conditions, boiled or froze at certain temperatures, possessed certain useful cleansing properties, etc. In the same way our knowledge of acids advanced from 'acid = corrosive to certain metals, sour-tasting in dilution', etc., to 'acid = having the property of turning litmus-paper red', to 'acid = proton-donor'. Nevertheless the term 'acid' may be held to have referred to the same natural kind despite and across all these changes of descriptive paradigm, just as 'tiger' has continued to pick out the same animal species whether vaguely defined as a 'large, fleet-of-foot, cat-like creature with stripes' or with reference to its chromosome structure.

In this respect – so the argument goes – such names are 'truth-tracking' or 'sensitive to future discovery'.[5] That is to say, their usage at any given time might always turn out (now as in the past) to be based on a limited or partial knowledge of just what it is – scientifically speaking – that constitutes the kind in question. Very often it is a matter of superficial appearances, as in the case of 'gold = yellow, ductile metal' (which would also encompass iron pyrites) or – perhaps the most famous example – 'whale = large, water-spouting fish'. However this gives no reason to conclude (with the strong descriptivists or paradigm-relativists like Thomas Kuhn) that shifts in the range of identifying criteria from one theory or classificatory system to the next can at times be so drastic as to break the referential chain of transmission and leave us at a loss to compare theories in point of their descriptive accuracy or causal-explanatory power.[6] What leads philosophers to adopt this surely desperate position – i.e., the thesis of radical 'incommensurability' between paradigms – is their acceptance of Frege's cardinal precept that 'sense determines reference' along with the idea (which Frege sharply rejected) that the sense of any given term can only be specified in relation to the entire language, discourse or received body of knowledge within which it plays a role.[7] Thus scientists working before and after some major episode of theory-change must be thought of as inhabiting 'different worlds', or worlds that contain a whole different range of putative objects, properties, causal powers, microstructural features and so forth.

Moreover, we cannot talk of scientific 'progress' in this regard since the very criteria for what *counts* as an advance in knowledge are themselves relative to this or that paradigm and hence incapable of adjudication from some standpoint of objective (paradigm-transcendent) truth.[8] Besides, as Quine famously argued, observations are always to some extent 'theory-laden' and theories always 'underdetermined' by the best empirical evidence to hand.[9] In which case scientists can always save a cherished theory by pleading observational error, perceptual distortion, the limits of precise measurement, etc., or alternatively save some striking empirical observation – where it comes into conflict with a well-established theory – by making suitable adjustments elsewhere in the overall 'web of belief'. At the limit (as with certain well-known problems in the field of quantum mechanics) this might even entail some revision to the ground-rules of classical logic such as bivalence or excluded middle.[10] However there is something decidedly suspect about an argument that leaves no room for such basic normative conceptions as those of good observational warrant or accordance with our best theoretical beliefs as judged by the standards of valid logical (e.g., hypothetico-deductive) inference.[11]

Hence a main attraction, for some, of the Kripkean 'new' theory of reference: that it offers a means to avoid this unpalatable upshot of wholesale paradigm-relativism or 'incommensurability' across different theories, languages or conceptual schemes. For if reference is fixed independently of any descriptive criteria that happen to apply from one to another paradigm then we can perfectly well explain how a term like 'electron', once introduced through the inaugural act of naming, continued to pick out the same referent despite some otherwise radical revisions to its range of defining properties or imputed characteristics.[12] Thus pioneer usages were no doubt descriptively and theoretically wide of the mark when assessed against our present (quantum-based) understanding, as was Niels Bohr's 'planetary' model of electrons orbiting the nucleus before he abandoned that model in favour of a quantum-theoretical approach.[13] Indeed, the earliest deployments of the term were so devoid of specific theoretical or descriptive content that they served as just a handy way of referring to 'whatever it was' among the range of putative microphysical objects that produced, e.g., those accidentally discovered remote luminescent effects which would later give rise to technological developments like the cathode-ray tube.[14] Yet it is still the case that we can speak of those early physicists as referring to a certain kind of subatomic entity – the *electron* – and also as having come up with different, more-or-less adequate theories and descriptions concerning it. For what the Kripkean account of reference-fixing entitles us to claim is that the pioneers set this process in train through an inaugural act of naming ('let us call "electron" the kind of thing that would explain these otherwise mysterious phenomena') and that the name then stuck – referentially speaking – despite its radical redefinition with the advent of quantum mechanics. By the same token, we can credibly assert that the ancient Greek atomists were already talking about the same sort of thing that present-day physicists talk about – and which achieved something like an adequate conceptual status with the advent of Daltonian chemistry – even though they (the Greeks) arrived at their theory on the basis of a purely a priori conjecture devoid of empirical or properly scientific warrant.[15]

Thus philosophy of science can be saved from its own sceptical devices by acknowledging (1) that descriptive attributes don't go all the way down, (2) that early usages are 'sensitive to future discovery', and (3) that in the case of genuine (as opposed to empty or fallacious) object-terms their reference is preserved across even the most revolutionary episodes of theory-change. That is, the term 'phlogiston' now survives as nothing more than the name for a nonexistent stuff that once figured (along with 'dephlogistated air') in a false theory of combustion while the term 'oxygen' has retained its referential good standing since we have adequate grounds to suppose that oxygen really exists and provides the best explanation of just what occurs in that process. This despite the fact that Priestley and Lavoisier – proponents of the two rival theories – conducted experiments that proved each correct by his own theoretical lights and which could arguably serve (on descriptivist grounds) to support Kuhn's case for the paradigm-relative nature of scientific truth-claims.[16] However such ideas will appear less plausible – indeed decidedly *outré* – if one adopts the alternative Kripkean approach and takes it that the reference of genuine (as distinct from factitious or illusory) natural-kind terms is truth-tracking and fixed by their referring to entities of just that sort.

Other instances are more problematic since they offer some leeway for reconstruing the object-terms or ontological commitments of an earlier theory in keeping with subsequent advances in scientific knowledge. Thus pre-Einsteinian talk about the 'ether' – the pervasive, intangible substance that was thought to explain the passage of light and other forms of electro-magnetic radiation throughout the universe – can be taken as roughly coreferential with post-Maxwellian talk about the 'electro-magnetic field'.[17] Although the ether was shown not to exist as a result of the Michelson-Morley experiments, still there is a case (so the realist might argue) for applying this retroactive principle of charity or for treating such talk as descriptively void but referentially on the right track. And again, while Black's 'caloric' hypothesis turned out to involve a false supposition – i.e., the existence of a likewise intangible fluid medium whereby to explain thermal conductivity and related phenomena – still it can be shown to have played a crucial part in developments that led to the theory of specific heat.[18] In these cases – the latter especially – any Kripkean approach would need to be qualified so as to incorporate at least some elements of the rival (descriptivist) account. Otherwise, of course, there could be no explaining how two distinct terms with different senses and with a role in radically different physical theories might nonetheless be construed as referring to 'the same' (or at least to strongly analogous) kinds of physical phenomena. Thus some philosophers have put the case for viewing the Kripkean approach not so much as an ultimate solution to problems thrown up by the Frege-Russell account but rather as a theory which allows – indeed requires – some additional descriptivist component.[19] Still they would mostly argue that Kripke's proposal is one that goes far toward resolving those problems and that it offers the best way forward not only for metaphysically oriented debates in philosophical semantics but also for epistemology and philosophy of science.

II

These ideas are widely contested – not least by adherents to the 'old' descriptivist paradigm – but have all the same exerted a powerful influence on recent philosophical debate. In particular they have led to a revival of causal realism (i.e., the claim that certain kinds of object necessarily and of their very nature possess certain properties, dispositions or causal powers) for which a main source is the Kripkean treatment of issues in modal logic. Other thinkers – Putnam chief among them – have shown more willingness than Kripke himself to press the argument in this direction. Thus Putnam has proposed a number of ingenious thought-experiments designed to drive home the realist point that meanings 'just ain't in the head'.[20] That is to say, what fixes the truth-conditions for our various statements concerning the physical world is not the range of descriptive criteria by which we pick out objects of this or that kind, but rather the existence of just such objects with just such uniquely identifying structures and properties. The best-known case has to do with a space-traveller from Earth to Twin-Earth who finds, on arrival, that everything looks the same as back home, including the existence of large quantities of water which fills up the lakes, falls as rain, boils and freezes at identical temperatures, etc. The only difference is that – unbeknownst to him – Twin-Earth 'water' (as referred to by the natives) has the molecular constitution XYZ, rather than H_2O.[21] So when the traveller exclaims with evident delight 'Lots of water around here!' he must surely be thought to have got it wrong – to have been misled by superficial or phenomenal appearances – since the stuff in question is *not* the kind of stuff that he and other Earthlings standardly (correctly) refer to as 'water'. And of course the scenario can be turned around by supposing a traveller from Twin-Earth to visit Earth and likewise misidentify Earthian 'water' as just the same stuff that exists in such abundance back home, unaware as she is – not having performed the requisite chemical analysis – that this stuff is in fact H_2O and not XYZ.

There are many variations on a kindred theme in the recent literature, some (like Putnam's) designed to refine, extend and reinforce the basic realist point while others – as I have said – adopt a more qualified approach by attempting to accommodate certain arguments from the descriptivist quarter. Then again, philosophers like Tyler Burge have argued that there is no reason in principle to restrict the Kripke-Putnam approach to natural kinds such as tigers, acids, gold, water or electrons. For the same considerations should apply just as well to artefacts or objects that don't occur naturally but which, nonetheless, have their reference fixed through an inaugural act of naming and thereafter passed down through a communal 'chain' of transmission that ensures a sufficient degree of continuity despite any shifts in their range of descriptive criteria.[22] This is not to say – crucially – that the correct usage of such terms depends on the individual speaker's possessing an expert or scientific grasp of what it is that uniquely identifies the object concerned. Thus the traveller to Twin-Earth is deceived by appearances *whether or not* he happens to know that Earthian water has the molecular structure H_2O. What makes him wrong about its Twin-Earthian counterpart is the fact that there are some experts back home – physicists or chemists – who do possess that kind of expert knowledge and to whom the wider community defers should any question arise with regard to anomalous cases such as 'heavy water' or borderline (say, highly polluted or otherwise non-standard) samples of the kind. Putnam calls this the 'linguistic division of labour' and takes it to explain how someone – like himself – who has problems in distinguishing beech trees from elms can nonetheless deploy those terms with a good degree of referential assurance.[23] Any issue with regard to their correct usage could always be resolved by appealing to the relevant specialist, i.e., arborological sources.

No doubt there is a sense in which arguments of this sort require that the basic position be modified so as to acknowledge the reference-fixing role of those various descriptive attributes or criteria that effectively decide what should count as expert opinion. All the same the Kripke-Putnam position is by no means undermined since it still provides the best means of explaining how elms and beeches – or Earthian and Twin-Earth 'water' – can indeed be picked out as distinctive kinds whose salient (or kind-constitutive) features are those implicitly referred to when competent speakers use the terms in question. Thus Putnam's not knowing how to tell the difference between the two sorts of tree is made up for by the fact of his knowing that others know, just as – from a chronological perspective – we can claim that people were referring to such things as *gold*, *water*, *acids* or *electrons* at a time when even the most expert sources could not have provided an adequate account of their constituent structures or properties. To this extent the 'linguistic division of labour' is the equivalent, in synchronic terms, of the idea that such early usages should properly be viewed as 'truth-tracking' or 'sensitive to future discovery'.[24] What is more, according to Kripke, it is a matter of a posteriori necessity that this should be the case, that is, a necessary truth about *gold*, *water*, *acids* or *electrons* that they possess just those structures or properties that they do in fact possess, whatever the range of differing descriptions applied to them since way back when the terms were first introduced. The same would apply to terms such as Twin-Earth 'water' if we suppose the possible world in question to be one where certain natural kinds do in fact (necessarily) possess a whole range of quite distinct atomic, molecular or genetic features. However it is crucial to Kripke's argument – at least from the realist standpoint – that we have to draw a line between *logically* possible worlds, i.e., those that we are able to conceive or postulate without contravening some transworld necessary axiom of logical thought, and worlds wherein the range of possible departures from our own is subject to various specified physical constraints.[25] For without this distinction there could be no warrant for the basic Kripke-Putnam claim, i.e., that a posteriori truths about the way things stand with respect to natural kinds (or this-world operative laws of nature) are also necessary truths in so far as they could not be otherwise in any world physically compatible with ours.

As I have said, such arguments have not gone unchallenged by philosophers within the analytic community. They are stoutly opposed by a sceptic like Quine who regards modal logic as a needless liability, rejects all talk about 'possible worlds' as a piece of sheer metaphysical indulgence, and adopts a naturalized (physicalist) epistemology that finds no room for such extravagant ideas.[26] On the other hand they are taken to the limit – and beyond – by a modal logician such as David Lewis who argues for the literal reality (as distinct from the merely hypothetical or counterfactual existence) of all those logically possible worlds that fall within the limits of rational conceivability or which don't involve any pair of contradictory propositions.[27] Thus, for Lewis, there is an endless plurality of worlds in which every contingent this-world truth is negated, so that (for instance) Julius Caesar didn't in fact cross the Rubicon, or kangaroos weren't in fact equipped with heavy tails which prevent their unfortunate tendency to topple forward at every step. These worlds are just as 'real' as our own but non-actual (and hence, to us, epistemically inaccessible) since they just happen not to be the world that we actually inhabit.

On this view we should think of 'actual' by analogy with indexical, deictic or token-reflexive terms like 'I', 'here', 'now' or 'today', that is to say, terms which intrinsically involve some reference to a given speaker at a certain time or place of enunciation. So just as there are manifold times and places that lie beyond our first-person indexical grasp, so likewise there are numerous alternative worlds whose reality is in no way affected by the mere fact that they have not been actualized in our own experience or that of persons who share our particular world. To suppose otherwise – so Lewis suggests – is the kind of parochial prejudice that must ultimately lead to downright solipsism or the refusal to credit any reality other than that which we are able to cognize from our own spatio-temporally restricted viewpoint. He also points out that if we want to be realists about mathematics then we shall have to accept that there exist certain abstract objects and associated truth-values of which we can indeed have knowledge even though they belong to a realm that by very definition cannot be accessed by any quasi-perceptual means of epistemic contact.[28] And since mathematics is the best (most secure) kind of knowledge we possess there must surely be a place for

Lewis's real but non-actual worlds together with numbers, sets, classes and other such abstract entities. Thus we should not be over-impressed by any argument on commonsense (actualist) grounds that rejects the reality of all those possible worlds and, along with them, the only conception of mathematics that doesn't reduce to some form of shifty conventionalist or fictionalist doctrine.

Lewis is a brilliantly gifted exponent of what remains – as I have argued at length elsewhere – an exorbitant and hugely implausible hypothesis backed up by all manner of ingenious argumentation.[29] It is one that has its origins in Leibniz – the progenitor of possible-worlds talk as a device for spelling out the implications of modal logic – and which might be taken to find support (albeit from an equally exorbitant quarter) in the 'many-worlds' interpretation of quantum mechanics.[30] However Lewis-style 'realism' is a far cry from the arguments advanced by Kripke and early Putnam with regard to the fixity of reference across all worlds compatible with ours in the relevant (e.g., physical or historical) respects. That is to say, it exploits a certain strategic blurring of the Kripkean distinction between transworld necessary truths such as those of logic and mathematics and truths that hold good as a matter of a posteriori necessity, i.e., in virtue of the way things stand with regard to our actual world. The former have to do with statements that *could not possibly* have been falsified no matter how the laws of nature lay or how events turned out in our particular world, while the latter have to do with statements whose truth-value is determined – and their reference fixed – by just such intramundane laws and events. In short, what is distinctively *realist* about modal realism of the Kripke-Putnam type is its insistence on drawing that line and thereby preventing the tendency of thought to stray over into worlds of counterfactual supposition which acknowledge no constraints on the capacity of reason to conjure up any range of alternative 'realities' subject only to certain basic logical axioms, e.g., that of non-contradiction. For this leads to such a downright profligate ontology – such an endless multiplicity of worlds all enjoying the same ontological status – that it tends to undermine the kinds of counterfactual-supporting argument ('had x not occurred, then neither would y; therefore x was a causal factor in the occurrence of y') that play a central role in scientific, historical and other sorts of causal-explanatory reasoning.[31]

Indeed there is a sense in which Lewis's extravagant hypothesis comes close to Quine's likewise extravagant doctrine of ontological relativity, that is, his idea that the objects or entities posited by different conceptual schemes are as many and various as the schemes themselves, and extend all the way from brick houses on Elm Street to numbers, sets, classes, centaurs and Homer's gods.[32] As I have said, Quine takes a dim view of modal logic since it seems to involve unacceptable consequences, such as that if it is a necessary truth that '9 is greater than 7' then it is also a necessary truth that 'the number of planets is greater than 7'.[33] Yet of course the latter is a contingent fact about the way things stand in our particular region of the universe while the former is a truth-of-definition accordant with the rules of elementary arithmetic. In which case – he argues – we should stick to the first-order quantified predicate calculus and eschew the kinds of misconceived modal reasoning that lead to such unfortunate (logically repugnant) results. However this objection can be turned back – on the Kripke-Putnam modal realist account – by distinguishing the order of transworld necessity that applies to certain truths of logic and mathematics from the order of a posteriori necessity that applies to certain truths about the physical world that we actually inhabit. Moreover we can thereby resist Quine's conclusion that there is simply no difference, in point of 'reality', between the various sorts of object that have figured as posits in various (e.g., commonsense, mathematical, scientific, religious or mythical) conceptual schemes. For one could argue that this pyrrhic conclusion is forced upon him – in large part – through Quine's refusal to apply just the kinds of reality-preserving modal distinction that would allow a more adequate treatment of metaphysical, ontological and epistemological issues. Besides, his point about the number of planets – that modal locutions run into trouble when it comes to distinguishing necessary from contingent truths – is one that sits awkwardly with Quine's dependence on modal distinctions by way of enforcing just that logical point.[34]

That is to say, there is a sense in which modal logic – contrary to received opinion – has a fair claim to be more basic to the process of rational (truth-preserving) argument than the first-order predicate calculus on which Quine supposedly builds his case. For that case cannot hold up except on the assumption that there exist necessary truths (like those of mathematics) and contingent truths (like that concerning the number of planets) which have to be distinguished on pain of falling into gross philosophical error. Thus:

[g]iven that logic is concerned . . . with formulating principles of *valid* inference and determining which propositions *imply* which, and given that the concepts of validity and implication are themselves modal concepts, it is modal logic rather than truth-functional logic which deserves to be seen as central to the science of logic itself. . . . From a philosophical point of view, it is much sounder to view modal logic as the indispensable core of logic, to view truth-functional logic as one of its fragments, and to view 'other' logics – epistemic, deontic, temporal, and the like – as accretions either upon modal logic (a fairly standard view, as it happens) or upon its truth-functional component.[35]

All the same these advantages are thrown away if modal realism is pushed to the point, as in Lewis's theory, where it invites the Quinean charge of sheer metaphysical extravagance by maintaining the existence of all those non-actualized but equally 'real' (since logically possible) worlds. Indeed – as I have said – this argument comes out pretty much on a par with Quine's ontological-relativist idea that what is real *just is* what is 'real' (within a given conceptual scheme) for all that we can possibly know, judge or ascertain.

Nevertheless, Lewis has a strong case when he recruits mathematics in support of his modal-realist claim that there must be certain transworld necessary truths that go beyond anything knowable by means of perceptual acquaintance or epistemic contact. To reject this claim is to end up in the sceptical position of those (anti-realists mostly) who declare that 'nothing works' in philosophy of mathematics since we can *either* have a notion of objective, recognition-transcendent truth that would place it forever beyond our epistemic reach *or* a conception of mathematical knowledge that equates truth with our best methods of proof or verification.[36] In which case we should have to conclude that there exist a great range of well-formed but as-yet unproven theorems – like Goldbach's Conjecture that every number is the sum of two primes – that are neither true nor false since we lack (and might never produce) an adequate proof procedure. Or again, we should find ourselves driven to endorse the surely absurd conclusion that Fermat's Last Theorem was likewise devoid of an objective truth-value during the three centuries of intensive work before Andrew Wiles came up with his celebrated proof. More than that: we should be quite at a loss to explain just what it was that rendered previous attempts inadequate with certain ruling metaphysical preconceptions – most of all in Dummett's work – that it tends to adopt an across-the-board (no matter how logically nuanced) verificationist approach that treats such issues as largely irrelevant in comparison to its major thesis. Nevertheless – I would argue – they are of the utmost importance if we want to get straight about basic questions like the role of mathematics in the physical sciences or how it can be that so seemingly abstract a branch of enquiry could have offered so much in the way of applied theoretical, predictive and explanatory power. Thus, in Eugene Wigner's memorable words: '[t]he miracle of the appropriateness of the language of mathematics for the formulation of the laws of physics is a wonderful gift which we neither understand nor deserve'.[44] To which the anti-realist will standardly respond with some version of the sceptical dilemma, i.e., that we can either have a notion of objective mathematical truth that *ipso facto* transcends the utmost capacities of human epistemic grasp or a scaled-down conception whereby nothing counts as a truth-apt mathematical statement unless it lies within the compass of our knowledge or available proof-procedures. Yet this is no answer to Wigner's problem except in the scientifically and philosophically disreputable sense of treating that problem as one best shelved for want of any ready solution. What modal realism seeks to provide is an answer which respects the distinctive kinds of knowledge that pertain in the formal and the physical sciences and which also takes account of their distinctive relationship to issues of objectivity and truth. To this extent it offers a welcome alternative to the kinds of blanket anti-realist doctrine that have largely dictated the agenda of recent epistemological debate.

Such arguments need to be worked out in detail with respect to those specific areas of discourse – from the formal sciences (such as logic and mathematics) to the various natural-scientific disciplines – where a realist approach will necessarily involve different kinds of ontological commitment. That is to say, it will require a good deal of specific fine-tuning as regards the existence of objective truth-values and the issue as to how this claim can be squared with the possibility of our acquiring knowledge concerning them. No doubt there are deep philosophical problems here, especially – as sceptics are quick to point out – in the paradigm case of mathematics where there might seem to be a flat choice between objective or recognition-transcendent truth and knowledge as a matter of provability by the

and that might yet conceivably turn out to reveal a flaw in Wiles's reasoning.

III

Of course Lewis's argument would count for nothing with those, like Dummett, who take an anti-realist view of mathematics and other areas of discourse. On their account (as we saw in Chapter 1) there is no making sense of the claim that statements can possess an objective truth-value quite apart from our capacity to find it out by some empirical or formal method of verification.[37] Thus Goldbach's Conjecture – along with a great many others unproven theorems – would fall into Dummett's 'disputed class' of statements that are neither true nor false, as distinct from merely undecidable according to our best, most advanced or sophisticated proof procedures. This conclusion follows logically enough if one accepts Dummett's anti-realist case for the impossibility of recognition-transcendent truths, that is, his idea that any 'gaps in our knowledge' must entail the existence of corresponding 'gaps in reality'. Furthermore it is one that in principle applies across each and every area of discourse from mathematics, logic and the physical sciences to history and ethics. Thus it excludes any modal conception, such as Lewis's, which embraces not only a realist outlook with regard to abstract entities like those of mathematics and the objective (even if unprovable) truth-value of statements concerning them but also a belief in the reality of all those non-actual yet logically possible worlds and their various constituent features.

Now there is a lot to be said, so the realist about mathematics might feel, for Lewis's robust attitude in this regard and his insistence that if anything is to serve as a guide in such matters then it had better be our grasp of just what is required in order to make good sense of mathematical truth-claims. Yet she might well balk at the further liability introduced by Lewis's outlook of intransigent realism with regard to possible worlds and his suggestion that the case for mathematical realism stands or falls with that for the reality (as distinct from the logical conceivability) of any and every such world. Here again there is a sense, as emerged in the comparison with Quine, that by taking so extreme or ontologically profligate a view Lewis runs the risk of drowning the realist baby in the metaphysical bathwater. At any rate his version of realism is far removed from the Kripke-Putnam emphasis on distinguishing contingent from necessary truths and – among the latter – those that possess analytic (transworld) necessity from those that hold as a matter of a posteriori warrant. Only thus can the realist hope to produce the kind of argument that would challenge the case for anti-realism advanced by thinkers like Dummett, that is to say, an approach that treats every area of discourse as having no room for truth-apt statements whose objective truth-value transcends the limits of recognition or verification.

It seems to me that realism stands in need of such defence since we shall otherwise be wholly at a loss to explain a great many aspects of everyday as well as scientific knowledge and enquiry. Anti-realists often make much of the so-called 'argument from error', i.e., the claim that we can never be justified in asserting the truth of our current-best theories when we know that by far the greater proportion of scientific 'knowledge' to date has eventually turned out false, or else been shown (like Newton's theories of space-time and gravity) to possess only a restricted scope of application.[38] So why should we think that our own epistemic situation is in any way different from that which has prevailed up to now? However the realist can turn this argument around by remarking (1) that any talk of past errors presupposes our possession of other, more advanced or adequate truth-standards; and (2) that the recommended attitude of due humility concerning our present state of knowledge entails the supposition that we might yet be wrong according to (what else?) objective criteria of scientific truth and falsehood.

Thus the realist case is in no way compromised – indeed much strengthened – by renouncing any claim to what Nicholas Rescher calls 'the ontological finality of science as we have it'.[39] Moreover there is the 'no miracles' argument which holds that we should always go for the least far-fetched or credibility-straining explanation, and should hence be sceptical of any approach – like anti-realism in philosophy of science – which would make it nothing short of a miracle that erroneous ideas should somehow have produced such a wealth of accurate predictive data and successfully applied scientific results.[40] In which case, according to Putnam, we have good reason to believe that 'terms in a mature scientific theory typically refer' and that 'laws of a mature scientific theory are typically approximately true'.[41] This goes along with the case for 'convergent realism' or the claim that, even if our best theories so far

have fallen short of the truth, nevertheless they are demonstrably on the right track in so far as all the evidence points toward their having picked out a range of entities (such as 'molecules', 'atoms' and 'electrons') whose role is indispensable to further research. Thus science may be taken as converging on truth at the end of enquiry to the extent that its theories are increasingly borne out by the best evidence to hand.

The anti-realist might readily accept all this and yet maintain – on prudential grounds – that we had much better treat atoms and suchlike as useful posits for the sake of upholding some empirically adequate theory, rather than leap to the premature conclusion that 'atoms' actually exist.[42] To which the realist will once again reply that such objections miss the point since realism in philosophy of science is itself a candidate hypothesis to be judged – like scientific theories – on the strength of its explanatory virtues or its capacity to offer a plausible account of our knowledge of the growth of knowledge. That it does so better than rival hypotheses is a claim borne out by the above-cited range of arguments plus those various considerations from modal or possible-worlds logic which, as I have suggested, provide strong support for a causal-realist approach. That is, they explain how the reference of terms (including theoretical terms or names for 'unobservables' like atoms or electrons) is maintained across sometimes quite drastic episodes of scientific paradigm-change; how knowledge accrues through the discovery of ever more detailed microstructural or depth-explanatory attributes; how theories can turn out wrong (or only partially valid) with the advent of later, more advanced or better corroborated theories; and again – most crucially for the realist – how the truth-value of well-formed statements or hypotheses might always transcend our present-best knowledge or means of verification. In short, they offer strong grounds for maintaining that the burden of proof falls squarely on the anti-realist despite the current trend toward regarding anti-realism as something like a default position in epistemology and philosophy of science.[43]

It is unlikely that sceptics will be won over by any amount of argument along these lines, whether through scientific case studies designed to vindicate the claim of convergent realism or through the sorts of evidence that Putnam provides with his thought-experimental variations on the theme of naming, necessity and natural kinds. Anti-realism is a doctrine so deeply bound up

best methods to hand.[45] All the same the sceptic will be hard put to argue against all the evidence to date that we should take a purely nominalist, instrumentalist or fictionalist view of mathematical statements and treat their role in the development of physical theories as just a kind of lucky fluke. More plausible is the case for regarding such 'abstract' entities as numbers, sets and classes as having to do with our acquired capacity for generalization from the everyday experience of bringing objects under this or that system of counting or group membership.[46]

Of course it is then incumbent on the realist to explain how a conception of this kind – classically adopted by empiricists like J.S. Mill – might be reconciled with the objectivist view of mathematical truth as always potentially transcending the limits of human cognitive grasp. Hence, as I have said, the anti-realist claim that we have to choose between a plausible epistemic account on which 'truth' must be conceived as lying within the scope of human knowability and a strictly unworkable alethic account on which knowledge must forever fall short of objective truth. Yet it equally remains for the anti-realist to offer some convincing account of how one can adopt the view that 'numbers don't really exist' while assenting to the proposition that 'there are two prime numbers between 11 and 19'. Or again, they will have a problem in making the case that all statements about elementary particles should be viewed as nothing more than useful (instrumentally efficacious) fictions while nonetheless declaring with the utmost confidence that 'the charge on every electron is negative'. What does seem clear – despite these philosophic qualms – is that one cannot make sense of the history of the physical sciences to date except on the assumption that mathematics has played a chief role in that history and hence that there must be some intrinsic (however elusive or conceptually recalcitrant) relation between mathematical truths and truths about the physical world. Wigner gives voice to the widespread sense of bemusement in this regard when he writes that 'the enormous usefulness of mathematics in the natural sciences is something bordering on the mysterious and . . . there is no rational explanation for it'.[47] But his remark is less than helpful if taken – as sceptics would readily take it – to entail that no such explanation could ever in principle be had. After all, one need not be any kind of Pythagorean mystic or subscriber to Hegel's idealist doctrine that 'the real is the rational' in order to think that mathematics must have some explicable purchase on those various physical phenomena that it is able to describe, predict or explain with such extraordinary power and precision. The Kripke-Putnam approach via modal logic and the causal theory of reference offers a means of laying such sceptical doubts to rest by meeting them point-for-point across the range of current anti-realist challenges.[48]

However it is equally important, from the realist's standpoint, to maintain a firm sense of the crucial distinction between epistemo-logical issues on the one hand and ontological issues on the other. This applies in particular to arguments with a modal, counterfactual or 'possible-worlds' dimension – such as those discussed above – where the distinction is very easily blurred. For then – as we have seen – there is a danger that any confusion in this regard will turn out to license either a generalized scepticism concerning the very possibility of objective, recognition-transcendent truth or else the kind of promiscuous ontology that multplies world upon world of unactualized but nonetheless 'real' possibilia. In the rest of this chapter I want to introduce some pertinent ideas from the currently active and widespread interdisciplinary movement of thought which goes under the name of critical realism.[49] Those ideas will be taken up later on and developed in various related contexts of discussion. For the moment what chiefly concerns us – to repeat – is the distinc-tion between ontology and epistemology, along with the necessity of drawing it in such a way as to render compatible two (as it might seem) conflicting or contradictory claims. These are, first, that the truth-value of our statements, theories, hypotheses, etc., is fixed objectively by the way things stand quite apart from our best state of knowledge concerning them; and second, that veridical knowledge can yet be achieved through the kinds of reliably truth-conducive method and procedure developed by the various sciences.

IV

Clearly this whole issue turns on the question as to whether realists can put up any adequate (or non-self-refuting) argument to just that effect. Their best shot, it seems to me, is the doctrine of transcenden-tal realism (henceforth 'TR') which figures among the most basic tenets of the critical-realist project, and which sets it apart from most other present-day approaches to philosophy of the natural and social sciences.[50] This can best be explained by unpacking both terms, seeing how they fit together, and contrasting this specific usage of the phrase with other (on the face of it) similar proposals from theorists of various persuasion. 'Realism' I have discussed at some length already but will here characterize more specifically with regard to the present context of debate. It is the claim that there exists a real-world domain of physical objects, events, structures, properties, causal powers and so forth which decide the truth-value of our various statements or theories and which cannot be treated as in any sense dependent on our current-best or even future-best-attainable state of knowledge concerning them. It thus comes out very strongly against an epistemic (knowledge-relativized) conception of truth and very strongly in favour of an alethic (truth-based and objectivist) account of knowledge. This thesis may be qualified to some extent, e.g., as regards certain items (like transuranic elements, synthetic DNA proteins, or subatomic particles produced in supercolliding accelerators) whose existence is indeed a result of applied techno-scientific know-how. However – so the TR argument runs – their production is subject to various physical constraints (such as those of subatomic charge, chemical valence or molecular bonding) which define the range of potential realia and hence determine the scope and limits of effective human intervention. What is crucial here is the complex dialectical relationship between, on the one hand, those 'transfactually efficacious' laws of nature that depend not at all on our various kinds of controlled observation, experimental set-up, manipulative technique, etc., and on the other those non-naturally occurring (but equally law-governed) entities that show up under just such specialized, e.g., laboratory, conditions.[51] We can thus make full allowance for the role of human agency in bringing these developments about while nonetheless maintaining a realist position with regard to the scientific object-domain along with its intrinsic structural features, dispositional properties, causal powers and so forth.

Thus one chief sense of the term 'transcendental' in critical-realist parlance is the sense: 'pertaining to an order of objective reality and a range of likewise objective truth-values that may always in principle transcend or surpass the limits of human knowledge'. To this extent TR comes out firmly opposed to any positivist, empiricist, instrumentalist or other epistemic approach that would reject the idea of verification-transcendent truths, even if – as in some recent versions of the case – what counts as 'verifiable' is defined in terms of idealized rational acceptability or epistemic warrant 'when all the evidence is in'.[52] However there is a second, more 'technical' sense which goes back to Kant's distinctive usage of the term in his *Critique of Pure Reason* and which has to do with the conditions of possibility for knowledge and experience in general. That is to say, it involves a transcendental deduction which accounts for our capacity to acquire such knowledge or to have such experience in terms of certain strictly a priori intuitions or concepts (e.g., those of time, space and causality) that alone make it possible for the mind to impose an intelligible order on the otherwise inchoate flux of sensory impressions.[53] This was Kant's answer to Humean scepticism, or the philosophic 'scandal' (as he saw it) of a radical empiricist outlook that despaired of achieving any adequate solution to the problem of knowledge. Rather we should see that Hume's quandary need not – could not – arise if philosophy turned its attention to those constitutive powers or faculties of mind which enabled us to bring phenomenal (sensuous) intuitions under concepts of understanding. Where previous thinkers had gone so disastrously wrong – empiricists and rationalists alike – was in failing to observe this cardinal requirement, and hence falling foul of Kant's dictum that 'intuitions without concepts are blind' while 'concepts without intuitions are empty'.

Such was the 'Copernican revolution' that Kant claimed to have brought about in epistemology and philosophy of mind. On his account it marked the epochal switch from a mistaken, dead-end, scepticism-inducing concern with what reality is like quite apart from our knowledge of it to a scepticism-allaying concern with how reality must appear to us, given the various a priori forms and modalities of human knowledge. Thus, for Kant, the main purpose of transcendental reasoning is to deduce just that range of necessary presuppositions with regard to the structure of phenomenal experience that provide a common framework for our understanding of objects and events in the physical domain and also for our self-understanding as conscious, reflective beings whose identity depends upon our sense of enjoying a continuous spatio-temporal existence. This latter is what Kant refers to as the 'transcendental unity of apperception', i.e., the synthesizing power of mind which – however elusive its nature – must be taken as the basic precondition for any such awareness. Moreover it ensures that our phenomenal intuitions of space, time and causality *cannot but* correspond to the way things stand in reality since reality *just is* – so far as we can possibly know – the way it is represented through those pregiven forms of jointly intuitive and conceptual grasp. So knowledge must confine itself strictly to the limits of phenomenal experience if it is to have any hope of defeating the Humean sceptic, or of closing the otherwise unbridgeable gulf between an order of objective or mind-independent (hence unknowable) reality and whatever lies within our epistemic grasp.

To be sure, reason – as distinct from understanding – finds itself impelled to transgress those limits and to posit the existence of a noumenal domain (that of 'things-in-themselves') which by very definition cannot be known. Such is, once again, the transcendentally deduced condition of possibility for any notion we can frame – or any scientific theory we propose – with regard to the 'external world'. However it can serve only as a Kantian 'regulative idea', that is, a source of guidance or orientation for our various cognitive endeavours, rather than playing a constitutive role in the acquisition of knowledge. Hence the title *Critique of Pure Reason*, epitomizing Kant's point that where reason oversteps its appointed bounds – where it presumes to give knowledge of that which can only be thought – then it runs into all manner of dead-end antinomies or contradictions. That is to say, we can *think* of knowledge as aimed toward an ideal (limit-point) conception of truth at the end of enquiry but can never actually *achieve* such knowledge since it would bring us out on the far side of human attainability. Hence also Kant's claim to have resolved the Humean problem of knowledge by managing to reconcile a full-scale doctrine of 'transcendental idealism' with a somewhat less developed but still (as he argued) indispensable outlook of 'empirical realism'. In support of the former Kant enlists pretty much the entire conceptual apparatus of the First *Critique*. As concerns the latter his arguments are philosophically unconvincing and do little to support the alethic realist's claim that there exists both a mind-independent (objective) reality and also – in consequence of that – a great range of to us unknown (perhaps unknowable) truths.

Indeed, one can trace all the vexing dilemmas of present-day epistemology to the radical cleavage thus opened up between Kant's 'transcendental idealism' and 'empirical realism', along with his likewise problematical attempt to explain how the manifold of sensuous intuitions can be somehow 'brought under' concepts of understanding. Transcendental Realism breaks the hold of those dilemmas by adopting the alternative that Kant ruled out since he considered it another manifestation of the tendency of reason to overstep its proper (i.e., regulative) limits and lay down the knowledge-constitutive terms and conditions of cognitive enquiry. That is to say, it critiques Kant's critique by maintaining (along with the alethic realist) that truth might always – now as heretofore – transcend or surpass our utmost epistemic powers while nonetheless holding *this itself* to be a matter of knowledge borne out by the history of science to date and by our grasp of the complex dialectical process through which science progressively converges on truth under various determinate (e.g., material, techno-scientific and socio-economic) conditions.[54] This makes it 'transcendental' in the Kantian sense of deriving from thought about the very possibility of scientific knowledge and progress in general but also in the non-Kantian realist sense of allowing us to know – not merely 'think' – how such claims can be warranted or justified.

One source of its explanatory superiority in this regard is the fact that critical realism allows for an adequately complex or 'stratified' account of the relationship between subject and object, knower and known, or cognitive agency (in a strong sense of that term) and the various physical domains wherein that agency is exercised. Thus it makes a chief point of avoiding the kinds of deadlocked dualism that have taken such a firm and disabling hold on the discourse of epistemology from Descartes, through Kant, to the present day. This is where critical realism marks a decisive advance beyond theories – whether in the natural or the social and human sciences – which endorse some version of the standard dichotomy between causal explanations on the one hand and, on the other, approaches that emphasize the rational or normative character of scientific thought. That is to say, it makes due allowance for the constant, many-levelled interaction between physical processes, laws of nature and the various ways in which these become manifest through experiment, observation and theory.[55] Where much philosophy of science goes wrong is by ignoring this dynamic reciprocity between knowledge and the object of knowledge, and hence running into a familiar range of epistemological quandaries. Among them is the positivist fetishization of 'facts', 'sense-data', 'observation-statements' and so forth, as if these latter could be somehow disjoined from the kinds of theoretically informed observation or experimental set-up which allow them to emerge under certain physically specifiable conditions. Thus scepticism is merely the flip-side or reactive counterpart of a positivist dogmatism that allows no commerce – no room for this productive two-way exchange – between 'context of discovery' and 'context of justification'.[56] In which case logical positivism/empiricism can best be seen as the latter-day version of an argument which goes right back to Hume's drastic disjunction between 'matters of fact' and 'truths of reason', and which is sure to insert its sceptical wedge whenever philosophy falls into this way of thinking.

Of course such arguments have long been raised against the logical-empiricist programme, not least by those – like W.V. Quine – who swung right across to the opposite extreme of a radically holistic theory premised on the twin doctrines of the 'theory-laden' character of observation-statements and the 'underdetermination' of scientific theories by the best available evidence.[57] They also play a crucial part in Thomas Kuhn's paradigm-relativist claim to the effect that, in some rather ill-defined sense of the phrase, 'the world changes' for thinkers living before and after a major change in the currency of scientific thought.[58] However such responses merely exacerbate the problem by relativizing the 'truth' of any given statement at any given time to the entire body of presently accepted beliefs, conceived as extending all the way – in Quine's famous image – from those at the logico-theoretical core to those at the empirical or observational periphery. In which case no belief is 'immune from revision' since even certain axioms of classical deductive logic – like bivalence or excluded middle – might ultimately have to be abandoned under pressure from conflicting empirical evidence, e.g., quantum phenomena such as superposition or wave/particle dualism.[59] From a TR standpoint these post-logical-empiricist developments should be seen as so many symptoms of the deepening crisis in mainstream analytic philosophy of science rather than as pointing a hopeful way forward from the various problems bequeathed by Kant. Thus they purport to overcome the dilemmas of logical empiricism but only at the cost of embracing a Quinean doctrine of wholesale 'ontological relativity' which finds no room for normative criteria of truth, rationality and progress.

Hence the alternative critical-realist proposal: that we reject the various failed solutions to the problem of knowledge deriving from Kant's likewise failed attempt to square his cardinal theory of transcendental idealism with a fig-leaf version of empirical realism. Rather we should take the route which Kant was at great pains to close off, i.e., that of transcendental realism or the thesis that truth might always exceed the limits of present-best (or even future-best-attainable) knowledge while nonetheless providing the standard by which all truth-claims must ultimately be assessed. What makes this possible – so the argument runs – is the process of constant dialectical exchange between theory, observation and experimental practice which leaves no room for those scepticism-inducing dichotomies that afflicted the logical empiricist project and thereby opened the way to such developments as Quinean and Kuhnian paradigm-relativism. These latter doctrines can be seen to result from a sceptical overreaction to the fact that scientific theories always operate at a certain remove from the various complicating factors (e.g., interference by external forces or other kinds of disturbing influence) which can never be taken fully into account by any theoretical science. Such idealizations – like that of the frictionless solid plane or the inviscid and irrotational medium of fluid mechanics – are the price one pays (necessarily so) when advancing hypotheses beyond the limits of empirical verification.[60] For the sceptic about scientific realism or 'laws of nature' they show that this price is most definitely not worth paying since every increase in theoretical or causal-explanatory power goes along with a proportionate reduction in the way of detailed descriptive or phenomenological yield.[61] That is, there is a regular law of diminishing returns whereby any putative advance in the scope and generality of scientific theories must entail a corresponding loss of empirical precision or accountability. In which case – so it seems – we are better off adopting a sensibly scaled-down (e.g., 'constructive empiricist') approach that renounces any claim with regard to the existence of real-world objects, properties or causal powers and instead makes terms with the limits thus imposed on our capacity for forming well-grounded scientific conjectures beyond the strict limits of empirical warrant.

On this view TR entails the downright contradictory pair of propositions (1) that every well-formed (truth-apt) statement has its truth-value fixed quite apart from our best knowledge concerning it, and (2) that veridical knowledge is yet within our cognitive grasp – perhaps at the ideal limit – through various well-tried methods of enquiry. Hence – to repeat – the pyrrhic conclusion embraced by some sceptics and anti-realists, namely that we can *either* have (some notion of) objective truth *or* the idea of 'truth' as epistemically constrained and therefore ex hypothesi knowable, albeit at the cost of ruling out any alethic (i.e., objectivist) conception. Transcendental realism rejects this as a false dilemma and one that has taken hold only in consequence of the widespread epistemic fallacy according to which it is strictly inconceivable – a species of logical nonsense – that truth should somehow transcend or elude the compass of optimized human knowledge. Such arguments sometimes go a long way toward granting the force of opposed realist intuitions, e.g., in Crispin Wright's elaborately nuanced proposals for 'superassertibility' and 'cognitive command' as criteria that approximate objectivist truth while keeping it within certain specified epistemic bounds and thus fighting shy of making that last concession.[62] Indeed the chief effort of recent work in this 'moderate' anti-realist vein has been to offer formulations of what properly counts as truth in some particular area of discourse which avoid the (supposed) sceptical nemesis of alethic realism and yet make room for some middle-ground approach on terms that the realist might be brought to accept.[63] However – from a critical-realist viewpoint – this amounts to yet another (albeit more refined or hedged-about) version of the epistemic fallacy. That is, it stops crucially short of acknowledging (1) the existence of a real-world (mind- and theory-independent) physical domain along with its sundry objects, structures, laws of nature, causal powers, etc., and (2) the various kinds and levels of human interaction with that physical domain whereby its affordances show up under given (e.g., observational or experimental) conditions.

Thus there is no problem for critical realism in maintaining *both* an objectivist (alethic or non-epistemic) conception of reality *and* an account of scientific practice that makes full allowance for the role of human agency in revealing certain processes, laws and causal properties whose manifestation (though not their reality) depends on our procedures for finding them out. This exemplifies the close dialectical relationship between TR as a matter of straightforward ontological commitment and the 'stratified' conception of reality as that which affords knowledge of the world through various investigative methods and techniques. In so far as these claims appear incompatible or downright contradictory it can only be on account of that deep-laid dualist mind-set that has characterized so many episodes of post-Kantian epistemological debate. From this point of view critical realism looks like just another effort to square the circle, that is, to explain how we can acquire knowledge of objective, hence mind-independent, hence strictly unknowable realia. From a critical-realist standpoint, conversely, such objections go to show that philosophy has been on the wrong track – and subject to periodic outbreaks of scepticism or anti-realism – since Kant introduced his fateful split between the realms of phenomenal (sensory-cognitive) appearance and noumenal (knowledge-transcendent) reality. If we can only break the hold of this dichotomy – one that has defined the 'problem of knowledge' for philosophers of many, often sharply divergent, views – then we shall see that TR involves not so much a squaring of the circle as an adoption of just that approach whose ruling-out by Kant has been the cause of so many subsequent epistemological woes.

This also involves drawing certain modal distinctions, as between the orders of contingent ('might-have-been-otherwise') fact, laws of nature which apply (necessarily so) to our own world and all others that physically resemble it, and 'transworld necessary' truths – such as those of logic and mathematics – which cannot be conceived as failing to apply in any possible world. Such arguments have been developed chiefly by modal logicians concerned to explicate the logic of necessity and possibility.[64] They have also been deployed by philosophers of science in order to provide an account of causal explanation in counterfactual-dependent terms, that is to say, in terms of what would (or would not) have occurred at some other, physically 'nearby' world in the presence (or absence) of certain antecedent and explanatorily relevant conditions.[65] Critical realism gives added substance to these often rather recondite and speculative claims through its stratified conception of reality and its firm grasp of the various ontological distinctions involved. It also does much to clarify the issue between a hard-line modal realist such as Lewis, who takes all those possible worlds to coexist, i.e., to stand ontologically on a par with our own, and 'actualists' who hold that modal talk is a useful heuristic device but who refuse to endorse any such (in their view) wildly extravagant doctrine.[66] For Lewis, as we have seen, 'actual' is a token-reflexive (or deictic) term that functions – in a similar way to words like 'I', 'here', 'now', 'tomorrow' and so forth – always with reference to some individual speaker in some specific time, place or context of utterance. Thus to call ours the 'actual' world is no more than to locate oneself in relation to just that range of spatiotemporal coordinates, causal regularities and laws of nature that happen to obtain in just those worlds that are physically compatible with ours. What it cannot rule out – unless at the cost of extreme ontological parochialism – is the real (though for us non-actual) existence of all those other possible worlds which differ from our own in certain specifiable respects. So when critics of Lewis charge him with indulging a grossly inflated ontology – when they protest that his distinction between 'actual' and 'real' gives rise to some absurd consequences – he can turn the charge around and ask by what right they deploy modes of counterfactual reasoning if not with reference to something more than a realm of merely abstract, i.e., unrealized, possibility. After all – Lewis argues – such reasonings must lack any genuine explanatory force unless they are taken to quantify over various possible (for us non-actual but objectively real) worlds wherein certain physical constants and laws of nature are subject to a process of controlled thought-experimental variation. Otherwise philosophers are getting their arguments on the cheap, that is, exploiting modal-counterfactual talk in a way that – as Russell famously remarked in a different context – has all the advantages of theft over honest toil.

Transcendental realism offers an approach that enjoys those advantages honestly and gives substantive content to modal claims while avoiding any Lewis-style recourse to the notion of endlessly multiplied divergent counterpart worlds. This it does, to repeat, by drawing a firm and principled distinction between real ('transfactually efficacious') physical constants or laws of nature whose workings are wholly independent of our various investigative methods and, on the other hand, whatever shows up through the deployment of increasingly refined, e.g., technologically enhanced, observational means. Thus it has no need for the kind of far-fetched speculative argument that would assert the reality of worlds which somehow exist in a realm of possibilia spatio-temporally disconnected from ours and hence entirely beyond our epistemic ken. Rather, the TR distinction falls out between objects, structures, properties and powers that pertain to the nature of this-world physical reality, objectively conceived, and the extent to which these are actualized – made manifest – through modes of applied scientific research. That is to say, the 'actual' is not (as in Lewis) a localized subset of those various, equally 'real' counterpart worlds that occupy the entire space of logical possibility but a product of certain specific operations – involving (say) electron microscopes, radio telescopes or supercolliding particle accelerators – which reveal certain otherwise inscrutable aspects or constituents of physical reality.

So TR is quite capable of sustaining a modal-realist approach with adequate counterfactual-explanatory resources but without having to venture beyond the limits of a plausible ontology. It also provides a strong alternative to various kinds of social-constructivist or paradigm-relativist thinking whose current appeal derives chiefly from their setting up a typecast, reductively characterized 'realist' (or 'positivist') opposition which bears no resemblance to the complex, dialectical and stratified version of realism developed by Roy Bhaskar and others.[67] Indeed its critique of such grossly simplified conceptions – along with their burden of unresolved problems and antinomies – has been among the most striking achievements of work in the critical-realist mode. In so far as TR plays a crucial role in that project (for reasons explained above) it should be seen as a major contribution to present-day, post-empiricist epistemology and philosophy of science. What it also brings out to instructive effect is the extent to which epistemological issues are deeply bound up with issues that have often been conceived as falling more within the scope of metaphysics and ontology. To be sure – as Kripke makes clear – it is important to maintain a vigilant sense of these distinctions if we are not to muddy the philosophic waters or risk the kind of confusion that results from treating substantive questions with regard to truth, knowledge and reason as if they were questions of a purely linguistic or logico-semantic import.[68] Indeed that confusion has been one major source of the various sceptical and anti-realist currents of thought which I have surveyed in the course of my first two chapters. However it should also have emerged by now – most pointedly through this discussion of critical realism – that metaphysical and ontological issues cannot but arise in the course of epistemological enquiry, that is, when we come to ask about the grounds of knowledge in rational, normative and justificatory terms. For if this is the point at which scepticism and anti-realism most typically get a hold (by drawing the supposed epistemological consequences of certain onto-metaphysical theses arrived at by a largely logico-semantic route) then any adequate realist response must surely do better on just that disputed terrain. In which case, as I have said, its most useful resources are those to be found in a combination of modal realism with inference to the best (causal or counterfactual-supporting) explanation and a transcendental argument from the conditions of possibility for our knowledge of the growth of scientific knowledge.[69]

CHAPTER 3

'FOG OVER CHANNEL, CONTINENT ISOLATED': EPISTEMOLOGY IN THE 'TWO TRADITIONS'

I

Up to now this book has been very much focused on the kinds of epistemological debate that have preoccupied philosophers in the Anglophone community, i.e., those who have defined their agenda either from within or – like the critical realists – from a standpoint specifically opposed to certain aspects of the mainstream analytic tradition. What I intend to do here (as promised in my Introduction) is broaden the focus to take in some epistemological perspectives from outside that tradition which nonetheless reveal many interesting points of resemblance as well as contrast. My approach – as before – will be through a mixture of thematic (topic-based) treatment and discussion of individual thinkers whose work has been especially influential. The title of this chapter – a legendary London *Times* headline from the early 1900s – suggests something of the hostile or downright dismissive attitude toward so-called 'continental' (post-Kantian mainland European) philosophy adopted by many thinkers in the mainstream analytic tradition until quite recently. My purpose is, therefore, to examine the rift between these two philosophical traditions and also – more constructively – to point up the signs of a growing rapprochement around various issues of shared concern. In particular I seek to show how certain problems that arose within the projects of logical positivism and logical empiricism (problems most famously brought to notice by W.V. Quine) have been addressed with great vigour and resourcefulness by continental thinkers, among them Edmund Husserl, Gaston Bachelard and Jacques Derrida.

At present there are many signs that some such revaluation is at last under way. Thus philosophers like Dummett are looking afresh at the issue between Frege and Husserl as concerns the status of mathematical and logical truths while analytic revisionists – such as John McDowell – recommend a return to certain Kantian insights, albeit through a highly selective ('naturalized' or 'detranscendentalized') reading of Kant. I suggest that these overtures, though welcome, are still premised on a narrow view of what counts as an adequate – 'analytically' acceptable – approach to issues in epistemology and philosophy of science. That is, they still inherit something of the logical-empiricist prejudice against any kind of epistemological argument that seeks to explain both the 'structure' and the 'genesis' of scientific concepts or theories, i.e., the processes of thought through which they were arrived at as well as the justificatory standards (inductive, hypothetico-deductive, falsificationist, etc.) by which they should properly be judged. It was chiefly for want of this genetic or epistemo-critical dimension that analytic philosophy at length gave way to various reactive developments, among them Quinean 'ontological relativity', Kuhnian paradigm-relativism, Richard Rorty's far-out linguistic-constructivist creed, and the 'strong' programme in sociology of knowledge. What is needed – I suggest – is a fuller recognition that these problems have arisen very largely in consequence of the artificial divide between developments in post-Kantian 'continental' and Anglophone 'analytic' thought.

II

Few philosophers nowadays – at least among the younger generation – would subscribe to the idea of 'continental' epistemology as belonging to an intellectual world quite apart from the mainstream 'analytic', i.e., chiefly Anglophone tradition. That idea held sway for around a half-century, from the 1930s heyday of logical positivism, through its modification at the hands of the logical empiricists, and thence to those post-1950 variants of the linguistic turn (influenced by late Wittgenstein) that found no room for the overly 'metaphysical' tendencies of continental thought.[1] Thus the positivists – Rudolf Carnap most prominent among them – took a strong line against what they saw as the inflated rhetoric and the meaningless pseudo-statements that characterized the writing of thinkers like Heidegger.[2] Less stridently, they regarded Husserlian phenomenology as a movement of thought which bore certain limited resemblances to their own but which strayed from the path of empirical method and logical rigour into various 'psychologistic' excesses.[3] The charge was subsequently taken up by others in the broadly analytic tradition who tended to endorse Frege's criticisms of Husserl on just this point.[4] This despite Husserl's strenuous insistence that his was a rigorously argued project of transcendental phenomenology which entailed a radical suspension or putting-into-doubt of all merely psychological attitudes, beliefs or modes of thought.[5] Most often the quarrel was played out along familiar British-empiricist versus continental-rationalist lines, with Cartesian dualism (and its notion of privileged epistemic access) figuring as the chief source of philosophic error.

Later on it became something like an orthodox article of faith among logical empiricists that continental epistemology had gone off the rails when it followed Kant – or at least certain passages in Kant's First *Critique* – and construed the theory of knowledge as having to do with a priori intuitions, 'concepts of understanding', and suchlike dubious appeals to the supposed self-evidence of first-person apodictic warrant.[6] Rather epistemology should stick with the scientific method which eschewed all forms of 'idealist' (subject-centred) metaphysics and which sought to give an empirically grounded and logically adequate account of our various processes of knowledge-acquisition. Nor was this attitude very much changed when Quine launched his famous attack on the two last 'dogmas' of old-style logical empiricism, namely its espousal of the Kantian analytic/synthetic dichotomy (which he purported to expose as altogether vacuous in logico-semantic terms) and its cognate idea that observation-statements or predictions could be checked one-by-one against discrete items of empirical evidence.[7] Quine's conclusion – his radically holistic claim that any statement or theory could always be saved 'come what may' by introducing certain adjustments elsewhere in the total 'fabric' or 'web' of belief – was widely perceived as signalling the end of logical empiricism in its early, confident phase. Yet he still came out very firmly in support of the empiricist position according to which the proper business of philosophy was to emulate the physical sciences by adopting a thoroughly naturalized (behaviourist) approach to epistemological issues and avoiding all forms of 'metaphysical' obfuscation.[8] Among these latter – so the argument went – was the typically continental idea that epistemology must have to do with intuitions, concepts or thoughts 'in the mind' of this or that individual knower. Similar objections were later raised by followers of Wittgenstein who took the view that any such appeal must involve some version of the 'private language' (or privileged epistemic access) fallacy.[9]

Still it is likely to strike anyone who has come across mentions of the 'Duhem-Quine thesis' in epistemology and philosophy of science that there must be some link between the two ('continental' and 'analytic') traditions which finds no place in this stereotyped account.[10] Pierre Duhem was a French physicist and mathematician by training whose interests subsequently turned to the philosophy and history of science. Nevertheless it was a cause of great annoyance to him that his work was known chiefly for its contribution to these latter (as he thought them) inferior and secondary disciplines rather than accepted as having made an important contribution to the advancement of physics and mathematics. This is not the place for a detailed account of the various obstacles and setbacks that Duhem confronted in his professional career and his dealings with the complex hierarchical structure of the French academic system.[11] More to the point for present purposes is the extent to which (ironically enough) his work pointed the way toward later developments which pressed much further in a strongly historicist direction. Indeed, it has been often been construed as lending support to a form of Kuhnian paradigm-relativism that Duhem would scarcely have endorsed, even though it can plausibly claim warrant in certain aspects of his thinking.[12]

His earliest publications (during the 1880s) were devoted to expounding Duhem's conception of thermodynamics as the best prospect for a unifying general theory that would elucidate the basic laws of physics and chemistry. At this stage his thought already manifested some of the features that would characterize his later 'philosophical' turn, among them a disdain for ontological commitments (such as atomism) which went beyond the empirical evidence and – concordant with that – a fixed aversion to any form of 'metaphysical' realism which claimed to reveal the ultimate nature of things or the underlying causal powers that explained phenomenal appearances. That is to say, Duhem inclined very strongly toward a Machian (positivist) view of scientific method as best devoted to 'saving the phenomena' (i.e., the empirical/observational data), and not yielding hostages to sceptical fortune by advancing realist hypotheses that could not be established by reference to those same data.[13] This is one reason why Duhem's philosophy of science has met with a receptive response among thinkers like Quine who likewise adopt an empiricist approach that eschews any surplus ontological commitment beyond that entailed by our acceptance of a certain, pragmatically efficacious conceptual scheme.[14] On this view there is no making sense of the idea that a physical theory might be verified or falsified through a crucial or decisive experiment which tested it directly against the evidence. On the contrary: we can always save some attractive theory in the face of discrepant empirical results by adducing the limits of precise observation, by invoking alternative 'auxiliary hypotheses', or by redistributing truth-values and predicates across the entire 'fabric' of currently held scientific beliefs. Then again, we can always conserve some anomalous empirical result by abandoning a hitherto well entrenched physical theory or – at the limit – suspending certain axioms of classical logic such as bivalence or excluded middle.

Hence the 'Duhem-Quine thesis' according to which observation-statements (even the most basic) are ineluctably 'theory-laden' and theories themselves 'underdetermined' by the best empirical evidence. This thesis has been subject to widespread debate and a good deal of criticism, the latter chiefly on the grounds that it appears to undermine the rationality of theory-choice and to deprive science of any normative standard by which to adjudicate rival truth-claims or hypotheses.[15] Also it comes rather sharply into conflict with certain of Duhem's working principles as a physicist, among them his theory of thermodynamics as providing a unitary framework – or grounding rationale – for the entirety of physics and chemistry. Thus some commentators have put the case for decoupling Duhem's from Quine's contribution to the thesis which routinely conjoins their names and thereby rescuing Duhem from any imputation of wholesale paradigm-relativism or ontological relativity. On the other hand this tends to play down the very marked leaning in just that direction evinced by some of Duhem's later work. The issue is further complicated by his book *German Science* which was published during the First World War and where Duhem indulged in a bout of patriotically motivated (at times crudely chauvinistic) cultural polemics.[16] Here he champions the 'typically' French preference for a fine-tuned balance of commonsense, intuition and rational procedure as against the 'typically' Germanic style of rigorous axiomatic-deductive thought. In support of this claim Duhem calls Pascal to witness on the two supposedly distinct mentalities – '*l'esprit de Wnesse*' and '*l'esprit géometrique*'– which he (Duhem) takes to characterize the French and German approaches to science. That this account produces some passages of near-caricature on both sides must no doubt be put down to the pressures of historical and political circumstance. All the same it exhibits, once again, the curious tension between Duhem's convictions as a working physicist and his thinking about issues in the history and philosophy of science. Thus it is hard to square his attack on those supposed Teutonic excesses with his elsewhere fiercely maintained commitment to the 'Gallic' (Cartesian) ideals of mathematical exactitude and logico-conceptual rigour.

These problems are raised in their sharpest form by Duhem's strong-revisionist account of early modern science and, in particular, its supposed radical break with previous, medieval or scholastic modes of thought. This had much to do with his Catholic faith and with Duhem's desire to push back the intellectual origins of scientific modernity so as to establish its dependence on – and continuity with – those earlier developments.[17] Central to his argument was the claim that Renaissance philosopher-scientists such as Leonardo da Vinci were drawing on a rich heritage of thought handed down by hitherto marginalized thinkers, among them Jean Buridan, Nicole Oresme and Albert of Saxony. Most scholars identify a marked change in his thinking around the years 1904–5 when he converted from something like the then orthodox 'clean break' (progressivist and anti-scholastic) view to a conviction that this was merely the result of deep-laid secularist prejudice, an outlook typified for Duhem by the French Third Republic and its anti-clerical campaigns. Just how far his subsequent work was motivated by theological as opposed to strictly scientific or historiographic concerns is a matter of widespread debate among Duhem's commentators. According to some – those of a broadly kindred persuasion – it enabled him not only to reconcile the claims of scientific knowledge and religious belief but also to achieve a more balanced, less partisan cultural-historical, approach. Others have seen it as a product of deep-laid doctrinal adherence which led him to espouse an outlook resembling that of Paul Feyerabend for whom the issue between the church authorities and astronomers such as Copernicus and Galileo was one that could not – cannot even now – be settled on 'purely' scientific terms.[18]

This interpretation is doubtless wide of the mark, given both the depth of Duhem's historical scholarship and his meticulous respect for the methods and procedures of scientific thought. Indeed his revisionism works most often to opposite effect by finding those methods and procedures strikingly anticipated among thinkers who had hitherto been consigned to the remote pre-history of modern science. Still there is a conflict in Duhem's work between, on the one hand, his commitment to the values of rigour, objectivity and truth and, on the other, his attraction to an instrumentalist doctrine which has at least something in common with the ruse whereby Galileo was required to affirm not the truth but merely the 'empirical adequacy' of the heliocentric hypothesis.[19] Thus a chief characteristic of Duhem's 'uneasy genius' – to cite the title of a study by one of his co-religionist admirers – was the constant striving to maintain a balance between these disparate elements in his thought.[20] So likewise with his effort to reconcile the claims of philosophy and history of science, the former conceived as having to do with the long-run scientific 'context of justification', while the latter is taken to concern itself solely with conditions obtaining in the original 'context of discovery'.[21] Here again it would be wrong to think of Duhem the physicist-philosopher as in any way committed – like the present-day 'strong' sociologists of knowledge – to collapsing that distinction and, along with it, the very idea that scientific truth-claims are subject to assessment by standards quite distinct from those deployed by social or cultural historians.[22] Nevertheless his work has sometimes been put to the service of arguments like these on account of its textbook association with Quine's radically holistic approach and hence – though Quine would just as strongly disown the idea – with Kuhn-derived doctrines of thoroughgoing paradigm-relativism.

Thus Duhem is a figure of particular interest for anyone seeking to unravel the tangled history of 'analytic' and 'continental' developments over the past half-century and more. Another is Alexandre Koyré, a Russian native and post-1917 exile whose complex intellectual trajectory took him via Germany to Paris and then (after the Second World War) to jointly held teaching posts in the US and France. Koyré is a thinker who defiantly resists classification according to any standard academic division of intellectual labour. He is best known as a philosopher-historian of early modern science, although one whose intense speculative bent and vast range of interests (in mathematics, physics, cosmology, philosophy, theology and various traditions of Neo-Platonic and mystical thought) place his work far apart from mainstream approaches to the subject. Nevertheless his writings have exerted a powerful influence, not least through their incisive originality of mind and their expansive vision of philosophy of science as a quest for universal yet historically emergent and culturally salient truths. *Etudes galiléennes* (1939) is the foremost example of Koyré's capacity to provide the most detailed and exacting analysis of scientific theories – in this case theories of movement, stasis and inertial force – while drawing out the kinds of problem and paradox that have preoccupied philosophers from Zeno to the present.[23] It is also typical of Koyré's work in the way that it treats these issues within a larger metaphysical framework that takes them to involve fundamental questions such as those first broached by the conflicting claims of Platonic and Aristotelian ontologies. His preference for Plato is everywhere apparent, above all in Koyré's realist philosophy of mathematics and his antipathy toward empiricist conceptions of scientific method.

This heterodox approach also emerges very clearly in his historiographic researches. Like Duhem, Koyré rejected the conventional view that genuine scientific knowledge got started only with the passage from 'medieval' to 'renaissance' modes of thought, that is, through a decisive enabling break with the legacy of hidebound scholastic doctrine which prevailed in the earlier period. Thus he made no sharp distinction between the sorts of theological issue (such as realism versus nominalism) that had so preoccupied medieval thinkers and the sorts of metaphysical issue that continued to emerge with undiminished force when science took its turn toward a broadly secularized worldview.[24] This also had to do with Koyré's attraction toward approaches like that of the anthropologist Lévy-Bruhl who posited the existence of certain collective mind-sets (*mentalités*) or dominant modes of thought, knowledge and perception. It was further reinforced by his reading in nineteenth-century hermeneutic philosophy and his consequent sense of the problems involved in negotiating differences of cultural outlook or deep-laid metaphysical commitment. Yet he never went anything like so far in a sceptical-nominalist direction as later thinkers – notably Michel Foucault – who treated all knowledge and the objects thereof (in particular those of the life-sciences) as cultural constructs which had their place only within this or that period-specific 'discourse', framework or conceptual scheme.[25] Nor was he by any means a paradigm-relativist in the Kuhnian sense, at least if one interprets Kuhn at face value when he claims that 'the world changes' for scientists working before and after some major revolution in thought.[26] Such notions go clean against Koyré's belief that science is indeed a continuing venture of discovery and that differences of mind-set – however profound – can nonetheless be rendered intelligible from a sufficiently informed historico-philosophical viewpoint. Indeed it was Koyré's enduring realist conviction – no doubt influenced by his studies in scholastic philosophy – that scientific knowledge was properly aimed toward discovering the essence of things rather than contenting itself with merely nominal definitions. Again this brought him out sharply at odds with the then-prevalent mode of positivist thinking in Anglophone epistemology and philosophy of science which confined itself strictly to the analysis of statements in terms of their verifiation-conditions and which steadfastly eschewed any such recourse to otiose 'metaphysical' or 'essentialist' talk.[27]

Hence Koyré's uncommon receptiveness to certain previously marginalized currents of thought – among them Renaissance hermetic philosophies (Paracelsus), Romantic mysticism (Boehme) and various nineteenth-century Russian proto-existentialist ideas – all of which he sought to bring within the compass of a unified history of thought. At the same time – and despite this seemingly hybrid and unfocused range of enquiries – his chief motive was to vindicate the claims of mathematics and the physical sciences as aimed toward a truth which transcended the socio-cultural vicissitudes of time and place. One indicator here is the fact that, during his early years, Koyré pursued intensive courses of study with thinkers as diverse as Henri Bergson (in Paris) and the mathematician David Hilbert (in Göttingen), as well as with Etienne Gilson, the great scholar of medieval thought and theology. This clearly impressed him with the need to go beyond conventional, academically defined areas of special expertise while nonetheless respecting those essential standards – of truth, objectivity and conceptual rigour – that characterized mathematics and the physical sciences. Another great influence was Husserl's project of transcendental phenomenology, which Koyré first encountered while still living in his native Russia and with which he continued to engage – even if (very often) from a sharply dissenting viewpoint – throughout his subsequent sojourns in France and the USA. From Husserl he took the idea of philosophy as a rigorous, reflective, self-critical activity of thought which suspended (or bracketed) our commonsense beliefs and thereby sought to reveal the underlying, a priori, and hence universally valid structures of knowledge and experience.[28] Nevertheless Koyré – like Husserl himself – tended to oscillate between this austere conception of philosophy's task and an approach that acknowledged its ultimate dependence on modes of intuitive self-evidence which had more to do with our being-in-the-world as historically and culturally situated agents.[29]

This helps to explain the great impact of Koyré's work during that period of pre-war French intellectual debate when thinkers like Sartre were attempting a synthesis of Husserlian transcendental with Heideggerian existentialist phenomenology, and these in turn with an understanding of Hegel mediated by Kojève's strong-revisionist reading.[30] What Koyré most strikingly brought to this debate was a grasp of its sources much further back in the history of thought. Thus he criticized certain elements in Husserl's work, among them the strain of transcendental idealism which emerged most clearly in the *Cartesian Meditations* and which struck him as a falling-away from the vocation of rigorous, scientifically disciplined enquiry.[31] In making this argument Koyré had recourse not only to the evidence of modern (post-Galilean) scientific thought but also to the Thomist theological tradition which likewise – albeit for different reasons – rejected any notion of human knowledge (even at the limit of idealized rational acceptability) as the ultimate arbiter of truth. Here again one can see how the productive tensions in Koyré's thought were also a source of its greatest strength at a time when philosophy was torn between various competing and (on their own terms) irreconcilable tendencies. Koyré was a realist in so far as he maintained – in company with some medieval thinkers – that science could deliver objective knowledge of a mind-independent physical reality. Moreover – and to this extent at least he agreed with Aristotle – that reality consisted of objects, properties and causal powers whose essential nature was such as to determine whether or not scientific enquiry was on the right track.

Thus Koyré's epistemological approach was squarely opposed to any form of instrumentalist thinking – like that of Duhem – which relativized truth to the powers and capacities of humanly attainable knowledge. That is to say, he shared Duhem's great aim of reawakening philosophers to the range and vitality of medieval thought, while stressing just the opposite (realist) aspects of what he took to constitute its chief and enduring legacy. Still Koyré never ceased to emphasize that scientific knowledge always had recourse to a far greater range of sources, analogues and modes of comprehension than could ever be explained by a doctrinaire adherence to the precepts of scientific positivism. Hence his attraction to hermeneutic approaches, among them Wilhelm Dilthey's idea of those different 'worldviews' or *Weltanschauungen* which at the deepest level shape our conception of physical reality. Along with this went his claim that modern science had by no means shed its 'metaphysical' commitments – as argued by hard-line positivists – but on the contrary continued to enlist such resources so as to render its truth-claims and theories intelligible.[32] At the same time Koyré held out firmly against the kind of instrumentalist approach that resulted not only from Duhem's strain of theologico-metaphysical thinking but also – strangely enough – from the outlook of radical empiricism adopted by a hard-line physicalist such as Quine with whom his name is routinely conjoined in discussions of the 'Duhem-Quine' thesis concerning the underdetermination of theory by empirical evidence and the theory-laden character of empirical observation-statements. What enabled Koyré to avoid this paradigm-relativist upshot was his espousal of a basically Platonist outlook which aspired to transcend the epistemic contingencies of scientific knowledge at this or that stage in its advancement to date.

No philosopher in recent times has done more to uphold the claims of scientific rationality and truth while taking on board such a range of arguments from (seemingly) opposed viewpoints. Thus his critique of positivism for its anti-metaphysical prejudice went along with his equally trenchant critique of those idealist – 'metaphysical' – currents of thought which paid insufficient regard to the manifest achievements of physical science. By the same token Koyré can now be seen as a thinker who did much to bridge the gulf between various emergent orthodoxies, among them the postures adopted by adversary parties to successive rounds in the so-called 'science wars' or 'culture wars' debate. These have typically pitched adherents to an outlook of hard-line scientific realism against advocates of a cultural-relativist or social-constructivist approach that would treat all scientific truth-claims as nothing more than products of this or that short-term ideological *parti pris*.[33] What Koyré held out was the prospect of achieving a perspective atop these particular kinds of academic or interdisciplinary dispute. Just how far he succeeded in that enterprise is a question that can scarcely be settled so long as the debate is conducted in terms that reproduce the same professionally motivated conflict of interests. At very least it may be said – on the evidence of his copiously detailed and rigorous enquiries – that Koyré's work points a way forward from some of the more sterile or deadlocked disputes in recent epistemology and philosophy of science.

III

No doubt this also has something to do with Koyré's complex intellectual formation through exposure to those various currents of thought encountered in the course of his itinerant early career. For there is – to repeat – something distinctly askew (at least in geo-cultural terms) about a faultline that is supposed to run between the European mainland and Anglo-America when in fact so many of the analytic founders from Frege and Wittgenstein to Carnap, Neurath, Schlick, Reichenbach and Hempel were natives of Germany or Austria. That their influence on Anglophone philosophy came about in large part through the intellectual diaspora created by Nazi persecution is of course a large factor here but one which should not be allowed to obscure the existence of deeper continuities.[34] Besides, it is now acknowledged – even by devoted students of Frege like Michael Dummett – that Husserlian transcendental phenomenology had a genuine claim to logical rigour and that its attempts to explicate the a priori structures and modalities of human knowledge and experience cannot rightfully be put down to any kind of psychologistic aberration.[35] Rather, what sets Husserl's project apart from the mainstream analytic approach is his seeking to account for both the 'structure' and the 'genesis' of knowledge, that is to say, both the element of 'absolute ideal objectivity' that distinguishes the truths of mathematics or logic and the process of reasoning by which such truths are arrived at through various stages and episodes of human enquiry.[36] So there is a line of thought that clearly links Kant and Husserl in the quest for some means of articulating truth with knowledge, or some way to overcome the problem – much discussed by recent analytic philosophers – of how one can reconcile a realist (or objectivist) conception of truth with an epistemology that brings such truth within the compass of human understanding.[37] The pyrrhic conclusion drawn by some – that this constitutes a strictly insoluble dilemma – is enough to suggest that analytic thinkers may indeed have important lessons to learn from Husserl's phenomenological researches.[38]

Thus current moves toward a certain rapprochement between the two traditions may be taken as a sign that analytic epistemology is beginning to question its erstwhile insistence on maintaining a sharp distinction between 'context of discovery' and 'context of justification'.[39] That is to say, it is now more widely accepted that issues of truth, knowledge and epistemic warrant need not, after all, be treated in rigorous quarantine from issues concerning the genesis of theories or the history of scientific thought.[40] There is still much resistance – understandably enough – to approaches which abandon that distinction altogether by equating 'truth' with the currency of belief at any given time and hence with certain dominant forms of social, political or ideological interest. Such ideas very often have their ultimate source in Nietzsche and their proximate source in Michel Foucault's ultra-sceptical 'archaeologies' of the natural and human sciences.[41] Still they find plentiful analogues in the more sceptically inclined branches of post-analytic philosophy where this particular strain of 'continental' influence is often conjoined with a pragmatist conception of truth as what's 'good in the way of belief' and a 'strong'-descriptivist approach to epistemological issues.[42] Hence the view that, since 'reality' is always under some description or other, therefore objectivity drops out of the picture along with the distinction between genuine knowledge and socially acceptable belief. However, these are claims that may be found on both sides of the supposed Great Divide and which have drawn much criticism on philosophic grounds from 'analytic' and 'continental' thinkers alike. Indeed one could argue that analytic philosophy in the wake of logical empiricism was left with few resources by which to challenge the kinds of radical critique advanced by sceptics such as Quine or paradigm-relativists such as Kuhn. What it lacked – in comparison with the post-Kantian continental tradition – was any adequate account of those various knowledge-constitutive modes of perceptual, cognitive and theoretical activity whose role had been so sharply devalued by adherents to the mainstream analytic line.

This is one reason for the marked revival of interest in Kant among philosophers (like John McDowell) who see Kantian epistemology – or at least certain aspects of it – as pointing a way beyond the unresolved problems with logical empiricism, notably its failure to provide any adequate normative account of knowledge.[43] In retrospect it is clear that the analytic turn against a priori truth-claims of whatever kind had much to do with post-Kantian developments in mathematics and the physical sciences. These included – most strikingly – the emergence of non-Euclidean geometries and then of a relativistic space-time conception that showed them to be not just logically conceivable (as Kant had allowed) but a basic component of our current-best physical theory.[44] Thus analytic philosophers have tended to treat Kant's claims about the a priori status of Euclidean geometry and Newtonian physics as a cautionary instance of what goes wrong when notions of intuitive self-evidence or apodictic warrant are accorded such privileged treatment.[45] Hence, no doubt, the widespread (though mistaken) idea that Husserlian phenomenology was likewise hobbled by its over-reliance on a method of 'pure eidetic inspection' that took no account of such limits to the scope of a priori reasoning in general. However it can more plausibly be argued – very much in keeping with Husserl's approach – that progress in these fields has most often come about through a joint application of intuitive, conceptual and scientifically informed modes of reflective understanding. Which is also to say that any doctrinaire veto on philosophy's attending to the phenomenological dimension of scientific enquiry is sure to result in a deficient grasp of the complex interplay between the various factors that make such progress possible.

So there is a strong case for thinking that one major cause of the much-touted 'crisis' in post-analytic epistemology is the failure or refusal of its precursor movements – logical positivism and logical empiricism – to take those factors into account. Whence the more extreme varieties of sceptical thought (such as the 'strong' sociology of knowledge) that have sought to exploit the credibility-gap between a narrowly empiricist or logicist conception of scientific method and the kinds of question that typically concern historians and sociologists of science.[46] After all, these developments are just as much beholden to Kuhnian paradigm-relativism and Quine's thesis of ontological relativity as to any influence from the 'continental' quarter. Indeed one could instance Husserl's great book *The Crisis of European Sciences and Transcendental Phenomenology* as the first to diagnose this widening gulf between, one the one hand, an unreflective and unself-critical positivism which lacked any adequate philosophical grounding and, on the other, a reactive movement of thought (again with its source in Nietzsche) which totally rejected the values of reason, truth and objectivity.[47] Husserl's was a long-range historical perspective going back to various nineteenth-century debates about the role of scientific knowledge and enlightened rationality *vis-à-vis* the claims of hermeneutic understanding or immersion in the 'lifeworld' of humanly intelligible values and beliefs. If his approach tended very often to vacillate between these two priorities it is nonetheless clear that Husserl – writing during the period of emergent Nazi domination in Europe – took a stance squarely opposed to any form of irrationalist or counter-Enlightenment reaction.

The same can be said of those Frankfurt-School critical theorists (such as Jürgen Habermas) who defend the 'unfinished project of modernity' against its current detractors by examining the various orders of truth-claim – or the different spheres of validity – that have separated out within the discourse of the physical, social and human sciences.[48] Thus, according to Habermas, it is vital to conserve the most important, i.e., critical and progressive, impulses of Enlightenment thought while deriving those emancipatory values from a theory of 'communicative action' based on the idea of free and equal exchange between all parties with access to the relevant (more or less specialized) information sources. In which case philosophy can take on board the whole range of anti-foundationalist arguments brought against more traditional forms of epistemology by proponents of the present-day 'linguistic turn' and yet maintain a principled commitment to the standing possibility of truth and progress in the scientific, ethical and socio-political spheres. This approach abandons the old subject-centred epistemological paradigm, but does so – crucially – without yielding ground to the kinds of cultural-relativist thinking that have often been advanced by followers of Wittgenstein or by those who appeal to 'language-games' or 'forms of life' as the furthest we can get in the quest for validating grounds, reasons or principles.[49] Again, as with Husserl, this project has some useful lessons to impart in the context of current Anglophone philosophical debate and – more specifically – when set against the widespread sense of a crisis afflicting epistemology in the wake of old-style logical empiricism. What it offers is a wider, more historically informed diagnosis of just those problems and a range of highly developed arguments for redeeming what was lost through philosophy's turn to inadequate (e.g., positivist) conceptions of knowledge and truth.

At any rate there is no warrant for the claim – put about by many during the latest renewed outbreak of 'science wars' controversy – that cultural relativism is a type of disease spread chiefly through unprotected contact with mainland-European sources.[50] In so far as there is any truth in this claim it applies only to a limited range of such sources, among them Foucault's genealogies of power/knowledge, post-structuralist claims about reality as a purely linguistic or discursive construct, and Lyotard's sweeping postmodernist pronouncements about the end of 'grand narratives' such as that of scientific truth at the end of enquiry.[51] Then again there is Heidegger's likewise sweeping diagnosis of modern techno-science as the predestined outcome of western (post-Hellenic) metaphysics and its drive to dominate nature and thought through an epochal forgetfulness of Being.[52] Yet such ideas, as I have said, have their close analogues in much that has transpired in recent Anglophone epistemology and philosophy of science, not least the somewhat improbable attempt – by Rorty among others – to enlist Heidegger's depth-hermeneutic approach in the service of a highly selective reading that tallies well enough with a homegrown pragmatist outlook.[53] Also there are various close affinities between the kinds of work produced by 'strong' sociologists of knowledge and hermeneutic thinkers in the Heidegger-to-Gadamer line of descent.[54] All the same the idea that post-Kantian 'continental philosophy' is chiefly responsible for this cultural-relativist turn is a claim that cannot stand up to scrutiny if one takes full account of its sources in Wittgenstein, Kuhn, American pragmatism, and other influences nearer home. Hence – to repeat – the growing recognition that partisan attitudes have tended to produce a grossly distorted perspective and indeed that some of the most powerful arguments *against* cultural relativism are due to thinkers in that 'other' tradition.

IV

Nor is this shifting pattern of response by any means restricted to the work of German philosophers and critical theorists. For there has also been a marked revaluation of French developments in epistemology and philosophy of science, including the work of two eminent philosopher-historians – Gaston Bachelard and Georges

Canguilhem – whose thinking can again be seen to cut across any simplified account of the analytic/continental divide.[55] Thus Bachelard adopts a critical-rationalist approach which lays chief stress on the capacity of scientific thought to achieve advances in knowledge through the critique of naive (commonsense) ideas and also of certain a priori intuitions and concepts to the extent that these have proved an obstacle to progress. In this respect his thinking clearly owes much to the mathematician and physicist Henri Poincaré who likewise considered such counter-intuitive developments as non-Euclidean geometry to have placed sharp limits on the role of a priori reasoning in science. At the same time Bachelard retains an interest in those processes of thought – individual and collective – through which scientific revolutions occur and which always involve some productive conflict between what appears self-evident to reason or commonsense perception and what constitutes a challenge to received ways of thought. Hence his various case studies of this complex dialectic and its working-out through the history of scientific paradigm-change. Where Bachelard's approach differs most markedly from Kuhn's is in stressing that such changes can always be justified – retrospectively at least – in terms of more adequate conceptual grasp and a definite advance in the ability of science to describe, predict or explain some given range of empirical phenomena. Thus once again – at risk of labouring the point – 'continental' philosophy of science turns out to provide strong grounds for resisting the cultural-relativist drift that has characterized some developments in post-1970 Anglophone thinking.

There is another side of Bachelard's work that may explain why this aspect has so far received rather less than its due share of attention. Here he explores the heuristic role of analogy and metaphor in episodes of scientific paradigm-change, that is to say, their capacity to produce insights which could not have been achieved without some creative-exploratory leap of thought whereby it was possible to express new concepts or hypotheses in a more-or-less familiar language. This aspect of his thinking might seem to promote a Nietzschean view of science – or of 'truth' in general – as nothing more than a host of sublimated metaphors and images whose origin has now been forgotten and which thus manage to pass themselves off as veridical concepts.[56] However Bachelard also insists on the process of 'rectification and critique' whereby such metaphors are progressively refined, developed and rendered fit for the construction of adequate scientific theories. Among his best-known examples is the cellular theory of organic tissue, one that started out as a metaphor with strongly marked affective connotations – including that of the beehive as an emblem of co-operative labour – but was then subject to more rigorous forms of conceptual elaboration. Or again, the tetrahedral image of the carbon atom possessed just the kind of intuitive appeal that enabled physicists to grasp it as a good working model, but then to move on – through stages of more refined scientific research – to a point where that model proved inadequate for their purposes.

Bachelard's work focused mainly on cases from the history of modern physics whereas Canguilhem – his student – specialized in studies of biology and the life sciences. Their approach may fairly be described as 'continental' in so far as it takes detailed account of the genesis of scientific theories or the kinds of thought-process that are typically involved in the production of scientific knowledge. To this extent it stands within the rationalist tradition, descending from Descartes, which conceives knowledge as involving the possession of 'clear and distinct ideas', arrived at through a properly disciplined exercise of a priori reason. However it also marks a break with that tradition by insisting that such clarity can only be attained through the constant critique of supposedly self-evident truths which may otherwise constitute an obstacle to scientific progress. Thus Bachelard firmly rejects any version of the Nietzschean ultra-sceptical idea that 'truth' is nothing more than a pale residue of those various metaphors, images and anthropomorphic figures of thought that philosophers vainly strive to overcome through their delusive conceptual labours. While such metaphors often play a formative role in the genesis of new theories that role is left behind – or their metaphoric status transcended – if the theory concerned proves to be knowledge-conducive and not a scientific dead-end. Hence the distinction between *histoire sanctionée* and *histoire perimée*, the former denoting those concepts and theories that can be seen to have made some real contribution to the progress of scientific knowledge, while the latter denotes those that have proved incapable of any such further advance.

This distinction finds a parallel in recent arguments put forward by Anglophone philosophers in the wake of logical empiricism who seek a more epistemologically nuanced account of the way that science may approximate to truth even in the case of theories that are nowadays regarded as empirically false.[57] Thus the 'phlogiston' theory of combustion may be taken to belong very firmly to *histoire perimée* – since the term 'phlogiston' is referentially void along with all statements containing it – while other theories may well have been superseded and yet lay claim to having played some crucial role in the development of later, more adequate scientific accounts. Among them are Black's 'caloric' theory of heat which we now take to be false in so far as it referred to a non-existent fluid and intangible substance that supposedly explained all heat-related phenomena, but which afterwards paved the way for the theory of specific heat and hence belongs to the history of 'sanctioned' (knowledge-conducive) hypotheses. Or again, we now take Einstein's Special Theory of Relativity – along with the Michelson-Morley experiments – to have shown pretty much beyond rational doubt that any talk of the 'luminiferous ether' is likewise referentially void and incapable of supporting truth-apt statements. Still there is a case for working on the principle that such talk can best (most productively) be interpreted as referring to the electro-magnetic field defined by Maxwell's equations.[58]

These particular examples have been worked out in detail by philosophers of science whose agenda is set by problems and concerns within the broadly 'analytic' tradition. Yet the fact that they converge so strikingly with Bachelard's epistemo-critical approach is further evidence that philosophy of science, like science itself, exhibits a pattern of progressive approximation to truth which cuts across any such merely parochial or academic lines of demarcation. Thus – in mainstream analytic terms – *histoire sanctionée* has to do with those developments that properly belong to the scientific 'context of justification' whereas *histoire perimée* is fit matter for a sociological approach whose sole focus is the 'context of discovery'.[59] On this account the history of false (discredited) theories can best be deployed by way of instructive contrast to the various well-tried procedures – of empirical testing, the framing of apt hypotheses, inference to the best explanation, etc. – that have marked out the progress of scientific knowledge to date. However what is most distinctive about Bachelard's thought is the way that it seeks to combine these perspectives and thus to explain both the provenance of scientific theories and the extent to which they have proven capable of further 'rectification and critique'. That is to say, it rejects any doctrinaire version of the 'two contexts' principle that would draw too sharp a distinction between, on the one hand, issues of method and justificatory warrant and, on the other, questions concerning how scientists have gone about their work under certain historically changing conditions. For it is Bachelard's claim – as against such a drastically dualist approach – that there is much to be learned about the process of scientific knowledge acquisition from a detailed study of the various spurs and obstacles to thought that have typified periods of pre-revolutionary crisis or incipient theory-change.

Here again it is worth noting how strongly this contrasts with Kuhn's paradigm-relativist notion that conflicting theories and truth-claims are strictly 'incommensurable' since any change of theory will always bring about a shift in the accepted range of putative physical realia along with some consequent revision to the standards of rational accountability and evidential warrant.[60] Thus Bachelard would clearly reject any argument for treating (say) Priestley's phlogiston-based and Lavoisier's oxygen-based theories of combustion as belonging to two such different 'worlds' – or Quinean ontological schemes – as to rule out any comparative assessment on rational or truth-evaluative grounds. Such ideas can best be explained as resulting from a widespread reaction against the kinds of narrowly procedural approach that sought to reconstruct the 'logic of scientific enquiry' from a standpoint of abstract or idealized method wholly unconcerned with questions beyond its strict philosophical remit. Indeed it was just this prescriptive narrowing of focus – most evident in the programme of logical empiricism – that provoked not only the Kuhnian thesis of paradigm-incommensurability but also the 'strong'-sociological approach whereby all theories, past and present, should be treated on a strict 'principle of parity' as regards their truth-content.[61]

Such claims go well beyond the sensible allowance that different scientists at different times and in different social-intellectual contexts have taken likewise very different views of what constitutes good, i.e., reliably knowledge-conducive, scientific method. Rather they suggest that we always do wrong to judge any past (presumptively false or discredited) theory according to standards which just happen to be those of our own, more 'enlightened' or 'advanced' state of knowledge. If these ideas currently find a source in the work of French postmodernist thinkers like Jean-François Lyotard or Heidegger-influenced hermeneutic theorists then they are just as much a product of the Wittgensteinian 'linguistic turn' or the Kuhnian doctrine of radical paradigm-relativism.[62] What they share is an outright rejection of that subject-centred or foundationalist epistemology which they take – albeit for different reasons – to have produced a long series of false turns or insoluble dilemmas. However it is clear from Bachelard's practice of so-called 'applied rationalism' (*rationalisme appliqué*) that thinking can combine a qualified acceptance of certain Cartesian precepts with a full recognition of the various ways in which it can be led into error through over-reliance on the witness of a priori intuitions and concepts.[63]

Bachelard therefore concurs with Husserl about the need to take account of both 'genesis' and 'structure' in any project of epistemological enquiry that seeks to explain the growth of scientific knowledge while also respecting those distinctive standards (of empirical warrant, conceptual rigour and explanatory power) which properly pertain to the scientific 'context of justification'. In this respect their thinking contrasts sharply with various sceptical-relativist currents within recent Anglophone epistemology, among them (as I have said) those that took rise from the demise of logical empiricism. Moreover, there is plentiful evidence in the writings of Jacques Derrida – especially his early work on Husserl and his Bachelard-influenced analyses of metaphor in the texts of philosophy – that Derridean deconstruction inherits something of the same epistemo-critical agenda.[64] At any rate it stands well apart from those other movements in recent French thought (post-structuralism, postmodernism and the Foucauldian 'genealogy' of knowledge) that adopt a highly sceptical approach to such issues. Thus when Derrida presses hard on various antinomies in Husserl's project – chief among them that of 'genesis' and 'structure' – he does so always with the utmost analytic rigour and with a keen sense of their taking rise from deep-laid yet conflicting necessities of thought which cannot be put down to mere confusion or failure of conceptual grasp. Likewise, when he instances the 'undecidability' of certain propositions with regard to the role of metaphor in philosophical discourse, this term is not deployed in a loose or ad hoc way (= 'vagueness', 'ambiguity', etc.) but explicitly with reference to Gödel's proof that any formal system complex enough to generate the axioms of elementary arithmetic will contain at least one theorem that cannot be proved within the system itself.[65] Such is also the 'logic of supplementarity' that Derrida finds everywhere at work in the texts of Rousseau and others, a logic that is pursued with no less rigour and tenacity for its contravening certain classical axioms, i.e., those of bivalence and excluded middle.[66]

To be sure there are various likely reasons for the widespread antipathy to Derrida's work among analytic philosophers, not least his extreme stylistic virtuosity and frequent recourse to oblique, intertextual or rhetorically complex modes of presentation. However it probably has much to do with ignorance of the relevant background, i.e., those developments in mainly French philosophy of mathematics and science that undoubtedly played a formative role in Derrida's early intellectual development. Also, like many 'continental' philosophers, he rejects the idea – the typically 'analytic' idea – that conceptual problems are most usefully addressed by tackling them head-on and without any reference to earlier thinkers who raised them in a different idiom or formal mode. Thus Derrida engages these problems through a close reading of canonical texts which poses questions of the utmost significance for epistemology and philosophy of language and logic but is apt to strike analytic philosophers as an oddly roundabout – even (some would say) a downright evasive – manner of treatment. Still this approach has some powerful arguments on its side, among them the case for philosophy as a continuing dialogue between past and present and (besides that) the sheer unlikelihood that some fresh-minted technical idiom should at last have resolved a whole range of recalcitrant problems which had hitherto defeated the best efforts of so many well-qualified minds. Also there is the fact – as I have mentioned above – that analytic philosophy has exhibited a marked tendency to treat those problems in such a way that they either resurface with undiminished force (*vide* logical empiricism) or else are delusively conjured away through a Wittgensteinian 'therapeutic' approach that most often leaves them firmly in place. What Derrida brings out to striking effect is the element of intellectual hubris involved in either conception and the need for a constant critical engagement with texts that continue to provoke questions unanswered by the latest swing of philosophic fashion. Indeed one could argue that the whole idea of a deep rift between the two traditions had its source in that narrowly positivist conception of scientific method whose reactive upshot was precisely the turn toward notions of truth as relative to some given paradigm, language-game, discourse or conceptual scheme.

V

Now at last there are signs, belated but welcome, that philosophers in the broadly analytic camp are beginning to question this skewed perspective on the history of post-Kantian epistemological thought. For it is increasingly clear that the deficits of logical positivism/empiricism had to do with just the kinds of philosophical concern that have figured centrally for thinkers in that 'other' (i.e., mainland European) line of descent. Among them – crucially – is the question whether issues of knowledge come down to issues of first-hand epistemic warrant. This was the question that divided philosophers like Neurath and Schlick in the debates around 'old-style' 1930s logical positivism, namely their disagreement as to how far scientific truth-claims could be cashed out in terms of a phenomenalist (sense-datum) language which nevertheless eschewed any recourse to 'subjectivist' or 'psychologistic' modes of thought.[67] It is also a question that has continued to preoccupy thinkers in the recent analytical tradition (such as McDowell) who have ventured the idea of a return to Kant – albeit a 'naturalized' or 'detranscendentalized' version of Kant – as holding out the prospect of deliverance from all our epistemological woes.[68]

However these suggestions are often advanced in a spirit of ground-breaking novelty as if nothing much had happened on the 'continental' side since Kant first proposed them, or as if the whole history of post-Kantian thought – from Fichte and Schelling, via Hegel, down to Husserl – represented nothing more than a local aberration from reputable standards of truth, rationality or common-sense warrant. Yet it is not hard to see how the problems with McDowell's revisionist reading of Kant – his strenuous attempt to dismount from the 'seesaw' of logical empiricism – are exactly those which first came to view in the quarrel between Fichte's subjective idealism (his idea of the world-constituting Ego) and Schelling's all-encompassing conception of nature as the ultimate source and ground of knowledge.[69] Recent 'rediscoveries' of Hegel by various analytic philosophers have exhibited a similar curious tendency to recruit Hegel for their cause as if by some fortunate alighting on a thinker whose work could be unproblematically enlisted without taking due account of its fortunes in that other (mainland-European) tradition.[70] What these overtures chiefly have in common is a failure to acknowledge that the issues in question have received a great deal of detailed, rigorous and philosophically acute treatment from 'continental' thinkers in the line of descent from Husserl to Derrida. Indeed there is something decidedly myopic about recent claims – on the part of these and other analytic revisionists – to have moved beyond the problems with old-style logical empiricism by invoking a duly 'naturalized' version of arguments from Kant and company in order to talk philosophy down from its delusions of epistemological grandeur. For if one thing is clear from a careful reading of Husserl and Derrida it is the fact that those issues cannot be set aside – or be made to appear just a species of 'metaphysical' delusion – through the standard (Wittgenstein-influenced) technique of treating them as so many pseudo-problems that result from our chronic 'bewitchment by language'. Rather they are problems which *necessarily* arise for any project of thought that attempts to resolve the classic antinomy between truth as a matter of 'absolute ideal objectivity' and truth as lying within the compass of attainable human knowledge.

Such is the issue that Derrida engages throughout his early writings on Husserl, an extensive and highly sophisticated body of work that is now beginning to receive something like its due share of scholarly and critical attention.[71] A crucial text here is his lengthy Introduction to Husserl's late essay 'The Origin of Geometry' where Derrida pursues the antinomy between 'structure' and 'genesis' which results from Husserl's attempt to explain the possibility of objective mathematical truths as somehow resulting from a sequence of discoveries with their own historical and culture-specific conditions of emergence.[72] Thus he shows that Husserl's entire project is riven by these two contradictory imperatives, i.e., the requirement that geometry should on the one hand be conceived as possessing a character of timeless, eternal, a priori truth, while on the other it involves the 'reactivation' of certain cardinal insights that have made up the history of geometrical thought from Euclid to the present day. In particular Derrida brings out the problems that result from any striving to secure the apriority claim when confronted with developments – such as non-Euclidean geometry – which would seem to place large obstacles in its way. That is, they demonstrate the existence of alternative geometrical schemes which undermine Kant's argument for Euclid as *the* great exemplar of truths arrived at through a process of sheerly indubitable a priori reasoning on the conditions of possibility for knowledge and experience in general. What chiefly distinguishes Derrida's approach to these issues is his raising them via a commentary on Husserl that acknowledges both the exemplary rigour of Husserl's various formulations and – quite consistently with that – the points at which phenomenology runs up against constitutive problems or aporias in its own undertaking.

This is also, as we saw in Chapter 2, a main topic of debate amongst analytic philosophers who ask (often without much hope of a satisfactory answer) how it might be possible to reconcile the claims of an objectivist or verification-transcendent conception of mathematical truth with those of an epistemic account that would bring such truth within the compass of existing or attainable human knowledge.[73] Here it is worth noting that Derrida takes due stock of the well-known exchange between Husserl and Frege on the status of truths in the formal sciences and the strict necessity – as Frege saw it – to redeem such 'absolute ideal objectivities' from any taint of empirical grounding or 'psychologistic' provenance.[74] Indeed I would suggest that Derrida's way of raising these issues allows him to advance far beyond the kinds of debate that have marked the subsequent history of mainstream 'analytic' responses to Husserl, from Gilbert Ryle's recycling of the standard 'psychologism' charge to Michael Dummett's avowedly more even-handed but still highly partisan (i.e., pro-Fregean) line of approach.[75] Thus Derrida is at once more alert to the tensions that characterize Husserl's project and more aware of the ultimate source of those tensions in the strictly inescapable conflict between 'structure' and 'genesis', or mathematical truth objectively conceived and mathematical knowledge conceived as accruing through a process of enquiry with certain clearly marked historical stages. This is why Derrida's reading of Husserl on the antinomy of 'genesis and structure' has a strong claim to engage these matters with greater pertinence and depth of conceptual grasp than is achieved by those analytic thinkers who content themselves with saying, *tout court*, that 'nothing works' in philosophy of mathematics.[76] Moreover his reflections on the problematic status of a priori truth-claims are pursued in a way that contrasts sharply with the approach adopted by philosophers who either reject such claims out of hand or arrive – like Putnam – at the pyrrhic conclusion that the sole candidate for a priori status is a trivially self-evident proposition such as 'not every statement is both true and false'.[77] For if one thing is clear from Husserl's immense labours of phenomenological enquiry – despite their intrinsic blind-spots or aporias – it is the need for thought to engage these problems in a way that adequately captures their deeper import for philosophy of the formal and physical sciences. What emerges from Derrida's work on Husserl is the impossibility of carrying through that programme announced by the logical positivists and empiricists, i.e., the attempt to treat such issues from a standpoint wholly unencumbered by Kantian (presumptively outmoded) epistemological concerns.

Just lately, as I have said, this realization has prompted some analytic philosophers to propose a return to Kant, albeit through a 'naturalized' revisionist reading which rejects his entire apparatus of transcendental argument and thereby drastically curtails the scope for a priori knowledge of whatever kind.[78] All that is required – according to McDowell – is a grasp of the basic Kantian point that there is simply no need for all those vexing dichotomies to get a hold (mind and world, subject and object, concept and intuition, logical form and empirical content) if we can just stop thinking in such obscurantist terms and dismount from the dualist seesaw. For we should then see that the mind's 'spontaneity', i.e., its active role in our various processes of knowledge-acquisition, is in no way separable from the mind's 'receptivity', that is to say, its (supposedly) passive registration of incoming sensory stimuli. Rather they are so closely interinvolved each with the other that in truth it is a mistake – and one with philosophically disastrous consequences – to speak of them as if those terms referred to distinctive powers or capacities of mind.

Thus logical empiricism can best be viewed as the latest episode in a long history of post-Kantian epistemological dilemmas that have always shown up in a similar form, i.e., in some version of the scheme/content dualism or the idea of knowledge as a matter of bringing sensuous intuitions under adequate concepts.[79] If we can just get rid of that bad Kantian legacy – resulting as it does from his unfortunate attachment to 'transcendental' modes of thought – then we can see our way clear to retrieving what is of genuine value about Kant's critical project, namely its refusal to concede even a notional separability between mind and world. Yet there are large problems with McDowell's argument, not least the fact that it rests this claim on a reading of Kant which merely substitutes one dualism for another, that is, Kant's talk of 'spontaneity' and 'receptivity' for his talk of 'concepts of understanding' *vis-à-vis* 'sensuous intuitions'.

Thus it offers no help in dismounting from the seesaw, especially since the passages in Kant's First *Critique* having to do with 'spontaneity' and 'receptivity' are among the most convoluted and obscure to be found anywhere in that work. Hence – to repeat – the various tortuous attempts to make sense of them by a long line of thinkers from the German idealists to Heidegger and (indeed) McDowell himself. My point is not at all that these efforts have been wasted because there is no genuine 'problem of knowledge' of the kind that Kant so vainly though valiantly sought to resolve. Rather it is to make the case that any subsequent attempt to resolve Kant's problem – and to do so on terms that avoid falling into the same dualist trap – had better go by way of a close engagement with that mainland-European tradition of thought wherein it has received by far the greater measure of detailed and philosophically adequate treatment.

No doubt McDowell is right when he claims that the dead-end of logical empiricism had to do with its failure – or adamant refusal – to address the sorts of issue that Kant exposed in those highly suggestive yet problematic passages of the First *Critique*. Yet there is something odd about the notion of returning to Kant as if *de novo* and without taking account of developments in that 'other' (continental) tradition. Of course this approach has much to do with the typically analytic belief that philosophical problems are there to be addressed (and hopefully resolved) quite apart from whatever has been said on the topic by earlier thinkers who lacked the resources of present-day linguistic or conceptual analysis. Hence the bemusement – or downright exasperation – of many analytic philosophers when confronted with Derrida's regular practice of devoting such minute textual scrutiny to recalcitrant passages of Kant or Husserl that cannot be construed in terms amenable to any such straightforwardly problem-solving approach. However it has become increasingly clear since the heyday of logical empiricism that the problems with mainstream analytic philosophy arose in large part through its refusal to engage with just the kinds of issue that have long preoccupied thinkers in the mainland-European line of descent. Most of all these concern the status of *a priori* truth-claims in mathematics and the formal sciences, the relationship between genesis and structure in matters of epistemological enquiry, and the question – so crucial for Husserl and Derrida – as to how any argument for the existence of 'absolute ideal objectivities' (such as those of logic and mathematics) can be reconciled with a plausible account of their discovery through acts of human cognitive or epistemic grasp. In each case, as I have suggested above, it requires only a shift of terminological register to see how similar issues have arisen in the discourse of post-1950 analytic philosophy. Yet there remained, until recently, a prevalent belief – on both sides – that these traditions of thought had become so completely divorced since that first parting-of-the-ways after Kant that the rift could not possibly be mended by any amount of good-willed ecumenical work.

Now at last there are signs that this situation is beginning to change, with thinkers such as Dummett proposing at any rate a partial reassessment of the issue between Frege and Husserl, and others – like McDowell – venturing the thesis that analytic philosophy might have got off on the wrong foot through its failure to heed the more important lessons of Kant's critical philosophy. However this rapprochement is still envisaged very much on terms laid down by the dominant agenda of an analytic discourse which may be thought to have lost its way in certain respects but which none the less reserves the right to decree what shall count as an adequate (analytically acceptable) reading of various alternative source-texts. Hence the strong element of revisionism – that is to say, of selective uptake and adaptive treatment – that has so far marked these cautious attempts to break with the old 'two cultures' mind-set. Hence also the impression that McDowell and others remain very much in the grip of those problems bequeathed by logical empiricism, even – or especially – when making the case for a more open-minded or non-sectarian approach. What is needed at this stage is a fuller acknowledgement that 'continental' epistemology and philosophy of science have explored certain areas – and yielded certain crucial insights – that possess their own distinctive standards of validity and truth. These regions of enquiry were firmly closed off from the interest of most analytic philosophers as a consequence of Frege's much-publicized dispute with Husserl and the resultant idea – propounded by Ryle among others – that the project of transcendental phenomenology was in fact just a species of thinly disguised psychologism.[80] In so far as that received wisdom is now being challenged from various quarters the prospects seem fair for a less biased and more philosophically productive engagement with the issues concerned.

CHAPTER 4

RESPONSE-DEPENDENCE: WHAT'S IN IT FOR THE REALIST?

I

In Chapters 1 and 2 I outlined a number of prominent debates in present-day 'analytic' epistemology – chiefly that between realism and anti-realism in their various forms – so as to provide readers with some useful points of orientation through this complex philosophical terrain. Chapter 3 took off in a somewhat different, 'continental' direction although I hope with sufficient references back to establish the various resemblances and contrasts between these two traditions of thought. What I propose to do now is develop some remarks from earlier chapters with regard to the idea of a response-dispositional (or response-dependent) approach to the kinds of problem encountered on our journey so far. The chief claim for this approach – briefly put – is that it holds out the prospect of a 'third-way' alternative, one that can satisfy realist demands for truth as something other (and more) than epistemic warrant or optimized rational acceptability while meeting the anti-realist's objections on all the main points at issue. I shall then go on (in Chapter 5) to reconsider some of these issues in light of yet another recently emergent theory although one that can trace its source back as far as Aristotle, namely the idea of a virtue-based epistemology. Thus the remainder of this book is very much focused on the various ways in which philosophers during the past decade-or-so have sought to find new answers to old and – as one might by now be tempted to conclude – strictly insoluble problems. My own (realist) view is nothing like so bleak since I put the case that they mostly take rise from a regular confusion between ontological and epistemological issues which cannot but lead to some such sceptical outcome.

Let me first offer a brief introduction to the topic presently in hand. Response-dependence is an idea that derives chiefly from Locke's discussion of 'secondary qualities' such as colour, taste and odour. These are distinguished from Lockean 'primary qualities' – objective attributes like shape and size – by the fact that any standard of veridical perception or accurate judgement concerning them must incorporate some reference to how they strike a normal (perceptually well-equipped) respondent under certain, likewise normalized ambient conditions. This argument has lately been extended to other areas of debate where it is thought to offer a promising alternative to hard-line 'metaphysical' realism (or objectivism) on the one hand and various kinds of anti-realist, constructivist, emotivist, projectivist or cultural-relativist approaches on the other. Thus response-dependence (henceforth RD) theorists have proposed its application to subject-domains ranging from philosophy of logic, mathematics and the formal sciences to aesthetics, ethics, sociology and political theory. In each case – so its protagonists claim – this approach has the potential to resolve a good many longstanding and hitherto deadlocked philosophical disputes. However, I argue, that prospect is illusory since when the RD 'quantified biconditional' (explanation below) is applied to areas of discourse beyond the perceptual domain it either reduces to a trivial (tautologous) truth or else remains open to various kinds of sceptical or anti-realist construal. This chapter makes the case with particular reference to issues in ethical theory and the philosophy of mathematics. Along the way it discusses the source of these problems in Kantian epistemology and locates them in relation to John McDowell's revisionist reading of Kant, one that has much in common with the RD approach. I also offer a brief survey of the various sceptical (e.g., Kripkean) and anti-realist (Dummett-type) arguments that have prompted this line of thought, arguments whose force it is unable to deflect for want of any adequate realist grounding. Hence – in the concluding section – my alternative proposal for critical realism as the best, most resourceful and promising way forward from these various hyper-cultivated doubts and dilemmas.

II

The topic of response-dependence is one that has lately been developed – with varying degrees of doctrinal adherence – in the work of

Mark Johnston, Alex Miller, Philip Pettit, Mark Powell, Peter Railton, Crispin Wright and others.[1] On the one hand, I aim to give a long-range perspective which shows how this debate has its origin in problems that were first raised by philosophers from Plato to Locke, Hume and Kant. On the other, I examine their proximate source in a variety of sceptical or anti-realist positions that have achieved prominence in recent (post-1970) philosophy of language, logic, mathematics, science and ethics. Among the main topics of discussion here are Wittgenstein's widely influential attack on objectivist conceptions of mathematical truth;[2] Saul Kripke's so-called 'sceptical solution' to Wittgenstein's paradox about rule-following;[3] Michael Dummett's verificationist approach to mathematics and other areas of discourse;[4] and RD theories of various type which seek to avoid excess 'metaphysical' commitments by replacing talk of 'truth' with talk of 'warranted assertibility', or by adopting a limit-point conception of idealized epistemic warrant.[5] What these all have in common is the basic premise that, quite simply, it cannot make sense to posit the existence of objective, recognition-transcendent truth-values for statements of the kind in question since *ex hypothesi* they would lie beyond our furthest epistemic reach and would therefore possess no determinate (i.e., knowable or specifiable) validity conditions. In which case – so it is argued – we had better abandon the objectivist conception of truth since it can only give rise to scepticism at the point where thinking comes up against this block in the path of epistemological enquiry. As Michael Williams succinctly puts it: 'if the world is an objective world, statements about how things appear must be logically unconnected with statements about how they are'. And again: 'to realise our vulnerability to scepticism we need only recognise the simple logical point that our experience could be just what it is *and all our beliefs about the world could be false*'.[6]

Response-dependence theory has evolved very largely as an attempt to hold the line against epistemological scepticism by examining sundry areas of discourse – from mathematics and the physical sciences to ethics, aesthetics and the phenomenology of perception – and attempting to specify just how far they involve some strictly irreducible appeal to the standard of normal or idealized epistemic warrant. In the latter sorts of case (prototypically that of Lockean 'secondary qualities') the relevant criterion is one that takes the form of a quantified and duly provisoed biconditional which decrees what shall count as an adequate response or an instance of veridical perception. Such a sentence might run: '*x* is red if and only if perceived as red by any subject with normally functioning visual and cortical apparatus under standard lighting conditions, i.e., at midday in average weather and with no local source of optical effects that might cause some aberrant or hallucinatory response'. Of course a similar sentence can be constructed for other secondary qualities, such as: '*y* is sweet if and only if it tastes sweet to any subject with normal gustatory responses and in the absence of anything that would mask or disguise its flavour'; or '*z* is loud if and only if perceived as loud by any subject with normally responsive auditory equipment and barring any localized sound-sources that would heighten, diminish or distort that perception'. Thus the biconditional is quantified in the sense that it applies to *all and only* those subjects whose responses fall within a given (normalized) range of perceptual sensitivity and can thus be treated as a reference-point for other, i.e., deviant or borderline cases. It is provisoed in the sense that it must also make room for those various non-standard ambient conditions that explain how even a perfectly normal or perceptually well-equipped subject may sometimes get things wrong – misrecognize a colour, misidentify a taste, misperceive the volume or intensity of a given sound – when exposed to stimuli that can be shown to interfere with the normal process of sensory cognition.

Indeed the main effort of response-dependence theorists has been to specify first what should properly count as a normal (or optimized) set of ambient conditions for a given perceptual judgement, and second what complicating factors need to be reckoned with as possible causes of error. Sometimes this latter approach takes the form of devising ingenious counter-examples, such as that of a genuinely red object – one that *would* appear red to a normal observer under standard conditions – but which the normal observer nonetheless perceives (say) as coloured purple or violet due to its irradiation with light from a concealed internal or external source.[7] However the chief purpose is to specify these various provisos with maximum precision and thereby establish a class of perceptions or judgements which, although they lack objective (observer-independent) truth-conditions, can nonetheless be treated as subject to normative standards of veridical warrant. By so doing, its advocates believe, one can make a strong start in heading off those sceptical arguments that have often traded – at least since Locke – on the subjectivity of colour-perception and other such secondary qualities. Moreover, it provides a firm categorical basis for distinguishing between areas of discourse where this approach properly applies and areas of discourse (such as mathematics or the physical sciences) where, according to the realist, our statements must be taken as possessing an objective truth-value quite aside from the vagaries of human perceptual response or the scope and limits of epistemic warrant.

This is where RD theorists take issue with some of the more extreme varieties of sceptical doubt that have left their mark on recent philosophic debate. Thus, for instance, Kripke's 'sceptical solution' to the rule-following paradox is one that accepts Wittgenstein's anti-foundationalist claim to the effect that any standards of 'correctness' in arithmetical procedure can only be a matter of communal warrant or of getting things 'right' in accordance with a certain accepted way of performing tasks like addition or subtraction.[8] So we will standardly take a pupil to have grasped the 'rules' of elementary arithmetic if he answers '125' when asked 'what is the sum of the numbers 68 and 57'. And, conversely, we shall take him *not* to have grasped those rules if he produces some different (to us unacceptable) answer. Yet he might just be working on a different 'rule' that diverges from *our* understanding of addition – or what is meant by the '+' sign – but which is perfectly consistent on its own terms and produces a whole range of other results that have just as good a claim to be 'correct' by his own (albeit heterodox) criteria. So likewise, if we ask him: 'continue the number-series 2, 4, 6, 8 . . . ', and he responds with the answer: '10, 14, 20, 28, 38', then we shall tend to conclude that he just hasn't grasped the rule for continuing a number-series, or the standards of objective arithmetical truth that would have made it correct to respond: '10, 12, 14, 16', and so forth. Yet here again – Kripke argues – there is no excluding the alternative possibility that the pupil is applying a different rule, one that – if asked – he could perfectly well describe, explain or justify in terms which we should find wholly unacceptable (since they formed no part of our own arithmetical practice), but which he took to be simply a matter of following the relevant rule. (In this case the rule in question would be: 'add 2 for every number up to 10 and then make incremental additions of 2 at each stage in the series after that'.) This sceptical outcome follows, on Kripke's account, from the twin Wittgensteinian considerations (1) that there is no fact or introspectible truth about what speakers *mean* by the plus-sign that could ultimately serve to adjudicate in such a case; and (2) that any first-order rule like that for addition must in turn have some higher-level rule for its 'correct' application, and so on through an infinite (vicious) regress which disqualifies any realist appeal to standards of objective truth. In which case the only possible 'solution' is one that again takes a lesson from Wittgenstein in viewing our communal practices, procedures or shared 'forms of life' as the furthest we can get by way of justification for maintaining our own against the pupil's idea of what counts as properly or correctly following a rule.

In Crispin Wright's case the chief motive for adopting an RD approach is the hope of finding some alternative to 'Kripkensteinian' scepticism that would register the force of such arguments while yet making room for a realist-compatible conception of those areas of discourse where, intuitively, truth cannot be just a matter of conformity with accepted practices and norms.[9] However there are clear signs that he, like other RD theorists, is still in the grip of that presumed dilemma which Kripke exploits in order to drive a sceptical wedge between objective truth and what conventionally counts as such for members of some given rule-following community. Thus Wright – whose earlier work was devoted very largely to Wittgenstein's philosophy of mathematics – continues to express certain doubts and misgivings with regard to the objectivist idea that arithmetical rules can be thought of as extending in a 'super-rigid' way into areas beyond the reach of our present-best computational or proof-theoretic techniques.[10] Others, like Alex Miller, are willing to go somewhat further in a realist direction but only to the point of a 'humanized platonism' – Miller's term – which again stops short of acknowledging that certain well-formed but unproven mathematical statements (such as 'Fermat's Last Theorem is true', uttered before Andrew Wiles came up with his celebrated proof) possess an objective truth-value quite apart from best judgement or optimized epistemic warrant.[11] Nor is it in any way surprising that they should show themselves reluctant to endorse such a claim, given both the provenance of RD theory – its strong links with Dummett-style anti-realism – and the fact that this entire line of argument is one that inevitably slants their approach toward the right-hand rather than the left-hand side of the quantified biconditional. Thus the formula is standardly set up in such a way as to privilege issues of perceptual response or judgements arrived under normal (suitably provisoed) epistemic conditions over issues of objective truth or those that might more aptly be addressed by the methods of the physical sciences.

Indeed – I would suggest – one reason for this strongly marked bias in their thinking is the fact that so much of the current debate centres on Locke's idea of secondary qualities, those that are taken to 'exist', by very definition, only in virtue of our proneness to perceive them in a certain way rather than in virtue of some real-world, objective, physically specifiable property or attribute. Yet even here there is good scientific warrant for saying that Locke got it wrong and that colour-properties *along with our perceptions of them* can better be explained by reference to various branches of physical science, such as optics (theories of reflectance, wavelength-distribution, photon absorption and emission, etc.) and the neurophysiology of visual perception. In which case Locke's whole notion of 'secondary qualities' can be seen as a product of the limited scientific knowledge available at his time, just as we now have reason to reject his sceptical conclusion with regard to the existence of natural kinds or the prospect of our ever advancing from 'nominal' to 'real' definitions in our knowledge of the physical world and its constituent features. So there is something distinctly odd about the RD manner of conducting this debate not only with constant reference to Locke on the topic of secondary qualities but also in a way that treats that issue as a paradigm case with important implications for 'areas of discourse' outside and beyond the standard Lockean range. Hence – I suggest – its predisposed bias toward meeting the anti-realist challenge in areas such as mathematics and the natural sciences on compromise terms that are just further grist to the sceptic's mill rather than on terms that the realist would accept as adequately answering the case.

III

This tendency to yield crucial ground to the sceptic even while avowedly rejecting their more extreme claims is one that emerges in many contexts of RD debate, from mathematics to the physical sciences, ethics and political theory. Of course the issues are posed somewhat differently from case to case, so that (for instance) a defence of ethical realism cannot proceed along just the same lines as a defence of realism in mathematics, logic or the formal sciences that challenges Kripke's sceptical 'solution' to the rule-following paradox. That is, any statement of the realist case with respect to some given area of discourse will need to take account of the precise sense in which truth for that discourse must be thought of as in principle transcending the scope and limits of normal response or accredited best opinion. Thus arguments for the objectivity of arithmetical truth won't carry over directly – or without some careful respecification of terms – into arguments for the objective character of certain moral judgements when based on a properly informed evaluation of acts, decisions and their real-world (human or other – maybe non-human animal) consequences.

I shall have more to say on this particular topic at a later stage. Meanwhile, let me note that despite the need for such an area-specific approach when these issues are engaged in any depth still there is a measure of common ground in so far as they each involve the basic question as to whether best opinion is *constitutive* of truth for this or that area, or whether – on the contrary – truth can be held accountable to standards that potentially transcend any such appeal to the deliverance of best opinion. This question takes on a particular urgency in the context of debates about legal authority and natural justice, as for instance in the recent (December 2000) intervention by the Republican-dominated US Supreme Court which effectively decided the outcome of a 'democratic' election in favour of the Republican presidential candidate (George W. Bush) who then turned out to have gained fewer votes in the key marginal state. On one view 'best opinion' is here identical with the highest *constitutional* authority in the land, that is to say, the Supreme Court and its ultimate (legally enshrined) authority to adjudicate in such matters. On another view there is still the further appeal to principles of natural justice or democratic right that would hold the Supreme Court's decision in this matter to have flouted those principles and hence to be in breach of its own constitutional warrant. So it is not just an opportunist play on words that associates the epistemological issue (what constitutes truth? best opinion or the way things stand in physical reality?) with the moral and socio-political issue (what is constitutionally just? a Supreme Court verdict or those standards of right conduct that properly apply in matters of collective human concern?).

Here it is worth remarking that another main point of reference for RD debate is Plato's dialogue *Euthyphro* where the question is precisely that of justice and whether or not there is any appeal beyond the deliverance of best opinion.[12] Euthyphro takes the view that what the gods approve is for that very reason morally good since the gods are optimally qualified to judge in such matters and hence to determine the criteria of goodness without possibility of error. Thus pious acts *just are* whichever acts the gods approve in their ultimate wisdom and there is simply no room for any challenge to their judgement that would hold them accountable to higher standards of goodness, justice or truth. For Socrates, on the other hand, pious acts are just those which intrinsically merit that description and the gods' approval should therefore be taken as a sign that they recognise virtue when they see it. So even if the gods are deemed to be infallible – always to exercise this absolute power of discriminating pious from impious or morally indifferent acts – still it is the case that their excellent judgement is measured by standards of objective moral worth rather than those standards being set or determined by their own excellent judgement. In Wright's words: on the Euthyphronist account the gods' evaluation 'enters in some constitutive sense into the determination of which acts are pious', whereas according to the realist 'gods are, by their natures, cognitively responsive to piety'.[13] Or again, as the realist would have it, 'the piety of an act is one thing, and the gods' estimate of it another, and it is merely that the gods are so fortunately endowed that the piety of an act need never elude them if they so choose'.[14]

It is not hard to see why this set-piece exercise in Socratic dialectic has become such a main reference-point for RD theorists, along with Locke on secondary qualities and Kripke on the rule-following paradox. What it brings into sharp focus is the question as to whether or just how far – for any given area of discourse – best opinion must be taken as constitutive of truth, or truth-claims subject to qualification through the various kinds of RD proviso that assert their dependence on normalized human (rather than godlike) perceptual capacities, epistemic powers, modes of evaluative judgement and so forth. Thus the issue turns – like much recent epistemological debate – on the realist's claim that truth is in principle recognition- and verification-transcendent, as against the anti-realist's claim that it cannot make sense to conceive of truth in this way since we should then be incapable of acquiring or manifesting any kind of knowledge.[15] For the realist truth is evidentially unconstrained, that is to say, 'conceptually quite independent of our standards of judgement' and something 'on which we impinge only in an (at most) detective role'.[16] For an anti-realist like Dummett, conversely, no statement is a genuine candidate for truth – or warranted assertibility – except in so far as we possess some evidence, criterion or proof-procedure which allows us to manifest an adequate grasp of its truth-conditions and hence a capacity to recognize and verify the statement concerned. Although Dummett is professedly no sceptic with regard to such matters his approach follows Wittgenstein (and thus lies open to the Kripkean sceptical challenge) in deploying this manifestation-argument, i.e., that the conditions for assertoric warrant are such as must always be expressible in terms of some accepted practice with recognized criteria for assigning determinate truth-values. For at this point the Kripkean can always respond, again with backing from Wittgenstein, that if indeed those criteria are all we have to go on – even in the case of elementary arithmetic or logic – then there is simply no answer to the rule-following paradox save the resort to his own sceptical-communitarian 'solution'. In which case – the realist will argue – we are confronted with a straightforward *reductio ad absurdum* of the anti-realist position and must therefore accept that nothing works in philosophy of mathematics except a full-scale, unqualified commitment to the existence of recognition-transcendent mathematical truths.

What the RD theorists attempt to do – roughly speaking – is split the difference between these antagonists (as between Socrates and Euthyphro) by supplying a duly provisoed version of the standard biconditional for each specific area of discourse where the issue is apt to arise. Thus they hope to avoid both the sceptical dilemma that supposedly results from adopting any full-fledged objectivist conception of truth and also the Dummettian idea that truth-values cannot possibly extend beyond the furthest limits of our power to ascertain or comprehend them. For there is, to say the least, something highly counter-intuitive about any argument that would count Fermat's Last Theorem neither-true-nor-false right up until the date when its proof was obtained and true thereafter just in case there are still competent mathematicians around and they don't suffer some outbreak of collective amnesia. Nor does it seem at all plausible that statements concerning unrecorded past events or events in some remote (epistemically inaccessible) region of the expanding universe should be thought of as lacking an objective truth-value just because we are in no position to find it out.[17] On the other hand RD theorists have an obvious investment in extending the range of candidate 'discourses' to which their approach can be suitably adapted or concerning which it has something useful to offer. Hence, as I have said, the marked tendency in RD debate to shift the emphasis from left to right of the quantified biconditional, with the result that more predicates can be treated as requiring specification in terms of normalized (or optimized) human response.

This tendency emerges most clearly in their treatment of ethical issues where some critics – Peter Railton and Ralph Wedgwood among them – have seen it as running dangerously close to the kind of subjectivist outlook expressed in Hamlet's cynical reflection that 'there is nothing either good or bad but thinking makes it so'.[18] That is, the typical outcome of an RD approach to any moral-evaluative predicate is to specify the conditions for its proper usage in terms which derive their normative warrant from the kinds of response that might be expected on the part of a suitable (morally competent) subject, rather than the kinds of behaviour, action, interpersonal conduct and so forth, that the ethical realist would surely regard as first-order candidates for such evaluation. Moreover, it tends to maximize the role of those distinctively human responses to the point where any argument concerning, say, the wrongness of wantonly inflicting torment on animals will be thought of as primarily a matter of our normal inclination to judge such actions wrong rather than a matter of the pain suffered by non-human sentient creatures. Thus the RD approach seems to come out in favour of a qualified anti-realist position in ethics which precludes the possibility that certain kinds of action are *intrinsically and objectively* wrong whatever the deliverance of best human judgement or the state of (maybe community-wide) consensus opinion. Hence Wedgwood's worry that it also licenses a view on which the highest constitutional authority in some given context – like that of the US Supreme Court – must be taken to determine (quite literally, to *constitute*) what counts as a valid judgement in matters of moral, judicial and socio-political concern.[19]

Of course the Euthyphronist can always rejoin that best judgement is *by very definition* responsive to the difference between right and wrong – as well as to the finest gradations on a scale of moral acceptability – and must therefore be considered incapable of error in arriving at a true evaluation. In which case, quite simply, the class of pious acts as defined by an objectivist about moral values would be extensionally equivalent to the class of pious acts as defined by someone (like Euthyphro) who construed moral values as dependent upon, or as constituted by, the gods' best judgement. However this conspicuously misses the point that we are here talking of human rather than godlike omniscient arbiters, which excludes any presumption of moral infallibility. Thus the extensional equivalence obtains only as a matter of stipulative warrant – 'best moral judgement *just is* what comes out right by all the morally relevant criteria' – and hence reduces to something very like a straightforward tautology. Otherwise the RD theorist can take a stronger Euthyphronic line and assert that moral attributes or predicates are response-dependent in a way that involves substantively specified human dispositions, priorities, concepts of social good, political justice, human or animal welfare, etc. This may seem to head off any charge that the quantified biconditional – along with its attendant range of context-specific provisos – is really nothing more than a trivially circular truth-of-definition disguised as an argument with substantive import for our thinking about ethical and social issues. But it then falls prey to the realist's other chief objection, i.e., that by filling out the right-hand side of the formula with all those *humanly specified* conditions and provisos the RD approach lends support to the idea that moral judgement is responsive to communally warranted criteria of right and wrong, rather than responsible to standards that may – in the case of certain communities – entirely elude their best, most developed capacities of moral thought. After all, there have been (and are) whole societies characterized by practices, beliefs, customs or 'forms of life' which are wrong or unjust not only in the sense that *we* presumptively more humane and civilized types are apt to consider them so but because they have involved an unacceptable degree of suffering, humiliation, class-prejudice, racial inequality, gender-bias, persecution of 'deviant' minorities, and so forth. Thus the RD approach is at risk of inviting the same sort of charge as is often levelled at 'strong' constructivist theories in the social sciences. That is, it tends to discount the reality of experience on the receiving end (so to speak) and thereby endorses a projectivist – or placidly consensual – account of moral values that exaggerates the role of accepted best opinion in determining what is right or wrong.

There is a similar tendency at work in other areas of RD debate where the biconditional is standardly set up in such a way as to privilege the claims of perceptual, epistemic or judgemental warrant over those of objective (recognition-transcendent or non-response-dependent) truth. As I have said, this results in large part from the fact that many thinkers who have adopted an RD approach have done so with a view to achieving some workable *modus vivendi* with the more extreme kinds of argument put forward by epistemological sceptics like Kripke or anti-realists like Dummett. In short, what these thinkers hope to provide is a suitably provisoed account of best judgement for each area of discourse which leaves no room for such doctrinal extremes since it acknowledges the full range of differing standards or criteria involved. So the task, as they see it, is to mark off those discourses at the objective end of the scale (e.g., mathematics) where the theory has least apparent purchase from those others (such as colour-perception) where it can plausibly claim to represent our best working intuitions in the matter. Or again, it is to specify just what differentiates moral discourse – where an objectivist approach has at any rate a strong measure of intuitive appeal – from a discourse like comedy where best opinion among people with shared cultural tastes and values is the most that we can reasonably hope for in the way of corroborative evidence. ('At first approximation', as Wright puts it, 'comic discourse is disciplined by the objective of irreproachability in the light of a community of comic sensibility.'[20]) Thus mathematics and comedy would stand at opposite ends of the scale and their truth-conditions or appropriate criteria would be distinguished all the more sharply through an RD analysis weighted toward the left-hand or right-hand side of the equation. However this is not how the approach most often works out since it carries an inbuilt right-hand bias – consonant with the basic RD thesis – which inevitably tends to shift the balance in favour of a treatment that attaches greater weight to the terms and conditions of human epistemic or judgemental response.

Hence Wright's puzzlement as to how we can conceive of a sentence as being 'undetectably true' unless there exists a rule which extends beyond the scope of our present epistemic grasp and is somehow able to confer truth upon it without 'any contribution from ourselves or our reactive natures'.[21] For, of course, when described like this, the realist position looks wide open to Kripke's sceptical challenge since it seems to entail a conception of truth as transcending our utmost possible knowledge and of rules as a kind of 'superrigid machinery' that churns out correct arithmetical solutions irrespective of whether we can follow them or not. To be sure, Wright evinces a certain impatience with Wittgenstein's 'sneers' about this so-called 'superlative conception of rules', perhaps because it has led to the opposite (Kripkensteinian) extreme of treating arithmetical truth as nothing more than a matter of assertoric warrant by the standards of some given – even if community-wide – consensus of judgement.[22] After all, as we have seen, it is just this drastically dichotomous way of conceiving the issue that has persuaded some thinkers – Benacerraf and Putnam among them – that 'nothing works' in philosophy of mathematics since we can *either* have the notion of objective truth (without the possibility of knowledge) *or else* the possibility of knowledge (without any notion of objective truth).[23] So one might expect Wright to adopt an alternative approach such as that of 'Gödelian platonism', i.e., a realist conception of numbers, sets, classes, functions, etc., which affirms their objective (recognition-transcendent) status while rejecting the wholly implausible idea that our knowledge of them must involve some kind of quasi-perceptual contact or mode of epistemic access analogous to our knowledge of objects and events in the realm of phenomenal experience.[24] It is just this strictly unintelligible version of the platonist argument – one with plentiful warrant from Plato – which has so bedevilled the debate about realism in philosophy of mathematics and other fields. However the advocates of response-dependence seem to have little time for the Gödelian alternative or indeed for any version of realism that would give due weight to the left-hand side of the quantified biconditional. For by so doing they would place sharp limits on the scope and relevance of an RD approach beyond those particular areas of discourse – like colour-perception – where it seems to work best.

Moreover, as I have said, there is room for doubt even here that a theory of (presumptive) 'secondary qualities' which leans so heavily on the Lockean account can claim any kind of *explanatory* power as distinct from its sheerly self-validating warrant as a truth about the logico-semantic or presuppositional structure of certain predicative statements. For instance, Mark Johnston – a leading early proponent of the theory – has more recently suggested that it cannot capture our standing intuitions in this regard since to say that something is red is *not* just to say that 'x is red iff [i.e., if and only if] x is disposed to look red to standard subjects in normal or optimal ambient conditions', no matter how detailed the range of provisos that are specified in that regard.[25] Rather, what it means is something more like: 'x is disposed to look red to standard subjects in standard conditions *because x* is red', where it is the redness of x – its actually *being* that colour – which explains why any subject with a properly functioning visual-cortical apparatus should see it that way in the absence of abnormal lighting or other such factors that would tend to distort or mislead their perceptual judgement. On Johnston's account, as Alex Miller remarks, 'it is impossible to a turn a sentence containing a true empirical explanation into an explanatory solecism merely on the basis of substituting expressions which are equivalent as a necessary and non-trivially a priori matter'.[26] And again: '[w]e cannot claim both that our concept of redness is response-dependent and that objects look red to standard observers in standard conditions because they are red. So, in order to hang on to the latter claim, we must jettison the former'.[27]

Miller disagrees and sets out to show that one *can* quite consistently hang on to both theses, i.e., that the quantified biconditional provides an adequate response-dispositional account of such judgements *and* that those judgements may be counted correct *because* object x has the property concerned, namely that which evokes attributions of redness in suitably qualified and circumstanced observers. However the issue between Miller and Johnston can be seen to turn more on their precise understanding of the RD thesis than on any radical difference of views with regard to its significance or purport. Thus, for Johnston, all that is needed is a rejigging of the quantified biconditional that would still give sufficient weight to the right-hand (RD-specified) list of provisos while taking more account of those left-hand properties (e.g., the redness of x itself) which normally evoke the appropriate response under suitable ambient conditions. In which case the amended formula would run: 'Subjects are able to sense a family of qualities had by a range of objects only if this empirical generalization holds: each of the subjects has a disposition which in standard conditions issues in the appearing of an object having some of its qualities (i) just when the object in fact has these qualities and (ii) partly because the object has these qualities'.[28] In other words their correctly (or reliably) *sensing* those qualities requires not only that the subjects concerned have the right kinds of sensory-perceptual disposition and bring it to bear under favourable conditions but also that their judgement is *objectively* warranted – x is indeed red – and at least partly explainable in terms of the physical qualities (or properties) in question. So where the normative element comes in is with the idea of 'sense' (like 'perceive' or 'recognize') as an achievement-verb or factive whose logical grammar entails the correctness of ascribing just that quality to just that object.

On the face of it this argument goes clean against any RD-compatible case for the constitutive role of optimized response or best judgement in determining what counts as a veridical perception of colour. Thus it seems to point toward a realist account that would eschew the phenomenalist appeal to Lockean 'secondary qualities' and insist rather that our best source of guidance in such matters is the kind of causal-explanatory account provided by the various relevant sciences of optics, neurophysiology, cognitive psychology and so forth. But this is not at all that Johnston has in mind, as can be seen from his casting the above-quoted passage in thoroughly phenomenalist terms, that is, as an 'empirical generalization' which holds for normal subjects under standard perceptual conditions and which involves their being reliably disposed to register 'the appearing of an object' with certain properties just so long as those requisite conditions are met. Besides, his whole way of framing the issue is one that retains the biconditional link or dependence-relation between properties and perceptual dispositions, and which hence leaves room for an RD construal albeit on modified (more realism-friendly) terms. So it is that Miller can work his way via a series of slightly reformulated biconditionals to the point where Johnston's 'missing explanation' argument turns out to entail no conflict with the RD thesis in something very like its original form. Thus '[t]he fact that standard subjects under standard conditions can sense or perceive the redness of things provides no reason for thinking that our concept of redness is not a response-dependent concept'.[29] However – to repeat – this conclusion follows only if one takes it that the 'missing explanation' concerned is the kind of explanation that must properly be specified in RD-compatible terms rather than (say) the kind of explanation that might result from applying our best current knowledge of optics, neurophysiology or even the phenomenology of perception as described in far greater depth and detail by philosophers such as Merleau-Ponty.[30]

IV

If Plato and Locke are the tutelary presences that loom largest in RD debate then Kant is another whose influence is strong even though his name very rarely crops up as an explicit point of reference. A more immediate source is McDowell's attempt to refurbish the arguments of Kant's First *Critique* in such a way as to talk them down from the heights of 'metaphysical' or 'transcendental' abstraction while retrieving what he takes to be their most important lessons in the context of recent epistemological debate.[31] Chief among these is the Kantian idea of knowledge as resulting from the interplay of 'spontaneity' and 'receptivity', the former conceived as the mind's active role in the process of knowledge-acquisition while the latter is thought of as ensuring its compliance with certain empirical constraints, thus placing due limits on its otherwise boundless freedom to interpret the world in accordance with its own subjective or projective devices.[32]

McDowell is insistent that we not mistake this active/passive dichotomy for anything more than a convenient *façon de parler*, one that is always at risk of betraying us back into bad old dualist habits of thought. Indeed it is just this notion of knowledge as involving an 'interface' or matching-up between mind and world, subject and object, or concepts and sensuous intuitions which McDowell holds chiefly responsible for most of the problems that have so bedevilled epistemology and philosophy of mind in the wake of logical empiricism. Yet ironically enough – as he cannot help but recognize – this whole post-Cartesian way of thinking is one that received its most powerful reinforcement from Kant's own description of knowledge as requiring that phenomenal intuitions be 'brought under' adequate or corresponding concepts. Moreover, Kant held that process to be somehow (mysteriously) accomplished through the exercise of judgement as a synthesizing power bound up with that of 'productive imagination', itself 'a blind but indispensable function of the soul, without which we should have no knowledge whatsoever, but of which we are scarcely ever conscious'.[33] So it was – through the influence of passages like this – that German philosophy after Kant embarked upon its drastically revisionist course, starting out with Fichte's subjective-idealist notion that reality 'itself' (and not just reality-so-far-as-we-can-know-it) could be understood only as the outward projection of a self-positing and world-positing Ego.[34] Still McDowell thinks that these passages may safely be set aside if we focus instead on Kant's cardinal point about the interplay of 'spontaneity' and 'receptivity' as strictly inseparable aspects of the process by which mind and world are always already brought together in the act of knowing. Thus to think of either as making an even notionally separable contribution is to fall straight back into the dualist fallacy which has plagued epistemology from the logical positivists, through Quine and Davidson, to those – like Rorty – who embrace a form of 'strong' descriptivist or constructivist doctrine which amounts to a version of Fichtean subjective idealism recast in present-day linguistic terms.

I have already (in Chapter 3) mentioned some of the problems that arise with McDowell's revisionist reading of Kant.[35] Chief among them is its constant tendency – despite his own reiterated warnings – to oscillate between the twin extremes of a 'spontaneity' that reaches all the way out (and thus makes world dependent on mind), and a 'receptivity' that reaches all the way in (and thus allows the mind no active role in our empirically acquired knowledge of the world). This in turn reflects the impossibility of separating Kant's doctrine of transcendental idealism from those other, supposedly less problematic components of his thought that McDowell – like Strawson before him – wishes to redeem through a selective reading of the First *Critique*.[36] However my main point here is that response-dependence theory has developed in part as a continuation of McDowell's attempt to overcome the subject/object dualism and, along with it, the 'problem of knowledge' conceived in terms of establishing some correspondence-relation between mind and world, concepts and intuitions, or truth-bearing statements and truth-making factual or objective states of affairs. This approach would be one that accorded a central role to the exercise of human judgement in its jointly 'spontaneous' and 'receptive' aspects, that is, a theory that made full allowance for the mind's active contribution while also acknowledging the kinds of constraint exerted by a due respect for the empirical evidence. It would therefore be an *epistemic* theory (like Kant's) in so far as it treated all truth-claims, hypotheses or empirical observations as ultimately subject to specification in terms of our various rational or cognitive powers and capacities. On the other hand – according to McDowell – it would allow no room for that trouble-making gap between 'mind' and 'world' that has pitched realists against anti-realists, or those who endorse an objectivist version of realism against those who fail to see how we can possibly ('realistically') conceive of truth as recognition-transcendent or epistemically unconstrained. These issues cannot arise, he thinks, so long as we accept the basic Kantian point that there is just no way of distinguishing the mind's 'spontaneous' contribution to knowledge from its 'receptive' openness to the world as given through various kinds of empirical experience. In which case the advocate of a duly naturalized (or detranscendentalized) Kantian approach has no cause to worry about the usual range of counter-arguments from a realist or objectivist quarter. Those arguments turn out to be just another version of that same old mischievous mind/world dichotomy which has skewed this debate at every stage from the post-Kantian quarrel between subjective and objective idealists to the current stand-off between epistemic and objectivist conceptions of truth.

However there is a fairly obvious sense in which McDowell – like Kant before him and the RD theorists after – comes down on one side of this quarrel and hence cannot make good his claim to have resolved it without prejudice to either party. That is, he adopts an epistemic approach wherein truth is dependent on the exercise of human judgement, and judgement in turn on those various powers or capacities of mind that involve various kinds of interplay between spontaneity and receptivity. Thus even in the case of 'purely' empirical knowledge – if indeed there can be any such thing – it is nonetheless essential, on McDowell's account, that spontaneity be always and everywhere in play if the givens of experience are to *count* as knowledge in any humanly intelligible sense. What McDowell wishes to avoid at all costs is the empiricist notion of the mind as somehow acquiring knowledge through its passive exposure to the incoming stream of 'sense-data', 'stimuli' or perceptual 'impressions'. Indeed – as I have said – he makes a strong case for thinking that this old, supposedly discredited, conception in fact lies behind a good many recent failures to resolve the epistemological issue, from the logical empiricists to Quine, Davidson and Rorty. Still there are large problems, from a realist standpoint, with McDowell's attack (following Sellars) on the 'myth of the given' as a chief source of all our epistemological woes.[37] For that attack gains much of its argumentative force from a counter-appeal to the mind's active role in synthesizing the data of experience through an exercise of judgement that must somehow be thought of (despite Kant's notable obscurity on the topic) as achieving the required match between sensuous intuitions and concepts. Yet this is to place the emphasis firmly on the 'subject' side of the bad old dualism, rather than on the 'object' side where realists would wish to place it. Nor can the issue be thought of primarily in terms of the dispute (as in Kant's day) between rationalist and empiricist theories of knowledge, or again – according to McDowell – between rival epistemologies that fail to recognize the joint contribution of 'receptivity' and 'spontaneity' in every act of judgement. For if one thing is clear about empiricist theories of knowledge from Locke and Hume to the present, it is the fact that they will always be squarely opposed to any realist or objectivist conception of truth that makes the truth-value of our observation-statements dependent on the way things stand with the world rather than on the way things stand with our sensory receptors, perceptual apparatus, Quinean 'surface irritations' or whatever.

Whence the famous (most would say abortive) effort by Schlick, Neurath and others in the Vienna Circle to construct a purely phenomenalist or sense-datum language that would restrict itself to reporting just those observer-indexed sensory episodes and eschew all reference to a notional 'reality' outside or beyond experience.[38] At any rate empiricism can scarcely be regarded as a strong candidate for ensuring that measure of objectivity or 'receptive' constraint upon the mind's 'spontaneous' powers which McDowell ascribes to it. All the more so since, on his own submission, receptivity cannot be conceived to exert such a needful constraining pressure *despite or against* those same spontaneous powers. Rather we should think of it as taking rise from within the sphere of spontaneity which is somehow capable of imposing this internal (yet seemingly external) check upon its own projective or quasi-autonomous world-creating powers. Thus it plays something very like the role that Kant attributes to the agency of moral will as a kind of self-thwarting internal imperative that issues from the subject as autonomous source of its own regulative precepts even though it bears down on that self-same subject as if from some source of moral authority outside and above the subject's merely 'pathological' wishes and desires.[39] McDowell at times goes pretty far along this path toward the kinds of paradox that Fichte exploited in his claim to push Kantian epistemology to its 'logical' (subjective-idealist) conclusion. 'If we restrict ourselves to the standpoint of experience itself', he suggests,

> what we find in Kant is precisely the picture I have been recommending: a picture in which reality is not located outside a boundary that encloses the conceptual sphere . . . The fact that experience involves receptivity ensures the required constraint from outside thinking and judging. But since the deliverances of receptivity already draw on capacities that belong to spontaneity, we can coherently suppose that the constraint is rational; that is how the picture avoids the pitfall of the Given.[40]

Yet then there seems no escaping the conclusion that reality is located *inside* that boundary which 'encloses the conceptual sphere', that is to say, something like the Fichtean idealist doctrine that reality is somehow a projection or creation of the mind's autonomous world-constitutive power. Thus in his efforts to avoid the empiricist 'pitfall of the Given' McDowell can be seen to swing right across – despite his contrary claim – to a standpoint that asserts the priority of 'mind' over 'world', or the need to acknowledge (as he puts it here) that 'the deliverances of receptivity already draw on capacities that belong to spontaneity'.

This may all seem pretty remote from the kinds of debate that typically preoccupy response-dependence theorists. That is, they tend to keep well clear of such 'old-style' epistemological issues and to press much further than McDowell with the claim that any question concerning the mind–world relation or the role of human judgement in various kinds of perceptual or cognitive deliverance can better be addressed through a careful analysis of the truth-conditions (or the duly provisoed standards of assertoric warrant) that pertain to this or that area of discourse.[41] Thus the RD theorists manage to avoid the sorts of complication that result from McDowell's strenuous attempt to retrieve what he thinks most valid and important about Kant's theory of judgement while rejecting what he sees as its unfortunate proneness to flights of metaphysical illusion. After all,

> Kant also has a transcendental story, and in the transcendental perspective there does seem to be an isolable contribution from receptivity. In the transcendental perspective, receptivity figures as a susceptibility to the impact of a supersensible reality, a reality that is supposed to be independent of our conceptual activity in a stronger sense than any that fits the ordinary empirical world.[42]

And yet, as we have seen, McDowell's effort to talk Kant down from these giddy heights is one that itself comes to grief – or runs into metaphysical quandaries of its own – when he tries to articulate just what is involved in the mutually dependent or co-operative interplay between spontaneity and receptivity. Thus it is scarcely surprising that the RD theorists (or those who have taken a lead from his work) should wish to avoid the kinds of problem that result from McDowell's halfway revisionist or moderately naturalized stance. Such is the idea that we can save a large part of Kant's doctrine – his 'empirical realism' and theory of judgement – while rejecting his 'transcendental idealism' and his notion of a 'supersensible reality' which somehow 'impacts upon' receptivity despite its belonging to a noumenal realm beyond the furthest reach of phenomenal cognition. For at this point, of course, we are back not only with the problem of Kant's comeuppance at the hands of Fichtean subjective idealism but also with the Platonist conception of truth as somehow both transcending our utmost powers of epistemic grasp and accessible to us through a quasi-perceptual mode of apprehension. So there is reason enough for the RD theorists to take a selective line with McDowell – just as McDowell does with Kant – and draw a discreet veil across those aspects of his thinking (precisely the Kantian aspects) which don't go far enough in their own favoured direction.

However, as McDowell rather acidly remarks about Rorty, 'cultivating a non-obsessive tone of voice isn't enough to show that philosophical obsessions are out of place'.[43] Thus the problems that are raised in Kant's First *Critique* cannot simply be made to disappear through a kind of linguistic-therapeutic counselling – whether in the Rortian or the Wittgensteinian mode – which declares them mere products of the 'bewitchment of our intelligence by language', or signs of our still being sadly in the grip of some old 'metaphysical' illusion.[44] That is to say, McDowell's wrestling with recalcitrant issues in Kantian epistemology is nonetheless important – and those issues nonetheless real – for the fact that it fails to deliver any answer that would (in Wittgenstein's famous phrase) 'give philosophy peace'. Nor can it be held that the problems are truly or effectively laid to rest when response-dependence theorists propose the use of a formal device – the provisoed and quantified biconditional – which claims to avoid all the well-known dilemmas of traditional epistemology while offering all that is required in the way of adaptability to various contexts of perceptual, epistemic or cognitive warrant. For this approach works out *either* as a trivial (self-confirming) thesis with respect to the assertibility conditions that normally obtain in those different 'areas of discourse' *or* as a stronger (but undeveloped) claim which, if pursued, would lead straight back to all the problems encountered by epistemologists from Kant to McDowell. Chief among them, I suggest, is the inbuilt tendency of any such epistemic approach – whether in the Kantian, the Kantian-revisionist or the response-dispositional mode – to relativize truth to the nature and capacities of human perceptual or conceptual grasp. What is thereby placed beyond rational comprehension (or supposedly reduced to a self-refuting paradox) is the claim that in many areas of discourse – mathematics and the physical sciences among them – truth must itself be construed as recognition-transcendent or epistemically unconstrained even though, as hardly needs saying, our knowledge of it must indeed be taken as subject to the kinds of limiting condition spelled out by epistemic theories.

V

It seems to me that response-dependence theory raises more questions than it is able to answer and that its answers for the most part take the form of a thesis – the quantified biconditional – whose explanatory power in any given case is inversely proportional to its generalized scope or its holding as a matter of purely *a priori* (definitional) truth. This is not to deny that the debate has raised interesting issues with regard to the diverse 'areas of discourse' – from mathematics to ethics – that have standardly figured as test cases in the RD literature. Yet it has done so mainly by throwing those issues into sharper relief rather than through its success in coming up with a third way between realism and anti-realism, or a solution to the rule-following paradox and other kinds of sceptical challenge. This failure has much to do with the way that RD theorists construe their own agenda, in particular their fixation on the Lockean topos of secondary qualities along with their constant reference to Plato as setting the basic terms of debate whenever such questions arise. The result is a distinctly skewed perspective which tends always to tilt the agenda away from any workable realist approach and toward a response-dispositional account that effectively prejudges the issue in its own favour.

This reflects the dominant RD assumption – most obvious in Wright – that on one point at least anti-realism has carried the day. That is to say, Dummett and others have shown the flat contradiction that exists between a truth-based objectivist *ontology* (of numbers, sets, physical items, properties, qualities, intrinsic moral values or whatever) and a realist *epistemology* that would somehow claim to put us in touch with that whole range of candidate items.[45] If this argument holds – if indeed it is impossible to conceive of truth as epistemically or evidentially unconstrained – then of course one alternative line of approach that is likely to seem attractive is the RD proposal for specifying various respects in which validity-conditions can be suitably tailored to the standards of best opinion or assertoric warrant. However its attractiveness will seem less obvious to the Gödelian platonist about mathematics who rejects that way of construing the issue, i.e., the idea of our somehow having *epistemic* contact with abstract entities like numbers.[46] From her point of view it is just another version of the pseudo-paradox foisted on realism by a false epistemology – a strange hybrid of Platonist and Lockean themes – which confuses two very different orders or conceptions of truth. Nor will it convince the causal realist who can happily accept the non-finality of scientific knowledge as we have it without letting go of the cardinal precept that our statements are viable candidates for truth just so long as they advance some definite claim about real-world (objectively existent) entities and their real-world constitutive properties.[47] In both cases the RD 'solution' will seem little more than a minor variant on the sceptical or anti-realist approach which relativizes truth to the scope and limits of humanly attainable knowledge.

That Wright himself has lingering worries about all this – especially as applied to the case of mathematics – is evident in his various later attempts to find some realist-compatible version of the basic RD approach that might resolve the Kripkensteinian rule-following paradox without going so far as to endorse an objectivist position with respect to any area of discourse, mathematics included. Thus he ventures the idea of 'superassertibility', conceived as applying to just those statements whose 'pedigree would survive arbitrarily close scrutiny', or whose truth would be sustained if all the evidence were in and assessed by a maximally competent subject under ideal epistemic conditions.[48] Nevertheless this proposal still fights shy of accepting the two most basic tenets of any realist conception, namely (1) that it involves some relation between a truth-bearer (the statement in question) and its truth-maker (that to which the statement veridically refers); and (2) that this relation can obtain – or the statement possess an objective truth-value – quite aside from whether or not we are now, or could ever be, in a position to judge reliably of its truth or falsehood. From a certain point of view there is nothing much at stake between the realist and the advocate of 'superassertibility' since they can both agree on the assignment of truth-values across a whole range of statements for which we have adequate evidence or epistemic warrant. Thus the realist will say: 'It is because certain statements (in the discourse in question) are true that they are superassertible', while the superassertibilist will retort: 'It is because they are superassertible that such statements are true'.[49] In other words the situation is much like that which obtains when the Socratic realist about moral virtue asserts that the gods approve pious acts because they (the gods) are by their very nature ideally responsive to piety while the Euthyphronist retorts that the gods' approval is just what determines (or constitutes) the piety of any given act. In each case the two parties can agree that the classes picked out – those of true statements or pious acts – are exactly coextensive despite their differing views on the priority issue. All the same this difference has large implications, as can be seen most clearly when Wright explains what it amounts to in terms of the current realist/anti-realist debate. 'Superassertibility', he remarks, 'is, in a natural sense, an *internal* property of the statements of a discourse – a projection, merely, of the standards, whatever they are, which actually inform assertions within the discourse'. And again, lest this point not register with sufficient force: '[i]t supplies no external norm – in a way that truth is classically supposed to do – against which the internal standards might *sub specie Dei* themselves be measured, and might rate as adequate or inadequate'.[50] In which case there would ultimately seem little difference – as concerns the main point at issue – between a superassertibilist conception of 'truth' premised on the notion of idealized epistemic warrant and a Wittgensteinian conception premised on the various discourse-internal criteria that apply (say) to arithmetical judgements or other such instances of rule-following behaviour.

Here, as so often, the debate is set up in terms which effectively create the very dilemma which the theory on offer is supposed to resolve. Thus when Wright characterizes the realist (or objectivist) position as entailing the idea of 'external norms' which would permit us to evaluate the truth-content of our various statements, discourses, practices, etc., *sub specie Dei* he is rigging the debate in just such a way as to foreclose any realist option other than the self-contradictory appeal to standards of knowledge (rather than truth) which transcend any grounds, reasons or evidence that we could possibly adduce in their support. A similar strategy is often deployed by thinkers of a more overt anti-realist persuasion – like Richard Rorty – who are apt to typecast the realist opponent as subscribing to a

'God's-eye-view' theory of truth which involves the nonsensical platonist idea of our somehow having quasi-perceptual access to ideal
verities that lie beyond the furthest reach of human cognition.[51]
However, as I have said, there is no good reason why the realist
should accept this mischievous portrayal of her own views on the
matter. Rather she can claim that it involves not only a confusion
between truth and knowledge (or truth and certainty) but also a tendency to fix upon just those episodes in the history of epistemological debate – from Plato to Locke and Kant – where that confusion
has been most strikingly apparent. Also it derives much of its
salience in present-day philosophy of mind, language and logic
from Kripke's ultra-sceptical take on the Wittgensteinian pseudo-
paradox about rule-following and the supposed absence of objective
standards (as distinct from agreed-upon communal norms) for
knowing what counts as a correct answer to some question in elementary arithmetic.[52] Such issues could only have taken hold or become
a main focus of philosophic interest through widespread acceptance
of the anti-realist thesis that, quite simply, it makes no sense to affirm
the existence of objective or recognition-transcendent truths. That
thesis in turn acquires much of its credibility – its force of apparent
self-evidence – from the unbridgeable gulf between mind and world
(or knowledge and truth) that will always reopen when those issues
are approached from a standpoint within the received range of
epistemological positions. Thus anti-realism in its present-day
(e.g., Dummettian or logico-semantic) form is the end-point of a
road that philosophy has long been travelling and whose course
has encompassed the widest divergences of empiricist versus rationalist or Lockean versus Platonist approaches to the problem of
knowledge.

Hence, as I have said, the pyrrhic conclusion that epistemology
is caught in a classic and unresolvable dilemma since it must *either*
lay claim (impossibly) to a knowledge of objective, recognition-
transcendent truths *or* renounce any such claim and settle for 'truth'
as nothing more than a matter of warranted assertibility according
to our best current knowledge.[53] Dummett may differ from Kripke
in maintaining that assertible utterances (thus defined) are fit candidates for the assignment of truth- and falsehood-values as opposed to
Kripke's more thoroughgoing sceptical view that their warrant comes
only from the fact – whatever sort of 'fact' it may be – of their playing
some communally recognized role in our various rule-following

practices.[54] All the same this difference amounts to very little when it comes to deciding whether (for instance) there is any objective truth of the matter concerning so-far unproven mathematical theorems like Goldbach's Conjecture or statements like that which asserts the existence of a duplicate solar system in some remote (epistemically inaccessible) region of the expanding universe. What these examples bring home is the extent to which scepticism has gained a purchase through the deep-laid assumption – across otherwise sharply divergent schools of thought – that the 'problem of knowledge' can only be addressed in terms that make some ultimate reference to the scope and capacities of human perceptual, epistemic or conceptual grasp. Yet if anything should count as a decisive reductio of this whole line of thought it is the fact that it has provided logically consistent and (to some) philosophically cogent grounds for withholding objective truth-values from the whole vast range of well-formed yet unverifiable statements like those instanced above. In so far as response-dependence theory has itself developed very largely in response to that same sceptical agenda it can perhaps best be seen as the propaedeutic to a full restatement of the realist case (along with its own specific range of provisos) as applied to each particular area of discourse where the theory has staked its claim.

VI

In this chapter I have discussed various kinds of counter-proposal, among them – most prominently – realism with respect to abstract (e.g., mathematical) objects, realism in ethics and political theory, and realist approaches to issues of causal explanation in the physical sciences. I have done so mainly because these are the sorts of argument that draw most attention from anti-realist thinkers such as Dummett and from those, like Kripke, who press yet further in a sceptical direction. They are also a primary point of reference for RD theorists who inherit much the same agenda and whose concern is more with the generalized (logico-metaphysical) debate about realism and anti-realism than with giving a detailed and nuanced account of how enquiry proceeds – or knowledge accrues – in different fields of investigation.

It is in just these respects that the project of critical realism holds out the best hope of advance toward an adequate epistemology for the human and social as well as the natural sciences. After all, one of that project's chief aims is precisely to show that philosophy is sure to run into problems of the type I have adumbrated here unless it adopts a properly 'stratified' approach to the different kinds or levels of explanatory method and procedure involved in various disciplines or subject areas.[55] This it can achieve only by allowing for the full range of reciprocal interactions between physical (real-world) properties and structures, causal powers, experimental situations, investigative methods, observational contexts, descriptive paradigms, explanatory theories and the level at which our understanding of these diverse factors is itself influenced by the social conditions of scientific and everyday knowledge production. Failing that, philosophy is destined to fall back into the kinds of vexing dualism that have marked so many episodes in its recent history, from logical positivism to Rortian 'strong' descriptivism, along with McDowell's revisionist take on Kant and – as I have argued – the scarcely less problematical claims of response-dependence theory.

Roy Bhaskar makes the point most succinctly in a passage from his book *Scientific Realism and Human Emancipation*:

> Facts are real, but they are historically specific social realities . . ..
> Fetishism, by naturalizing facts, at once collapses and so destratifies their generative or sustaining social context and the mode of their production, reproduction, and transformation in time, *ipso facto* dehistoricizing and eternalizing them. The fact form then acts so as to obscure, from scientists and non-scientists alike, the historically specific (cognitive and non-cognitive) structures and relations governing sense-experience in science.[56]

It is not hard to see how this critique of positivist or empiricist thinking might carry over to the various problems with response-dependence theory that I have diagnosed here. Thus a critical realist would be quick to point out that the RD approach, like Dummettian anti-realism, trades on a wholesale conflation of ontological and epistemological questions; that it fails to distinguish the 'intransitive' domain of physical (causally operative) structures and powers from the 'transitive' realm of human observation, intervention or experiment; and that it takes no account of those socially mediated aims and interests that characterize the various natural and human sciences at this or that stage of development.[57] She would also have a good deal to say about the role of collective human agency in bringing about those particular kinds of observational result which cannot provide any *direct* evidence of causal mechanisms or laws of nature, yet which still give adequate grounds for asserting their 'transfactually efficacious' character.[58] This allows room for a social conception of knowledge that accords full weight to economic, historical and cultural determinants but which stops well short of any Wittgensteinian or Kripkean appeal to communal life-forms (or 'agreement in judgement') as the end-point of justification. As Bhaskar puts it:

> [f]acts are indeed paradigmatic social institutions. They are *real*, in as much as but for them certain determinate states of the physical world, for which our intellectual agency is a necessary condition, could not occur. They are *social*, in as much as, though dependent upon human agency, they are irreducible to a purely individual production. But although all facts are social results, not every social result is a fact: facts are the result of specific cognitive, and especially empirically grounded, processes of social production.[59]

With few exceptions – among them the work of Philip Pettit[60] – the RD debate is a striking example of the broader 'analytic' tendency to bracket out just those mediating social factors that might otherwise prevent the chronic oscillation between an individualist (even solipsistic) approach to the 'problem of knowledge' and a full-fledged communitarian approach like Kripke's so-called 'sceptical solution'. What critical realism thus holds out is the prospect of explaining *both* how this situation arose (through a 'fetishized' empiricist idea of perceptual warrant with its origins in Locke) *and* how it might be resolved – or transcended – through a fruitful conjunction of ideas and methodologies from philosophy of the natural and the social sciences.[61]

The way is then open to expose some of the inadequately theorized premises of RD thinking, among them – as I have said – its residual attachment to those stark dichotomies bequeathed by the project of old-style logical empiricism. This critique would have resources in plenty for explaining the deadlocked antinomies induced by a deficient (reified or non-dialectical) conception of knowledge and scientific method *vis-à-vis* their social and material conditions of emergence.[62] Moreover, it would pinpoint precisely that curious Rortian jamming together of a hard-line causal-determinist doctrine as applied to 'unmediated' sensory data with the 'strong'-descriptivist notion that scientific 'truths' are as many and various as the culturally contingent theories, languages, metaphors or narratives in which they play a transient role.[63] Response-dependence theory is itself a response to such drastically dualist conceptions but one that falls short of providing an adequate alternative approach. This is nowhere more apparent than in RD exchanges on the topic of Johnston's 'missing explanation' argument, where accounts of what is missing (or not missing, or simply not required in order for the theory to work) are advanced purely as a matter of conceptual analysis and in total isolation from wider contexts of causal-explanatory argument.[64] Thus critical realism has a strong claim to represent the most cogent, developed and sophisticated set of resources for addressing the problems that continue to surface in present-day epistemological debate. What I have tried to do here is bring out those problems with reference to the mainstream analytic agenda while suggesting some ways in which critical realists might engage and contest that agenda. Now – in Chapter 5 – the focus switches to another line of thought that has lately seemed to promise a constructive way forward in these matters, namely the idea of a virtue-based epistemology. Here again I shall criticize some aspects of that approach while also seeking to convey what is most valuable, challenging and philosophically distinctive about it.

MAKING FOR TRUTH: SOME PROBLEMS WITH VIRTUE-BASED EPISTEMOLOGY

I

Let us take it as fairly uncontroversial that there are certain distinctive virtues – among them those of honesty, integrity, caution, openness to criticism, willingness to give up cherished beliefs in the face of conflicting evidence – that are knowledge-conducive in so far as they characterize competent, responsible and well-disposed epistemic agents. Let us further suppose that these virtues are intrinsic to any kind of enquiry that prizes the interests of truth above those of received opinion or consensus belief. Then again (more controversially) let us take it that truth-claims of *whatever* kind – across the whole range of disciplines or subject areas – are subject to evaluation in terms which *cannot but* involve some appeal to the exercise of just those jointly ethical and epistemic virtues. On this view there is no credible account of what knowledge amounts to except one that takes adequate stock of the various qualities, dispositions and aptitudes which motivate or characterize those who engage in such enquiry. After all, what criteria should we apply in this context if not the sorts of truth-promoting virtue – like those listed in my opening sentence – which can and should serve as an adequate safeguard against sundry forms of epistemic error or fallacious reasoning? Such is at any rate the thesis maintained by advocates of a virtue-based approach who often cite Aristotle in support of their case that epistemology cannot do without some appeal to *phronesis* or to the kind of cultivated practical wisdom that typically results in sound moral judgements and virtuous actions.[1] That is, there comes a point in assessing the worth of our truth-claims, evidential practices, inferential procedures, etc., where no purely formal or rule-based account can explain why some (and not other) such methods are reliably knowledge-conducive. What makes the crucial difference – these thinkers hold – is whether those rules or methods are applied in the right way, i.e., with adequate care, precision, attentiveness to detail, sensitivity to possible distorting or complicating factors and so forth.[2]

In which case it is no surprise that mainstream, non-virtue-based approaches to the problem of induction or attempts to provide some formalized account of the logic of scientific enquiry should so often have run into trouble when it came to providing justification for their own methods and premises. If one thing has emerged from the history of post-1950 epistemological debate – especially since Quine's famous attack on the two last 'dogmas' of logical empiricism – it is the fact that any such approach must be grounded in certain intuitive judgements concerning the best, most plausible or (although Quine would not have phrased it this way) epistemically virtuous means of squaring the empirical evidence with our standing ontological and theoretical commitments.[3] Christopher Hookway makes this point with regard to a curious passage from Quine's *Word and Object* where he appears caught between a crudely behaviourist (stimulus-response) model of knowledge-acquisition and a strong, though vaguely formulated, sense that something more is required by way of normative values or justificatory warrant. Thus, according to Quine,

[t]he sifting of evidence would seem . . . to be a strangely passive affair, apart from the effort to intercept helpful stimuli; we just try to be as responsive as possible to the ensuing interplay of chain stimulations. What conscious policy does one follow, then, when not simply passive toward this inter-animation of sentences? Consciously the quest seems to be for the simplest story. Yet this supposed quality of simplicity is more easily sensed than described. Perhaps our vaunted sense of simplicity, or of likeliest explanation, is in many cases just a feeling of conviction attaching to the blind resultant of the interplay of chain stimulations in their various strengths.[4]

What is so remarkable about this passage – as with much of Quine's writing on the topic of 'naturalized epistemology' – is its failure to resolve the active/passive antithesis, or the question as to how an agent-oriented language of willed 'effort', maximal 'responsiveness', 'conscious policy', deliberative choice between competing 'stories' and so forth, can somehow be reconciled with a language of 'passivity', 'chain stimulations', 'blind resultants' and suchlike behaviourist impedimenta. In other words it is the normativity problem that ensues from his adopting a radically empiricist approach, one which leaves no room for the idea that progress in knowledge might indeed be a matter of carefully reasoned, consciously pursued and rationally motivated theory-choice.

To be sure, Quine does on occasion allow himself to invoke such normative values – *vide* the passage cited above – but only as a passing concession and one that carries little weight in this context. Thus any 'feeling of conviction' we might experience with regard to some given construal of the evidence must itself be the 'blind resultant' of various sensory promptings together with our likewise passive registration of the 'strength' they acquire from associative linkage with other such enchained stimuli. What clearly drops out of this Quinean account – despite his muted suggestions to contrary effect – is the idea that normative criteria such as 'our vaunted sense of simplicity' or our quest for 'likeliest explanation' might involve something other and more than could ever find room in a thoroughly naturalized epistemology. Hookway interprets the passage from Quine as a frank acknowledgement that our various modes of reasoning (inductive, hypothetico-deductive or whatever) necessarily entail some ultimate appeal to the witness of 'immediate' – self-evident or prereflective – experience. Such experience carries its own epistemic warrant in so far as it cannot (and need not) be grounded in some further range of justificatory principles or grounds. Rather it involves modes of intuitive conviction that are 'phenomenologically immediate' in so far as they manifest a 'kind of salience' whereby certain 'inferences and propositions stand out as possessing particular epistemic values, as being relevant, in different ways, to our epistemic practices'.[5] From which point Hookway goes on – in company with other proponents of a virtue-based epistemology – to spell out the various particular attributes and qualities that characterize such practices at their knowledge-conducive best. Thus on his account – unlike Quine's – one can have all that is needed in the way of normativity while avoiding the problem of vicious regress ('rules for the proper application of rules for the proper application . . .', etc.) through an 'immediate' sense of what is right or fitting in this or that context of enquiry.

On the other hand, according to Hookway, there must be something more to this notion of 'immediacy' than a downright Quinean empiricist appeal to sensory promptings or the incoming 'barrage' of ambient physical stimuli. After all, it is just his point that any adequate theory of knowledge will have to make room for those epistemic virtues – of attentiveness, acuity, open-mindedness, respect for the evidence, consistency in reasoning, absence of dogmatic preconceptions and so forth – which provide the otherwise missing normative dimension. They are also what the virtue-theorist presumably has in mind when she claims that there is a crucial difference between the basic prerequisite of possessing good eyesight and the higher-level skill (or epistemic virtue) of applying one's visual-cognitive gift in such a way as to perceive salient aspects of some given situation or object. 'I shall enquire well', Hookway writes, 'only when I notice things that are epistemically relevant – only when what is epistemically salient tracks what is epistemically relevant.'[6] And if this is the case then we are justified in thinking that 'traits analogous to Aristotelian virtues may have a role here' since 'they guide the use we make of our skills and capacities in carrying out enquiries effectively'.[7] Only thus – he believes – can we hope to overcome the problem that has bedevilled so many attempts (from logical positivism down) to provide epistemology with an adequate normative or justificatory basis.

Indeed the problem in its basic form goes back to Hume and the absolute impossibility, as he thought, of ever establishing a rational connection between matters of factual or logical truth and matters of evaluative judgement.[8] However – so the virtue-theorist maintains – if philosophy can do no better than that by sticking to the old Humean agenda then the time has surely come for a decisive change of priorities. And if the sole alternative presently on offer is the Quinean option of pressing right through with Hume's sceptical argument and thus excluding all normative values in favour of a radically empiricist outlook then that change had much better be one that makes sufficient room for a virtue-based epistemology. Whence Hookway's conclusion: that 'there is an important role for states that are similar to ethical virtues in epistemic evaluation', and moreover that 'success in our enquiries requires us to have stable patterns of finding emotionally salient things that enable us to use our skills and other excellences effectively'.[9] For we should otherwise never get beyond the stage – the logical-empiricist stage – of specifying formal terms and conditions for the conduct of well-regulated epistemic enquiry while failing to explain what such enquiry involves by way of adequately trained perception or sensitive judgement when it comes to interpreting the 'raw' empirical data. Thus the virtue-theorists take Quine to have shown pretty much beyond doubt that logical empiricism was a failed enterprise, that is to say, one that ran aground on his arguments concerning the radically holistic nature of meaning and belief, the 'underdetermination' of theories by evidence and the 'theory-laden' character of observation-statements.[10] From which they conclude that something else has to fill the gap between evidence and theory, and moreover that nothing can do so – without giving rise to just another version of the same problem – except a virtue-based epistemology which restores a properly normative dimension to the quest for knowledge and truth.

Of course this approach meets with resistance from those who continue to maintain the distinction between *truth* as a matter of objective warrant and *truthfulness* as a matter of getting things right to the best of one's ability. Thus realists will argue that knowledge – properly conceived – is inseparable from truth and must therefore transcend any limiting conditions placed upon it by the appeal to our present-best range of truth-seeking endeavours.[11] However (so the virtue-theorist replies) their case has been significantly weakened through various counter-arguments lately advanced by sceptics of various persuasion. Among these latter are committed anti-realists such as Michael Dummett, paradigm-relativists like Thomas Kuhn, so-called 'internal' (or framework-relative) realists like the later Hilary Putnam, and – not least – the ingenious inventors of Gettier-type counter-examples which purport to show how knowledge can always come apart from a specification of justified true belief.[12] (I shall have more to say about the Gettier problem later on in this chapter.) Also there is the Wittgensteinian argument – pushed to the sceptical limit by Saul Kripke – that any rule for the conduct of correct reasoning in mathematics, logic or whatever field of enquiry will always be subject either to an infinite (vicious) regress or to the charge of trivial circularity.[13] Then again, there is the case put forward by some recent writers on this topic that scepticism gets a hold only through the realist's misguided (because self-defeating) claim for the objectivity of truth, that is to say, its radically non-epistemic or 'recognition-transcendent' character.[14] This line of argument derives its apparent knock-down force from the logical impossibility that we could ever be in a position to assert that some given statement was objectively true or false despite the fact that its truth-value might always in principle surpass our utmost powers of proof, ascertainment or verification. Realism stands forever 'under the shadow of scepticism' in so far as it opens an unbridgeable gulf between objectivist truth and humanly attainable knowledge.

In Chapters 1 and 2 I discussed what I take to be the central falla-cies in Dummett's and other, less sweeping or doctrinally committed versions of the anti-realist case. In Chapter 4 I suggested that recent attempts to defuse this issue – among them the response-disposi-tional approach adopted by thinkers like Crispin Wright – fall short of their aim since they end up either by endorsing anti-realism in a somewhat more nuanced form or by tautologically equating truth with the deliverance of optimized epistemic warrant or idealized 'best judgement'. However my main concern now is with a different, sharply contrasted line of thought which claims to shift the whole ground of debate and not risk succumbing to the same old dead-end epistemological dilemmas. On this view, to repeat, the only adequate response to scepticism or anti-realism is one that incorporates the epistemic virtues as a basic component of our various truth-seeking or knowledge-conducive practices. Those virtues – and their careful specification – are what make all the difference between a merely formal or procedural approach to the problem of knowledge and one that does justice to the normative values bound up with all kinds of genuine (i.e., disciplined, rational, open-minded, evidentially con-strained and well-motivated) enquiry. Thus we need to get over the received idea that if considerations like this are to play any role in our thinking about epistemological matters then they can do so only in a supplementary way, that is, once we have arrived at some ade-quate first-order theory of truth or knowledge and can then – should we wish – take account of the various traits, dispositions and virtu-ous characteristics that might serve enquirers to best epistemic advantage. This distinction is much like that between scientific 'context of justification' and socio-historical 'context of discovery', as upheld most zealously by the logical empiricists.[15] That is, it allows some limited role for talk about the epistemic virtues just so long as such talk doesn't stray over on to ground staked out by phi-losophy of science and epistemology in its more rigorous (scien-tifically accountable) forms. Yet, of course, this standard order of priorities – along with the presumption of methodological rigour – is

just what the epistemic virtue-theorists call into doubt. For, according to them, it is an approach that has manifestly failed to make good
its case (*vide* the travails of logical empiricism in the wake of Quine's
assault) and has thus given rise to all manner of reactive, i.e., sceptical and anti-realist trends.

II

Such arguments have had a good innings of late and indeed constitute
something like an emergent orthodoxy in the field of virtue-based epistemology. All the same their sources go much further back, as can be
seen from those passages in Kant's First *Critique* where 'judgement'
figures in a mediating role between the otherwise disparate realms of
sensuous (phenomenal) intuition and conceptual understanding.
These are some of the murkiest passages in Kant, not least because he
then feels compelled to explicate 'judgement' in terms of a yet more
obscure faculty, that of 'imagination', itself described as 'a blind but
indispensable function of the soul, without which we should have no
knowledge whatsoever, but of which we are scarcely ever conscious'.[16]
In Chapters 2 and 3 I suggested that all the main issues in post-Kantian
epistemology – on the 'continental' (i.e., mainland-European) as well
as on the 'analytic' side – have arisen in consequence of Kant's failure
to provide a more adequate, less floundering answer to the problem as
to how sensuous intuitions could be 'brought under' concepts of understanding. In the First *Critique* it is left pretty much unresolved, but is
then taken up – as many would argue, to no great clarificatory effect –
in the teleological doctrine of mind and nature that preoccupies Kant
in section two of the *Critique of Judgement*.[17] Thereafter it becomes
the chief dividing-point between subjective and objective idealists
(such as Fichte and Schelling) and a main focus for continuing debates
in the phenomenological tradition from Hegel to Heidegger.[18] Among
analytic philosophers it resurfaces, as I have said, in those problems
that beset the logical positivists and empiricists, and which have lately
been placed back on the agenda – albeit in a somewhat revisionist guise
– by new-born Kantians such as John McDowell.[19] At such points the
debate very often reverts (whether knowingly or not) to that juncture
in the history of thought where Kant took up the challenge of
Humean scepticism.

However, as we have seen, McDowell's purported solution can be
seen to run into all the same quandaries that emerged in the history

of German idealist thought after Kant. Chief among them is that of setting empirical constraints on the exercise of spontaneity while nonetheless allowing the mind sufficient scope for its active role in the process of judgement. For that role can easily expand to the point – as in Fichte's radical recasting of Kantian themes – where the sovereign Ego is thought of as somehow imposing those same empirical constraints through its own self-limiting yet world-constitutive activity.[20] Yet it can also contract to the point where judgement becomes nothing more than a passive registration of incoming sensory data and is hence deprived of what McDowell terms its 'responsible freedom' in the bringing-to-bear of normative or rational-evaluative standards. Thus among his main purposes is that of showing how important (though also how difficult) it is 'to see that we can have both desiderata: both rational constraint from the world and spontaneity all the way out'.[21] And again: 'I am trying to describe a way of maintaining that in experience the world exerts a rational influence on our thinking'.[22] However this realization needs to be balanced by an adequate account of the role played by spontaneity as an active power of judgement that reaches out into the world so as to bring it within the compass of attainable human knowledge. All the same, if we are ever to dismount from the seesaw, then '[w]e need to conceive this expansive spontaneity as subject to control from outside our thinking, on pain of representing the operations of spontaneity as a frictionless spinning in a void'.[23] What chiefly distinguishes McDowell's approach is his willingness to take these epistemological problems on board and to do so, moreover, with constant reference to just those aspects of Kant's thinking in the First *Critique* that have spawned such a range of conflicting interpretations.

Indeed this question of how to wrest a space for 'responsible freedom' in judgement – a space where reason can exercise its powers with due regard to empirical constraints – is one that has continued to vex philosophy in the mainstream analytic line of descent even where that tradition has expressly renounced any Kantian conception of knowledge as vested in certain a priori (transcendentally deducible) intuitions, concepts and categories. It is a problem that was briefly pushed out of sight by the logical-empiricist claim that enquiry could perfectly well proceed through the bringing of first-order empirical observations under higher-level (e.g., deductive-nomological) modes of reasoning whose validity was self-evident and hence required nothing more in the way of normative justification.[24] Quine's attack on the 'two dogmas' of logical empiricism set out to demolish this residual Kantian dichotomy while leaving a third dogma very firmly in place, that is, the idea that epistemology could be 'naturalized' by treating it – in behaviourist terms – as a study of how human beings typically respond to the 'meagre input' of sensory stimuli by producing a 'torrential output' of theories, hypotheses, explanations, etc., under given observational conditions.[25] This required nothing more than an extension of the methods and techniques of the natural sciences into an area which had hitherto (wrongly) been conceived as exerting a normative jurisdiction over just those methods and techniques. It then remained for Davidson to point out Quine's adherence to yet another covert dogma, i.e., his notion of empirical data as open to as many divergent interpretations as there existed ontological schemes or frameworks under which those data might be subsumed.[26]

Thus the old dualism emerged once again in the guise of a thoroughly contextualist theory that relativized truth or knowledge to the entire 'fabric' or 'web' of beliefs-held-true at any given time. Yet Davidson's proposed alternative approach was one that overcame this problem only by espousing a direct realist (or maybe radical empiricist) doctrine according to which, '[i]n giving up the dualism of scheme and world, we do not give up the world, but re-establish unmediated touch with the familiar objects whose antics make our sentences and opinions true or false'.[27] That is to say, it completely cut out any reference to the normative values or standards of responsible enquiry that a thinker like McDowell seeks to restore by way of countering the Quinean idea of a thoroughly naturalized (and hence, he argues, thoroughly inadequate) theory of knowledge. This opened the way for Rorty to claim – with presumptive Davidsonian warrant – that we can be as hard-headedly 'realist' as we like about (say) the causal impact of incoming photons on Galileo's eyeball while still maintaining that all such physical events are under some optional description or other. In which case, according to Rorty, the issue is strictly undecidable as between Galileo's 'observing' the moons of Jupiter and thereby 'shattering the crystalline spheres once and for all' and his opponents' taking those 'same' observations as merely introducing a further complication in the old Ptolemaic-Aristotelian astronomy.[28] So this whole chapter of developments can now be seen as having pushed so far in a naturalistic direction as to leave epistemology entirely bereft of normative or rational-evaluative criteria and hence prone to a reactive swing which views interpretation, in Rorty's phrase, as effectively going 'all the way down'.

Jaegwon Kim puts the case with specific reference to Quine but in terms that could just as well apply to Davidson, Rorty and other exponents of a naturalized approach that offers no adequate or principled defence against 'strong'-descriptivist arguments of this sort. In Kim's words, '[i]f justification drops out of epistemology, knowledge itself drops out of epistemology. For our concept of knowledge is inseparably tied to that of justification . . . Knowledge itself is a normative notion. Quine's non-normative, naturalised epistemology has no room for our concept of knowledge'.[29] McDowell is equally clear about this and makes the point, as usual, in Kantian terms which involve the necessity of distinguishing – though *not*, he would insist, completely divorcing – the role of causal 'impingements' on our sensory organs from the 'space of reasons' or normative justification. Thus: 'if those impingements are conceived as outside the scope of spontaneity, outside the domain of responsible freedom, then the best they can yield is that we cannot be blamed for believing whatever they lead us to believe, not that we are justified in believing it'.[30] Least of all can we hope for such justification – and here he agrees with Kim – from a Quinean naturalized epistemology which admits no normative criteria except those that are somehow supposed to derive from the process of knowledge-acquisition conceived in narrowly physicalist terms.

McDowell's great hope in returning to Kant – on a suitably detranscendentalized reading – is to redress this imbalance without setting up some further chronic oscillation. Thus he holds out the saving prospect of a fully sustainable state of equilibrium between the claims of empirical 'receptivity' and the claims of a 'spontaneity' that would give judgement adequate scope for its exercise of 'responsible freedom' while keeping it within empirically prescribed limits. In this way McDowell respects Kant's demand that reason should acknowledge certain necessary constraints on its proper sphere of jurisdiction – i.e., that it should not encroach on the domain of cognitive understanding where intuitions are 'brought under' adequate concepts – since otherwise it would become nothing more than a kind of speculative free-for-all or 'frictionless spinning in the void'. Yet this leaves unanswered another of the great problems with Kant's First *Critique*, namely that of explaining just how our empirically constrained and rationally guided knowledge of the world can be responsive to certain ideas of reason which must themselves be taken to inform (or to orient) every act of cognitive judgement but whose sphere of jurisdiction lies altogether outside and beyond the cognitive domain. Hence McDowell's keenness to avoid any hint that he might surreptitiously be trading on an appeal to Kant's idea of a noumenal realm whose existence we are constrained to suppose – as a matter of transcendental deduction from the conditions of possibility for knowledge and experience in general – but whose nature and properties inherently elude our utmost powers of cognitive grasp. This he takes to involve the claim of our somehow being able to manifest 'a susceptibility to the impact of a supersensible reality, a reality that is supposed to be independent of our conceptual activity in a stronger sense than any that fits the ordinary empirical world'.[31] So it falls prey at once to all the standard counter-arguments, among them the objection that this noumenal reality is held to transcend all the categories of cognitive (phenomenal) understanding such as that of physical causality, while it is nonetheless conceived as 'impacting' upon us in a quasi-causal manner or at any rate through some responsive disposition or 'susceptibility' on our part that enables us to register its impact.

In short, McDowell has good reason for wanting to keep this transcendental dimension of Kant's philosophy safely outside the picture and for wanting to retain just those components – like the idea of judgement as a seamless imbrication of 'spontaneity' and 'receptivity' – which (in his view) offer a promising way forward from the dogmas, antinomies or dead-end dualisms of current epistemological debate. However this solution is not to be had on Kantian terms since those terms are too closely bound up with the appeal to judgement as deriving its normative or rational-evaluative force from a 'space of reasons' outside the jurisdiction of cognitive understanding. Hence his curiously roundabout description of Kantian spontaneity-cum-receptivity as affording an alternative picture, one in which 'reality is not located outside a boundary that encloses the conceptual sphere'.[32] The negative construction – along with the complex Chinese-box-like imagery – seems to fight shy of explicitly endorsing the positive claim, i.e., that reality must be located *inside* the conceptual sphere. Still this is just what the passage must be taken to mean on any logical construal which – perhaps unkindly – makes no allowance for McDowell's paraphrastic efforts to avoid stating the case in such downright idealist terms. Moreover, it is an upshot that cannot be avoided whenever epistemology repeats the Kantian turn toward a theory that would render the truth-value of our various judgements or statements dependent on – or in some way conditioned by – our perceptual capacities, cognitive powers or extent of (however optimized) epistemic grasp.

III

So the question arises: can a virtue-based epistemology do any better in resolving these problems that have dogged the efforts of McDowell and others to devise a post-empiricist theory of knowledge which would (1) make good the normativity-deficit, and (2) avoid all the usual forms of set-piece sceptical challenge? That is to say, by introducing the epistemic virtues among its most basic criteria of justified true belief can this theory meet the whole range of objections – including Gettier-type counter-examples – which have so far created such a deal of trouble? Gettier's point, briefly stated, is that people can hold beliefs which are indeed justified and true, but which for various reasons intuitively strike us as not meeting the requirements for genuine knowledge.[33] Thus it might be that Alison, having been told that her friend Geraldine had won first prize in a local lottery, and having also observed ten lottery tickets in Geraldine's possession, went on to conclude – justifiably and truly enough – that the lottery winner had purchased ten tickets. However (so the story goes) it was not in fact Geraldine but somebody else – maybe Alison as yet unbeknownst to herself – who had *both* won the lottery *and* got lucky with one out of ten. So despite her subscribing to a true proposition and being justified in holding that belief on the evidence (i.e., her having actually seen Geraldine's tickets) we should not wish to say that Alison *knew* the relevant fact about the lottery winner.

Gettier and various commentators after him came up with a range of yet more complex and ingenious examples to similar effect, i.e., that Plato's definition of knowledge as 'justified true belief' was one that left room for just such doubts concerning its ability to capture our working intuitions in this regard.[34] On the other hand some took issue with Gettier's way of framing the analysis and argued, for instance, that he had skewed the whole debate by taking true beliefs to be 'justified' by the evidence even though that evidence was oblique, off-the-point, or (as in the case of Alison and Geraldine) actively misleading. Again, it has been suggested that the best way around these problems is a 'reliabilist' theory which requires that knowledge be adequately grounded in some causal nexus or concatenated chain of sensory-perceptual (or strong testimonial) evidence that puts knowers reliably in touch with whatever they claim to know.[35] However objections have been raised to this theory also since it leaves room for such *outré* yet philosophically cogent counter-instances as that of the motorist driving through Barn-Façade County who knows that the favourite local hobby is painting incredibly detailed two-dimensional roadside images of barns and who takes one of these to be what he is now seeing, whereas it just happens that he is passing the only genuine, three-dimensional barn in that part of the world.[36] So whereas an uninformed passerthrough who didn't know that this was Barn-Façade County would no doubt be straightforwardly deceived by appearances our cluedup motorist is double deceived since his knowledge leads him astray. Or again, take the opposite case of one who doesn't know about the local pastime and who therefore assumes that any barn-like object he comes across is indeed a barn, but who happens to encounter the locally unique real thing at some stage in his travels and thus identifies the object correctly despite his lack of the relevant information. Here we might well be inclined to say that his justified true belief doesn't amount to knowledge since the situation is such as to render it a product of ignorance concerning that crucial fact. Yet, as Brandom points out, it all depends on just how widely one draws the geo-cultural bounds to what counts as the region – so to speak, the epistemic cachement-area – within which these standards of veridicality are taken to apply.[37] Thus if the hobby was peculiar to Barn-Façade County and was practised rarely, if at all, in the state of which that county formed a part then the motorist in our last example might well be said to know (i.e., truly and justifiably believe on good, epistemically reliable or trustworthy grounds) that this was a real barn before his eyes and not a two-dimensional replica. But then again, if the hobby had a US-wide following and he was ignorant of this fact, having perhaps just recently entered the country from abroad, then most likely our intuition would go the other way and we should be less inclined to accord his true belief the status of genuine knowledge.

Such are at any rate some of the problems that have preoccupied philosophers in the wake of Gettier's article and whose lack of any ultimate, objection-proof solution in reliabilist terms (as shown by the series of examples above) has prompted the quest for a different approach with more adequate normative resources. It is in this context of debate that theorists have lately developed the idea of a virtue-based epistemology that would claim to provide just such resources and thereby equip the theory of knowledge with a fully worked-out and convincingly detailed justificatory dimension.[38] However this enterprise has problems of its own, among them – not least – the fact that it takes us back very squarely onto Kantian ground with regard to the relationship between epistemology and ethics. That is to say, it requires that cognitive interests (or those of conceptual 'understanding', in Kant's sense) be thought of as playing a secondary role *vis-à-vis* certain ethical values or precepts that should regulate the course of truth-seeking enquiry. Thus, for Kant, one means of bridging that problematic gap between sensuous intuitions and concepts of understanding is through the appeal, via 'judgement', to a supersensible faculty of pure reason that provides us with the practical 'orientation' in the absence of which our epistemic endeavours would lack any sense of directive or coordinating purpose.[39] From here it is but a short distance to those passages in the second part of the *Critique of Judgement* where Kant introduces his teleological theory of mind and nature as participating jointly in this purposive scheme of things and thereby pointing a way beyond the epistemological rift.[40]

That this doctrine creates more problems than it solves – even for some of Kant's best-disposed commentators – is scarcely surprising given its commitment to the notion of a preordained harmonious adjustment between mind and world. Thus it courts all those charges that Kant had been so anxious to avoid in the First *Critique*, among them – most patently – that of allowing speculative interests (which were all very well in their proper, i.e., theological or ethico-political domains) to encroach upon the realm of cognitive enquiry where the rule is that intuitions should always be brought under adequate concepts through acts of determinate judgement. Moreover, it extends the scope of 'aesthetic' experience – albeit in Kant's capacious sense of that term – to a point where ethics and epistemology alike are conceived as crucially reliant on certain ideas or analogues from the aesthetic domain such as that of our disinterested pleasure in the beautiful or our sublime apprehension of moral truths beyond the

reach of cognitive understanding. So it is hard to see how this pro-
leptic excursion through the Third *Critique* can leave us better
placed to negotiate either the epistemological quandary of the
Critique of Pure Reason or the kindred problem that arises with
Kantian ethics, that is, the problem of explaining just how the categorical imperative and maxims of practical reason may be thought
to apply – or to provide any guidance – in matters of complex, real-
world, humanly situated ethical choice.[41] In short, if these Kantian
dilemmas are anything to go by – and the case of McDowell rather
strongly suggests that they are – then perhaps there is reason to
doubt whether epistemology has much to gain from an ethics-first
or virtue-based account that courts similar objections.

No doubt it will said that this is to get things badly askew since,
after all, a chief claim of virtue-based ethics and epistemology is precisely that they manage to avoid the kinds of problem that result
from adopting such an abstract, formal or deontological approach.
Hence the well-known arguments advanced by critics of Kantian
moral philosophy – like Alasdair MacIntyre, Michael Sandel,
Michael Walzer and Bernard Williams – who otherwise have little
enough in common as regards their particular ethical or socio-
political views.[42] What unites them is the belief that virtuous acts,
practices, commitments and so forth cannot be subject to some legislative faculty that comes (so to speak) from outside and above, and
which thus lays claim to an order of validity quite apart from the
various customs or forms of life which provide their only possible
source of justification. Hence – they maintain – the curious form of
double-think into which Kant is forced by his attempt to uphold the
absolute autonomy of practical reason (that is, its indifference to all
merely 'pathological' or 'heteronomous' aims and desires) while
decreeing that true virtue consists in a willed subjection to the over-
riding dictates of 'the moral law within'. Thus they all take the view
that we can make no sense of ethical discourse except in so far as it
plays a role within some received tradition or communal life-form.
Where they differ – on a scale that runs, roughly speaking, from 'left'
to 'right' communitarian standpoints – is in the matter of just how
far they go toward rejecting the validity of any argument that would
question some given set of values or beliefs from an 'external', i.e.,
non-participant or critical perspective.

MacIntyre has remarkably swung right across from his early position according to which it was an ethico-political imperative to

challenge the prevailing 'self-images of the age' to a conservative doctrine that equates virtue with conformity to this or that communal narrative whereby moral agents can make coherent and satisfying sense of their lives.[43] 'Liberal' communitarians like Walzer find more room for social criticism as an exercise of independent thought and moral judgement while denying that such criticism could have the least force if it didn't appeal to a certain range of widely shared values and beliefs.[44] Elsewhere the debate is engaged between those (like Williams) who think that ethics can retain its critical edge without going in for high-toned Kantian moralistic talk and those – very often disciples of Wittgenstein in the social sciences – who reject the very notion that judgement can be exercised from a standpoint outside the various language-games or life-forms that provide the criteria for any valid (communally warranted) belief.[45] Thus the communitarians and the virtue-theorists have plenty of detailed disagreements as concerns the extent to which critical reason can legitimately claim to challenge the deliverance of communal best judgement. However they are united on one point at least: that it makes no sense – in epistemological or ethical terms – to adopt a position whereby truth in such matters might sometimes be thought to elude even the best-placed, most fully informed or epistemically virtuous enquirers. For it is a claim common to both parties that philosophy goes wrong – gives rise to all manner of insoluble problems – when it presumes to treat issues of knowledge and justification from a strictly impersonal (objectivist) standpoint and fails to take account of those interests, motives and guiding principles that characterize some (not other) modes of truth-seeking endeavour. Where they diverge is not so much on this basic point as on the question how far such virtues should be specified in terms of shared (community-wide) belief or rather in terms of distinctive qualities – like attentiveness, caution, open-mindedness or the courage to resist peer-group pressure – that more aptly apply to individual thinkers in particular epistemic contexts.

Thus the virtue-based account lays claim to providing a more adequate approach since it avoids both the kinds of problem that result from an overly formalized (or deontological) conception and the opposite risk of appearing to endorse a placidly consensual theory of knowledge or justificatory warrant. This it does – to repeat – by locating the norms of good epistemic practice in just those attributes that serve to mark out competent, good-faith, expert, perceptive and well-motivated enquirers from others whose practice can be shown to lack one or more of these cardinal virtues. Where traditional approaches run into trouble is by attempting to exclude or to marginalize such normative considerations and hence producing the kind of dilemma – the chronic oscillation or 'seesaw' movement so vividly evoked by McDowell – between irreconcilable extremes.[46] However it is far from clear that a virtue-based epistemology of the type recently proposed is any more successful than McDowell's in dismounting from the seesaw or achieving the desired equilibrium. That is to say, this approach can be seen to replicate the problems encountered by McDowell's Kantian version of the response-dependence argument, namely its tendency to fudge the issue with regard to the respective contributions of 'mind' and 'world' – or 'spontaneity' and 'receptivity' – in the process of knowledge-acquisition. Thus the virtue-based account conspicuously fails to explain how the quest for knowledge can take its bearings from the regulative notion of objective, verification-transcendent truth (and hence avoid a Dummett-type anti-realist upshot) while granting the epistemic virtues pride of place when it comes to assessing the personal qualities of those who engage in such pursuits.

To be sure, it offers a useful corrective to full-fledged communitarian theories – especially those with their source in late Wittgenstein – that would impute nothing more to the exercise of right reason or correctness in this or that rule-following practice than conformity with the norms laid down by some existing 'language-game' or shared 'form of life'.[47] From here, as we have seen, it is but a short step to Kripke's 'sceptical paradox' about rules for the application of rules and his 'sceptical solution' which merely restates the Wittgensteinian case that communal warrant – 'the way we do things' – is the furthest one can possibly get by way of epistemic justification.[48] A virtue-based approach has at least this signal advantage: that it offers a means of blocking the Kripkensteinian regress by maintaining that reasoners can think for themselves and apply certain standards (of intellectual probity, consistency, respect for the evidence and so forth) which are not just those of 'agreement in judgement' among members of some given community. All the same – I shall argue – it gets no further than McDowell, Wright or the advocates of response-dependence theory toward meeting the realist's basic objection, i.e., that truth can always come apart from 'best judgement' since even the most virtuous, intellectually disciplined and truth-oriented forms of enquiry may still (for whatever reason) fall far short of their aim.

Moreover recent debates in this area can be seen to have swung back and forth between a range of alternative positions (such as external-ism versus internalism in epistemology and philosophy of mind) which once again evoke McDowell's metaphor of the violently oscil-lating seesaw.[49] What I propose to do in the rest of this chapter is look more closely at some of these inbuilt tensions or deep-laid conflicts of priority that have so far marked the project of developing a virtue-based epistemology.

IV

Most significant here is the fact that this approach has partly grown out of, and partly emerged as a reaction against, the kinds of relia-bilist argument put forward by philosophers and cognitive theorists like Alvin Goldman. On their view the best way around all those old epistemological quandaries – such as Gettier's problem about closing the gap between 'knowledge' and 'justified true belief' – is to adopt a basically causal account whereby knowledge is taken to consist in beliefs arrived at through a process of cognitive enquiry which puts the knower reliably in touch with his or her information sources.[50] This is clearly an externalist approach in so far as it aims to cut out any normative appeal to whatever is supposed to go on 'in the minds' of properly equipped, duly qualified or intellectually responsible seekers-after-truth. It has the great advantage (so Goldman claims) of explaining how people can properly be held to know a great many things which they have not thought about or sub-jected to any kind of conscious critical scrutiny but which nonethe-less count as genuine (i.e., reliably produced and epistemically secure) items of knowledge.

Thus it tends to come out in marked opposition to any version of the hitherto dominant theory, from Plato to Kant and beyond, that would supply epistemology with a normative dimension conceived in terms of those inner goings-on – or well-regulated processes of thought – which make all the difference between *genuine* knowledge and inadequate (even if true and, as it happens, epistemically war-ranted) belief. For this is a distinction that makes no difference if one takes it, with Goldman, that knowledge *just is* the product of reli-ably truth-conducive processes of belief formation which require nothing more than that knowers should stand (or at some time have stood) in an appropriate causal relation to their various sources of evidence. Least of all are they required – as Kant would have it – to possess some kind of ultimate justificatory warrant that would derive their entitlement to make such claims from the transcendentally deduced 'conditions of possibility' for thought, knowledge and experience in general. Such arguments are beside the point in so far as they place impossibly restrictive (as well as metaphysically extravagant) conditions on what counts as genuine knowledge. Also, they tend to confuse matters by suggesting (again in Kantian fashion) that issues of good epistemic warrant cannot be treated apart from issues of right reason, these latter construed in strongly normative terms. Whence all the problems and vexing dualisms that have beset epistemology in the mainstream ('continental' as well as 'analytic') line of descent. Much better adopt a reliabilist approach that brings the whole topic back down to earth by attending to the various ways in which human beings actually acquire, process and assimilate knowledge rather than indulge such hopeless quests for strictly unattainable grounds and guarantees.

As I have said, this kind of argument has clearly had a large influence on the advocates of a virtue-based epistemology even though – just as clearly – their thinking departs from it in various crucial respects. Thus they share its opposition to any form of abstract, purely rule-based, or deontological approach that would locate the requirements for epistemic rectitude in a Kantian realm of internal ('autonomous' or self-imposed legislative) precepts quite apart from the sorts of virtuous practice that can and should typify our conduct in such matters. This broadly externalist emphasis goes along with their belief – contra Kripkean and other varieties of wholesale epistemological scepticism – that the relevant virtues should be manifest in our cognitive dealings with the world rather than confined to some private domain of strictly inscrutable goings-on in the mind of this or that enquirer. Thus reliabilism of the Goldman type has often been a point of entry for those among the epistemic virtue-theorists who started out dissatisfied with the way that such debates had typically gone, not least through Kant's lingering influence (as diagnosed by Quine) on the discourse of logical empiricism.[51] However there were certain aspects of this approach which failed to meet their demands, among them its adoption of a causal theory of knowledge that left no room for any but a notional (reductionist and underspecified) account of those normative values which had to play a role in the assessment of our various epistemic practices. To this extent

Goldman's theory was open to the same objections as Quine's hard-line physicalist programme, even though it offered far more in the way of explanatory resources for a robust, causally detailed description of what should transpire between the input and output stages of reliable knowledge acquisition. That is, it came to strike the emergent company of virtue-theorists as lacking in just the most crucial respect, namely a willingness to break with received, impersonal conceptions of the epistemic 'good' and to substitute a theory that identified such goodness with a range of adequately specified personal qualities, traits, or attributes. Indeed in his later work Goldman himself has gone some way toward meeting this criticism by developing a form of 'process reliabilism' which provides more explicitly for the inclusion of normative values and can therefore, he suggests, quite properly be regarded as a virtue-oriented approach.[52]

Still there are problems in reconciling any such causal theory of knowledge with the claim that certain epistemic virtues, defined in ethico-evaluative terms, must be thought of as playing a basic and prerequisite rather than a secondary or adjutant role in the process of its acquisition. They are problems familiar enough from the history of post-Humean debate on the fact/value distinction as well as from Kant's tortuous attempts to explain how the realm of cognitive enquiry – where phenomenal intuitions are 'brought under' adequate concepts through an act of determinate judgement – might yet coexist with a 'space of reasons' which leaves adequate room for the exercise of responsibility in making such judgements. Here again McDowell takes Kant to offer some useful advice just so long we sensibly discard all that otiose metaphysical (or transcendental) machinery and focus rather on his thoughts about the conjoint role of 'spontaneity' and 'receptivity' in all our knowledge and experience. Thus, according to McDowell's Kant, '[t]he idea of a faculty of spontaneity is the idea of something that empowers us to take charge of our lives'.[53] And again: 'Kant points the way to a position in which we can satisfyingly apply that idea to empirical thinking: we can hold that empirical inquiry is a region of our lives in which we exercise a responsible freedom, and not let that thought threaten to dislodge our grip on the requirement that empirical thinking be under constraint from the world itself'.[54] However – as I have argued – McDowell's detranscendentalized reading of Kant not only leaves out some crucial load-bearing parts of the Kantian system but also falls back, despite all his claims to contrary effect, into just the kind of dualism between 'receptivity' and 'spontaneity' (or 'empirical constraint' and 'responsible freedom') that he is so anxious to avoid. In which case the question remains: can a virtue-based approach to these longstanding epistemological problems come up with an answer that finally succeeds where so many others have failed?

Certainly this is the claim advanced by those, like Ernest Sosa, who have started out from a reliabilist position and then become convinced – for the kinds of reason summarized above – that any such approach is bound to fall short of capturing our best, most adequate concept of knowledge for want of a sufficiently developed normative component. Thus Sosa first presented his case for the epistemic virtues as basic to our thinking about issues of knowledge and justification in order to point a way beyond the deadlocked dispute between foundationalists and anti-foundationalists.[55] At this stage he conceived them as roughly analogous to perceptual powers like acuteness of vision or epistemic capacities – such as accurate memory or vividness of sensory recall – which still lent themselves plausibly enough to treatment in reliabilist (causal-explanatory) terms, albeit with some extra allowance for the exercise of discriminative judgement. Later on – in his book *Knowledge in Perspective* – Sosa took a large step further toward a virtue-first epistemology by distinguishing between the kind of knowledge that is presumably possessed by non-reflective (i.e., non-human) sentient creatures and the kind of knowledge that can justifiably be claimed by those, like ourselves, who are capable of such judgement.[56] His point is that what counts for *them* (the animals) as measuring up to the reliabilist standard of properly acquired, causally explicable dispositions to behave thus or thus in some given situation provides no remotely adequate standard by which to judge the epistemic status of human beliefs and truth-claims. These latter cannot be simply the upshot of reliably knowledge-conducive causal processes since human knowledge involves much more in the way of reflective, self-conscious and critical-evaluative thought. Thus what makes the difference in human terms between genuine knowledge and justified true belief is this additional component which can only be specified through a theory that allows for just that range of distinctively human epistemic virtues. Which is also to say that Goldman-style reliabilism meets its justificatory limit at the point where purely externalist explanations run out – as applied to human knowledge – and where one has to reintroduce the appeal to certain internalist (virtue-based) constraints on the range of beliefs that can reasonably count as candidates for epistemic warrant. After all, the mere fact that some given belief-state is produced in a human knower by some causally sufficient chain of sensory promptings or evidential inputs is in itself not enough to qualify that belief-state as in any way 'reliably' knowledge-conducive. Rather, what is involved is the further criterion that it should meet the conditions of reflective scrutiny and of the subject's being able – if so required – to offer some adequately reasoned account of just how and why they arrived at that particular judgement.

Here again it is worth noting that McDowell addresses the same issue and in terms of a similar distinction between the human realm of rational, reflective, self-conscious belief-formation and the non-human animal realm of causally efficacious inputs or sensory stimuli. Thus '[w]e need to recapture the Aristotelian idea that a normal mature human being is a rational animal, but without losing the Kantian idea that rationality operates freely in its own sphere'.[57] On the other hand this gives rise to the question – from a detranscendentalized Kantian perspective – as to 'how spontaneity [can] permeate our lives, even to the extent of structuring those aspects of them that reflect our naturalness – those aspects of our lives that we share with ordinary animals'.[58] Perhaps the thought is 'that the freedom of spontaneity ought to be a kind of exemption from nature, something that permits us to elevate ourselves above it, rather than our own special way of living an animal life'. However this goes clean against McDowell's naturalized reading of Kant as a thinker who can best (most charitably) be relieved of all that surplus-to-requirements metaphysical baggage. Hence the following somewhat wire-drawn passage where McDowell strives to keep these antinomies from emerging too plainly to view:

> [w]e do not need to say that we have what mere animals have, non-conceptual content, and we have something else as well, since we can conceptualize that content and they cannot. Instead we can say that we have what mere animals have, perceptual sensitivity to features of our environment, but we have it in a special form. Our perceptual sensitivity to our environment is taken up into the ambit of the faculty of spontaneity, which is what distinguishes us from them.[59]

My point is that Sosa's argument runs into a similar problem at just the stage where he attempts to make the case for a virtue-based as against a purely reliabilist (causal) epistemology in terms of the supposedly parallel distinction between properly human and non-human animal knowledge. That is, it takes for granted what many would deny on ethological as well as philosophic grounds: that we are in any adequate position to advance this claim through the appeal to concepts (like those of reflection, self-consciousness, 'spontaneity' or whatever) that belong so much to one particular – indeed distinctively Kantian – mode of philosophical discourse on the scope and capacities of human judgement. Besides, as I have said, it creates large problems for Sosa's residual attachment to a form of causal-reliabilist epistemology just as it does for McDowell's 'naturalized' yet still residually transcendental take on Kant.

V

Hence, I suggest, the problems that arise with the turn toward a theory of the epistemic virtues as a means of avoiding those earlier problems that had dogged debates in the wake of logical empiricism. Such was Sosa's leading claim in his 1980 article 'Knowledge and Intellectual Virtue' where he argued that this was the best, indeed the only way beyond the ultimately dead-end dispute between foundationalist and anti-foundationalist (e.g., coherentist or pragmatist) theories of knowledge. That issue could never be resolved, he now thought, except by adopting an altogether different epistemological perspective.[60] Still it is clear from the various disagreements which continue to arise amongst advocates, disputants and halfway converts that the virtue-based approach inherits all the same dilemmas that have characterized previous putative solutions, such as those of the response-dependence theorists and McDowell's revisionist reading of Kant.

Most crucial is the problem as to just what an epistemic virtue should be taken to involve if not – at its most basic – the realist acceptance that truth might always elude our best, most reliable or virtuous means of ascertainment. It is here (as I argued in Chapter 4) that the advocates of response-dependence lean strongly in an anti-realist direction despite their overt professions of even-handedness, and here also that McDowell draws the line against any alethic (objectivist) theory of truth that would place it outside and beyond the realm of jointly operative human 'receptivity' and 'spontaneity'. What the virtue-theorists claim to provide is an approach that avoids this problem by switching their primary focus of attention from the kinds of justificatory warrant possessed by our various statements, beliefs, truth-claims, theoretical commitments, etc., to the kinds of disposition – virtuous or not – that characterize epistemic agents. However this aligns them very squarely with the response-dependence (and hence, on my submission, the anti-realist) camp in so far as it equates truth with best opinion or optimized judgement among those pre-sumptively qualified to know on account of just these imputed qual-ities. Thus virtue-based theories must always at some point run into the realist counter-argument that they fail to acknowledge the objec-tive (recognition-transcendent) character of truth, whether as regards epistemological or ethical matters. That is to say, the realist in episte-mology will charge them with restricting truth to the scope and limits of human knowledge, no matter how attentive, open-minded or judi-cious the investigative process involved. And the ethical realist will likewise maintain that what makes an action right or wrong – what ultimately warrants our approval or disapproval – is the nature of that action when assessed in terms of its impact on those (whether human or non-human sentient creatures) whose lives it affects for better or worse.[61]

No doubt the virtue-theorist will quickly respond that her posi-tion is open to no such criticism since it makes full allowance for those epistemic virtues – of caution, self-criticism, acceptance of the non-finality of knowledge as we have it – which between them ensure an adequate respect for the standing possibility that truth might elude our present best truth-seeking endeavours. Yet these character traits, no matter how admirable, are still specified in such a way as to reverse the realist order of priority between *truth* conceived in objective (recognition-transcendent) terms and *truthfulness* con-ceived as the disposition, among suitably motivated agents, to regu-late their epistemic conduct in keeping with just such virtuous principles. To be sure, this theory can fairly claim to improve upon rival, e.g., reliabilist or deontological, accounts to the extent that it supplies the former with an otherwise missing normative dimension and also corrects for the latter's overly formal or abstractly rigorist approach. Yet it is far from clear – to invoke McDowell's metaphor one last time – that the virtue-theorist has thereby succeeded in dis-mounting from that particular seesaw. For one striking feature of recent debates in this area is the way that its proponents have tended to deploy some qualified version of reliabilism as a check upon the kinds of 'internalist' bias exhibited by deontological theories while nonetheless – like Sosa – reverting to some (likewise qualified) version of internalism so as to avoid the normativity deficit charged against straightforward reliabilist accounts.

Of course it may be said that this is just the virtue of virtue-based theories: that they refuse to accept the dilemma thus posed between a causal-reliabilist approach devoid of normative values and a deontological approach devoid of credible epistemic warrant. Instead they would claim to steer an alternative path which runs into no such problems since the notion of an epistemic virtue, suitably defined, is one that provides plenty by way of normative justification while relying not at all – or at least to no credibility-damaging extent – on deontological premises. All the same, as I have said, this claim is apt to look somewhat shaky if one asks wherein that justification is thought to reside and what precisely might count as an adequate definition of this or that epistemic virtue beyond the mere fact of its counting as such among those of a like mind. At this point the theorist has a choice between strengthening the internalist requirement – i.e., that agents should knowingly, consciously, reflectively and responsibly (rather than just reliably) apply such standards – and falling back to a reliabilist position that makes room for virtue-talk but only as a means of deflecting the standard counter-argument on normative grounds. Both positions have the merit of avoiding any recourse to that Wittgenstein-inspired line of thought which would have it that justifications run out – quite simply, that there is nothing more to be said – when one accepts that some particular way of proceeding has its place in our communally sanctioned range of language-games, practices or life-forms. By the same token they can both lay claim to offering a welcome escape route from the kinds of hyperinduced sceptical doubt (and the equally sceptical 'solutions') drawn out of Wittgenstein by Kripke and other exponents of the rule-following paradox.[62] Thus internalist approaches of the strong variety maintain that there exist certain normative standards – of rationality, consistency, intellectual caution and care to avoid erroneous results – which prevent such dilemmas from getting a hold. Meanwhile reliabilism makes the case that when our reasonings go right then this is explained by their exhibiting a justified (= causally explicable) kind of relation between epistemic input and cognitive output stages. However the fact that each provides an answer to Kripkensteinian scepticism is no guarantee that these approaches are capable of being reconciled, perhaps – as the virtue-theorists hope – through the adoption of a third-way alternative that would retain what is most useful about both while curbing their respective excesses. On the contrary: it appears from much of the current literature that they tend to pull in opposite directions and to create just the kind of chronic oscillation that typified McDowell's and other such failed attempts to restore reflective equilibrium.

Nor is this in any way surprising, given the strictly impossible role that the epistemic virtues are required to play in achieving that desired outcome. The strain was already apparent in Sosa's early suggestion that the intellectual virtues could be held analogous to reliably knowledge-conducive perceptual faculties such as good eyesight, acute hearing or tactile sensitivity.[63] For it is, to say the least, highly questionable that abilities like these which involve a large measure of what cognitive theorists would regard as modular or 'encapsulated' (i.e., quasi-automatic) processing can offer a legitimate basis for extrapolation to higher-level intellectual capacities such as abductive reasoning or inference to the best explanation. Indeed it is on just this crucial point that erstwhile proponents of the 'strong' modularity thesis (chief among them Jerry Fodor) have more recently scaled down their claims and denied that the thesis could possibly extend beyond those relatively specialized perceptual and cognitive functions that are capable of adequate specification in modular terms.[64] That is to say, the thesis conspicuously fails to account for other, more 'global' (non-encapsulated) processes of knowledge-acquisition that involve the exercise of rational-evaluative powers surpassing any purely formal or computational account.

Thus there is something distinctly askew about Sosa's claim that the intellectual virtues can best be understood by analogy with well-functioning modes of sensory-perceptual cognition. No doubt – as we have learnt from neurophysiologists and cognitive scientists – there is a vast amount of complex interpretative processing that normally goes on between the stage of passive sensory uptake (or Quinean 'bombardment' by incoming physical stimuli) and even the most basic stage of perceiving this or that object in our visual field.[65] Philosophers have drawn various lessons from this, among them Quine's doctrine that epistemology should be 'naturalized' – take a lead from the physical sciences – and seek nothing more than to offer a strictly non-normative account of how the 'meagre input' of sensory data gives rise to the 'torrential output' of scientific theories and hypotheses.[66] Then again, in a different key, it has often been adduced by Wittgensteinians, Kuhnians and others in support of the idea that perceiving an object is always a matter of 'seeing-as', or perceiving it under some particular 'aspect' depending on our various kinds of background knowledge or information. This latter line of argument has been pushed pretty hard, to the point where (again with warrant from Wittgenstein) it is taken to refute the very possibility of distinguishing between veridical perceptions and - delusory appearances, as in Norwood Hanson's case of the expert physicist who sees an x-ray tube where the neophyte sees only a very complicated kind of light-bulb.[67] Thus they are both 'right', according to Hanson, since they are seeing the object under different aspects and there is ultimately no ranking their perceptions on a common scale of correctness.

My point is that philosophers of very different persuasion – such as Quine and Wittgenstein – can enlist this scientifically demonstrable fact about the theory-laden character of perceptual data and deploy it in a way that effectively excludes all normative considerations. This in turn raises problems for Sosa's conception of the intellectual virtues as analogous to properly functioning modes of perceptual-cognitive response. For the best alternative to following either the Quinean or the Wittgensteinian path – and thus running up a large normativity-deficit – is to go in something more like Fodor's direction, that is, toward a theory which specifies certain innate ('modular') capacities of mind that are reliably knowledge-conducive and which therefore don't fall prey to holistic arguments whereby any given cognitive input is subject to manifold possible interpretations according to this or that range of background beliefs, suppositions, ontological commitments or suchlike. However, as I have said, Fodor's thinking has lately taken a somewhat different turn. Thus he still sees merit in the claim that certain specialized, e.g., sensory-perceptual, functions must be thought of as highly 'encapsulated' since otherwise they would be subject to all sorts of outside interference and unable to do their work with maximum speed and reliability. But he now rejects any version of the argument for 'massive modularity', i.e., the claim that *all* mental functions – from base-level processing of sensory data to high-level modes of abductive inference – can (or might eventually) be brought within the remit of a full-scale modular approach. As Fodor puts it,

> [r]eally massive modularity is a coherent account of cognitive architecture only if the input problem for each module (the problem of identifying representations in its proprietary domain) can be solved by inferences that aren't abductive (or otherwise holistic): that is, by domain-specific mechanisms. There isn't, however, any reason to think that it can. Empiricist treatment – namely, to assume that the domains of *all* cognitive processes are distinguishable in the sensorium – is wildly implausible outside perception (and not all that wildly plausible *inside* perception) . . . By all the signs, the cognitive mind is up to its ghostly ears in abduction. And we do not know how abduction works. So we do not know how the cognitive mind works; all we know anything about is modules.[68]

One may doubt whether things are really quite as bad with our understanding of abductive inference as Fodor here makes out, or that the problems it creates for a modular approach are problems for abduction per se. Indeed, as I have argued in earlier chapters, abduction – or inference to the best explanation – is among the most basic and well-established modes of scientific reasoning as well as the strongest source of arguments for a realist ontology and epistemology.[69] Still – to repeat – Fodor's change of mind on this topic *does* throw doubt on any theory of the 'intellectual virtues', like Sosa's, which treats them as analogous to well-functioning perceptual or sensory-cognitive processes. For this analogy assumes (as might be expected, given the provenance of epistemic virtue-theory in earlier reliabilist accounts) that there is no essential difference – such as Fodor maintains – between what goes on at the level of strongly modular or 'encapsulated' cognitive functions and what goes on when we engage in more complex modes of rational-evaluative thought. But if there is such a difference then it threatens to deprive those virtues of the normative (ethically oriented) character which they must be taken to possess if they are to count as such in any but a loose or misapplied sense of the term.

Hence perhaps Sosa's more recent tendency to de-emphasize the kinship between knowledge as a product of optimally functioning

perceptual processes and knowledge as the aim of virtuously motivated epistemic enquiry.[70] Thus he now requires that subjects should
not only form their beliefs through a reliable (knowledge-conducive)
relation to their cognitive inputs, evidential data, information
sources and so forth, but should also possess the reflective capacity
to grasp what it is about those same beliefs (and the process through
which they were acquired) that renders them epistemically virtuous.
However, once again, this brings him out on contested ground since
it involves an internalist – at times a distinctly Kantian – appeal to
standards of judgement or right reason that are thought of as exerting their normative force *over and above* any epistemic warrant sup-
plied by exposure to the right kinds of cognitive input. Yet it is a
central claim of his and other projects for a virtue-based epistemology that it should point a way beyond the kinds of philosophical
impasse that have marked the history of debate on this topic from
Kant to logical empiricism and its various successor movements. By
appealing to the epistemic virtues, so it is thought, one can shift the
terms of dispute so as to cut out that false disjunction between causally reliable sources of knowledge and ethically responsible ways of
construing the best evidence to hand. John Greco makes just this
claim when he argues that the normative deficit of Goldman-type
reliabilist theories can best be got over by introducing the further
requirement that, in order to possess 'positive epistemic status', a
subject's virtues must include their willingness to take responsibility
for whatever they advance in the way of purportedly veridical statements.[71] However this still leaves the virtue-theorist in something
very like the uncomfortable position occupied by McDowell and the
advocates of response-dependence as a solution to all our epistemic
woes. That is, it fails to resolve the issue between reliabilists and
internalists as regards what should properly count as an epistemic
virtue. For the theory is constantly tugged both ways – as so often
in the history of post-Kantian debate – between a primary emphasis on whatever grounds our beliefs in the deliverance of valid
perceptual-cognitive warrant and an emphasis on whatever constitutes the reason (the rational-evaluative justification) for believing or
thinking as we do. Thus the notion of an epistemic 'virtue' comes to
seem very much like a handy device for fudging the epistemological
issue or for shifting attention from deep-laid problems in philosophy
of mind and knowledge by adopting an alternative approach that
pushes those problems conveniently out of sight.

My case is not so much that virtue-talk has no place in epistemo-logical discussion as that it cannot take pride of place – as some of these theorists would claim – without shifting the focus from questions concerning knowledge and its justificatory grounds to questions concerning the motives, priorities and more-or-less virtuous dispositions of those who engage in its pursuit. Of course there are various ways of strengthening the conditions for what should properly count as a genuine and consistent (as opposed to merely flukish or transient) epistemic virtue. Among them are the criteria of reliably well-formed judgement, openness to persuasion by the strength of opposing arguments, and the 'positive epistemic status' that accrues from taking full responsibility for the content and soundness of one's own beliefs. Yet this still leaves room for the demurrer – at least from a realist standpoint – that what the virtue-theorists conspicuously fail to explain is the standing possibility of error even in the case of beliefs that fully meet these more robust validity conditions. That is, one can still get things wrong (objectively so) for want of some crucial piece of evidence or item of knowledge that would otherwise have led to a different (veridical) conclusion, despite having exercised those epistemic virtues to the utmost of one's intellectual powers.

Thus the problem here is the same as that which afflicts the advocates of response-dependence and others – like McDowell and Wright – who adopt a broadly kindred approach. On the one hand they can specify 'best judgement', 'idealized rational warrant' or 'optimal response' in such a way as to make those virtues *infallibly* truth-tracking, i.e., as *by very definition* incapable of error.[72] In this version their argument is perfectly compatible with a realist, objectivist or verification-transcendent view of truth but – by the same token – trivially circular and devoid of substantive (perceptual-cognitive or epistemic) content. On the other they can fill out the specification for what properly counts as an epistemic virtue with regard to those particular traits, qualities, intellectual dispositions and so forth, which are taken as reliably knowledge-conducive and hence as reliably serving to distinguish the sheep from the goats in terms of (what else?) epistemic reliability. But then we are back with the realist's standard objection, namely that this means restricting truth – or the range of truth-apt statements, hypotheses, predictions, etc. – to the scope and limits of human (no matter how optimized) perceptual and cognitive response.

VI

Marie McGinn states the case most succinctly by noting the 'intuitive disanalogy between ethics and epistemology'. This has to do with the inherent implausibility of any argument that makes the epistemic virtues (such as caution, disinterest, intellectual curiosity, openness to criticism and so forth) the ultimate arbiters or baseline criteria rather than a set of enabling conditions for attaining veridical knowledge. Thus, according to McGinn,

> [t]here is an idea of objectivity which may seem inescapable when it comes to assessing our beliefs about the world, but which has very little appeal applied to our ethical beliefs, and which is often associated with a subjectivist conception of the latter. This is the idea that there is an objective reality, completely independent of human beings, at which our beliefs aim and to which we require the results of our epistemic evaluations to correspond. Our sense that the question of the reliability of our epistemic practices is pressing surely turns on this intuitive disanalogy. For, in so far as belief formation is regulated by subjective criteria, it seems that I cannot reasonably take myself to have knowledge of the objective world *unless* I have reason to believe that my subjective criteria are a reliable guide to objective states of affairs.[73]

In this passage McGinn is specifically contesting Christopher Hookway's claim that knowledge must involve some 'immediate' experience or state of mind which constitutes its ultimate, self-evidential ground and in the absence of which there could be no breaking the closed circle or halting the otherwise vicious regress of justificatory arguments.[74] Such experience has to be characterized in subjective – even emotional – terms since these provide the only adequate alternative to formal, procedural or rule-based conceptions of epistemological rectitude which run into all the familiar problems pointed out by Kripke and others. Thus Hookway proposes a radically heterodox approach to these issues, one that would reverse the received (i.e., mainstream-analytic) order of priories and treat the emotions – or certain kinds of epistemically salient emotion – as taking precedence over any account of knowledge that stresses its impersonal, detached, emotionally *un*involved character. In which case it might be held that McGinn's objections don't apply to other, more distinctively virtue-based theories which involve no such dubious appeal to 'immediate' states of mind that by very definition cannot be assessed on cognitive or rational-evaluative terms. Yet it could also be held – justifiably, I think – that they *do* so apply since the virtues adduced, whatever their precise specification, are likewise construed as taking epistemic priority over any of the more traditional (objectivist) criteria for what constitutes veridical knowledge, as opposed to mere opinion or subjective belief. After all, it is just this leading claim that distinguishes virtue-*based* epistemologies from other (again more traditional) approaches that allow some room for the motivating influence of various personal traits or dispositions just so long as such allowance is properly confined to the epistemological 'context of discovery' and not permitted to stray over into the 'context of justification'.[75]

Thus McGinn's argument against Hookway also has a pointed relevance to the kinds of theory typically advanced by virtue epistemologists. Indeed one could slightly recast her final sentence so as to read: 'in so far as belief formation is regulated by [the virtues], it seems that I cannot reasonably take myself to have knowledge of the objective world *unless* I have reason to believe that my [epistemically virtuous] criteria are a reliable guide to objective states of affairs'. In other words these thinkers cannot have it both ways, on the one hand granting the virtues epistemic pride of place while on the other presuming that those virtues must – by very definition – be reliably knowledge-conducive and hence involve no conflict with the claims of realists and objectivists about truth. Or rather, they *can* adopt this line of argument but only at the cost (as with the response-dependence theorists) of trivializing their thesis by defining an epistemic virtue as 'whatever it takes' to ensure that our beliefs are reliably formed and the resultant knowledge necessarily truth-tracking. Here again, the virtue-epistemologist may think to avoid this circularity problem by offering a more detailed, specific and substantive account of what it *actually* (as distinct from just notionally) takes for a virtue to merit that name. However he will then have another awkward problem to confront, namely that the more substantive his specification of the virtues involved the more they will tend to compromise his claim for this approach as being perfectly compatible with a realist respect for the existence of objective (verification-transcendent) truth-values. That is to say, such theories may very well include among their list of salient virtues the disposition to believe that there *do* exist objective truths, that these are *not* response-dependent or in any way epistemically constrained, and (what follows logically from this) that the truth of such claims is itself altogether independent of the attitude, virtuous or otherwise, that epistemic agents may adopt toward them. However, once again, the virtue-theorist takes away with one hand what he holds out with the other since if he is right about the basic (constitutive) role of the epistemic virtues in all our processes of knowledge-acquisition then it is the attitude that really, fundamentally counts rather than any objective truth of the matter.

Although this might appear a no-lose position for the virtue-theorist (since he seemingly gets the last word either way) one could just as well argue that it is a no-win situation, or a double-bind predicament whereby his case turns out to be self-refuting on either construal. For in so far as the virtues take precedence over truth that case must default on its claim to respect our strong realist intuition that there exist a great number of (to us) unknown – perhaps unknowable – truths which lie beyond the grasp of even the most virtuous, epistemically well-disposed enquirer. Nor can this objection be countered by answering that humanly attainable knowledge, not objective truth, is what the epistemic virtues should properly be taken to promote and hence that the opponent gets things wrong – skews the whole debate toward a different agenda – by supposing that it raises the issue of realism versus anti-realism. For it is surely just the point of a virtue-based epistemology to address and resolve that issue through a redefinition of its basic terms which explains how truth can be brought within the compass of achievable (so long as virtuously motivated) knowledge. Yet this drives the virtue-theorist straight back onto the opposite horn of the dilemma, i.e., by requiring that truth be conceived as epistemically constrained even if at the ideal limit of what virtuous enquirers would (counter-factually) endorse as truth were they only to apply their powers of best judgement under optimal epistemic conditions. On the other hand it is hard to see what significant role the virtues can play if the theory is qualified so far as to admit the existence of objective (recognition-transcendent) truths which constrain them to a strictly infallible – rather than more-or-less reliable – truth-tracking capacity. For in that case there is nothing more substantive to the argument for a virtue-based epistemology than there is to a Euthyphronist construal of the RD claim which simply collapses the distinction between objectivist truth and epistemic best judgement.[76]

Yet if that distinction goes by the board then not only are the virtues left with no genuine (explanatory or justificatory) work to do but also it becomes an insoluble mystery how expert – well-informed and virtuously motivated – thinkers could ever have managed to get things wrong with regard to some erstwhile generally endorsed but now discredited item of belief. That is to say, the advantage of a virtue-based approach is inevitably compromised as soon as one asks how truth can come apart – as it so often has – from the standing consensus of best judgement at some given stage in the progress of enquiry to date.

This is just one of the problems that beset any argument for grounding knowledge (as distinct from the quest for knowledge) in an appeal to the epistemic virtues. Another, as I have said, is the tendency of such arguments to oscillate between a basically Aristotelian conception of those virtues which defines them chiefly with reference to the various knowledge-conducive practices wherein they play a salient role and a more Kantian (deontological) approach that treats them as subject to certain 'internal' checks and constraints. This latter requirement is most often introduced – as for instance by Sosa and Greco – by way of strengthening the normative component of virtue-based theories and marking their difference from straightforward reliabilist (Goldman-type) accounts.[77] It is also invoked, on occasion, as a means of preempting the likely objection that any theory, such as this, which ties the virtues to existing (communally sanctioned) practices is apt to work out as an uncritical endorsement of just those entrenched practices and a strong disincentive to anyone wishing to pursue some alternative line of enquiry. Of course this issue crops up in sundry forms across a great range of present-day debates, from political philosophy (where it pitches liberals against communitarians) to philosophy of science (where it turns on the question as to whether – or just how far – scientific truth-claims are subject to standards of communal or peer-group warrant). However the chief source of disagreement concerning virtue-based epistemologies is what some would regard as their overcommitment to a practice-based (Aristotelian) approach that pins its faith to those epistemic virtues which currently enjoy widespread acceptance, and which thus tends to preclude – or downplay – the possibility of holding them to critical account. Whence the danger, these critics maintain, of a slide toward the kind of Wittgenstein-influenced communitarian thinking whereby it simply *cannot make sense* to question or criticize the values and beliefs embodied in some given practice, language-game or communal 'form of life'.[78] No doubt there are important distinctions to be drawn, not least with respect to Aristotle's stress on those moral, intellectual and social virtues that conduce to the common good yet which cannot be developed except through an effort of self-cultivation on the part of well-disposed individuals. All the same it is clear from certain recent, conservatively inclined statements of the case for a neo-Aristotelian (virtue-based) ethics that the comparison with Wittgenstein has some force.[79] This applies even more to arguments for a virtue-based epistemology where any relativization of knowledge (or truth) to the standards of some given – no matter how virtuous – epistemic community will very quickly run up against strong objections from a realist quarter.

Such objections may gain added force from the fact that some advocates of this approach, among them Lorraine Code, have quite explicitly linked it with a 'socialized' conception of knowledge that stresses the communal character of epistemic norms and the extent to which scientific, historical and other sorts of truth-claim are always advanced against a background of shared values and beliefs.[80] Also it is joined, in her later work, to a feminist epistemology whereby the chief emphasis falls on those various gender-inflected discourses that effectively decide what should count as authorized, legitimate 'knowledge' according to dominant (i.e., male-oriented) standards of good epistemic practice.[81] Thus it is a question of assessing the relevant virtues in terms of their compliance or non-compliance with established societal norms, and of placing most value on those that resist hegemonic pressures even though – as the logic of her argument clearly requires – the latter must also make some appeal to an alternative (non-hegemonic) community of like-minded enqirers. To be sure, Code is equally insistent that epistemic agents should 'take responsibility' for their claims, that is to say, put them forward only on condition that (1) they have been arrived at through a duly reliable process of belief-formation; and (2) they have been subject to an adequate degree of intellectual and critical self-scrutiny. However – as so often with debates in this field – one is aware of the thinly disguised conflict between a way of thinking about the epistemic virtues that pulls in a communal or 'socialized' direction and a way of thinking that reverts to certain Kantian (internalist, rule-based or deontological) arguments. Moreover this conflict goes to the heart of any virtue-based epistemology since, as I have said, it shows that project to be caught in a strictly inescapable dilemma. For if the virtues are specified in sufficiently 'thick' (i.e., practice-specific) terms as to make good their leading claim then the theory runs close – uncomfortably so, one might argue – to the Wittgensteinian or, indeed, the 'strong'-sociological case that all knowledge is the product of certain practice-relative or communally sanctioned values and beliefs.[82] Yet if such criticism is met by embracing certain features of a deontological account then the resultant 'thinning' of those epistemic virtues will tend to deprive the theorist's position of its claim to offer a truly distinctive (and genuinely problem-solving) alternative approach. Thus 'you're damned if you do and damned if you don't', as Bart Simpson more pithily phrased it.

My own view – as will be evident by now – is that these problems arise through an over-extension of the virtue theorists' case which leads them to apply ethical criteria that have their proper role in the epistemic context of discovery to issues that belong very squarely within the context of justification. That is to say, there is no doubt that such criteria go a long way toward explaining what makes the difference between well-motivated, open-minded, conscientious and intellectually responsible modes of enquiry and others that exhibit none or few of these virtuous characteristics. More than that: the theory gives a strong account of just why those particular traits should be reliably knowledge-conducive and also why their polar opposites – partiality, dogmatism, ingrained prejudice, lack of intellectual scruple – should tend to promote distorted or erroneous beliefs. So much is indeed self-evident unless one adopts a cultural-relativist or 'strong'-sociological view whereby the distinction between truth and falsehood amounts to no more than that between beliefs which enjoy a high measure of social or peer-group acceptability and beliefs which (by common assent) lack any such status.[83] One major claim of the virtue-based approach is to show that such issues need not arise since the relativist's challenge only gets a hold through the failure of objectivist or proceduralist accounts to offer any adequate normative grounds for what qualifies as genuine, reliable or responsibly acquired knowledge. However this case will appear less convincing if one takes the realist's cardinal point that the objective truth-value of certain propositions may (now or forever) elude our best powers of epistemic discernment just as knowledge – by very definition – transcends any possible specification in terms of currently accepted best belief. If the virtue-theorist at this point retreats to the failsafe option of simply *equating* truth with best belief (since what makes it 'best' is precisely its infallible deliverance of truth) then the virtues can no longer have any but a notional or place-holder role in epistemological debate. Thus it seems to me – for the various reasons set out above – that they had much better restrict their claim to the context of discovery and not yield hostages to sceptical, relativist or anti-realist fortune by pressing it into the context of justification.

CONCLUDING SCIENTIFIC-REALIST POSTSCRIPT

I

Epistemology is a large and complicated subject – one that defies synoptic treatment in a book of this length – so I have had to be highly selective in my choice of particular topics for discussion. All the same, as I have argued, the entire debate can be viewed as a range of positions taken up with regard to the basic issue between realism and scepticism concerning the existence of an 'external' (objective or mind-independent) world that is *not* just a construct out of our various sense-data, conceptual schemes, paradigms, language-games, discourses, cultural life-forms or whatever. There is no philosophical answer to the sceptic in the sense of an answer that would finally quell such doubts and convince them on sheerly logical or demonstrative grounds that scepticism cannot make sense. G.E. Moore famously thought to provide such a 'proof of the external world' when, in the course of a Cambridge lecture, he held up one hand, pointed to it with the other, and asserted that everything followed from this basic demonstration that at least two objects could be known to exist on straightforward evidential grounds.[1] Any well-trained sceptic could make short work of Moore's purported proof, just as she could argue, *contra* Wittgenstein, that such doubts cannot be laid to rest merely by observing that they have no place in our communally sanctioned language-games or life-forms and must therefore be counted strictly unintelligible.[2] Indeed such arguments give the sceptic a handle for insisting that realism is nothing more than a certain, deeply acculturated habit of thought which provides absolutely no guarantee of its own veridical status. Still the realist may very well want to come back and ask whether arguments of this sort can be held to possess more rational warrant than appeals to the self-evidence of progress in various tried and tested fields of everyday experiential and applied scientific knowledge. That is to say, the burden of proof falls squarely on those who would reject the case for convergent realism, or for scientific method as our best guarantee that most of our theories or working hypotheses are on the right track, even though (as the realist will readily concede) by no means secure against any prospect of future revision or rejection.[3]

At this stage the sceptic routinely responds with some version of the 'argument from error', i.e., the claim that since so many erstwhile well-entrenched scientific theories have demonstrably *not* been on the right track therefore it is a safe bet that most of our currently accepted 'knowledge' will likewise turn out to be false, partial or based on inadequate evidence.[4] What this amounts to is a kind of sceptical meta-induction which turns the realist's argument back upon itself and demands why we should place any confidence in methods and assumptions – like inductive reasoning or the idea of scientific progress – that have suffered such a range of failures and setbacks throughout their history to date. But then, once again, the realist will ask: on just what grounds can the sceptic advance this case if not on the implicitly realist premise that we now have adequate scientific reason to count those earlier theories false, or to assert with good warrant that terms like 'phlogiston' or the 'luminiferous ether' no longer have any legitimate role in physical science? More than that: she can point out the difference between a term like 'phlogiston' that proved wholly devoid of referential content with the advent of Lavoisier's oxygen-based theory of combustion and a term like the 'luminiferous ether' which can be shown to have referred (albeit on a charitable or truth-optimizing construal) to what physicists would later describe as the 'electro-magnetic field'.[5] In other words there may be instances of quasi or oblique (as distinct from null or downright fallacious) reference where the term in question has played an important facilitating role in the development of a later, more adequate scientific theory.[6]

Thus the realist can put up a strong case – *contra* the wholesale sceptical argument from error – for the partial conservation of certain theories that have not (like the 'phlogiston' theory of combustion or Aristotle's concept of 'natural place' to account for the motion of falling bodies) relinquished any claim to describe or explain the physical phenomena concerned. After all, as Hilary

Putnam remarks, there is a certain 'grand indifference to detail' in the paradigm-relativist idea that Aristotle's theory made just as good sense on its own cosmological terms as later theories of gravitational attraction like those of Galileo or Newton. On Aristotle's account, if one travelled to the Moon and released a rock from some few feet above its surface then the rock would head straight off to Earth, thus seeking out its 'natural place' in the sublunary order of the elements.[7] Of course the relativist may stick to his thesis and choose to ignore its awkward implications when confronted with evidence such as that provided by NASA films of the first moon-landing, not to mention the entire existing body of astronomical theory and observational data. Or again, he could join the small but vociferous lobby which maintains that the landing never took place and that the film 'evidence' was faked as a means of boosting US scientific morale in response to Soviet advances. But he would then – it is fair to say – be opting out of scientific debate or leaving philosophy of science behind for the sake of quite different interests.

The same kind of argument can be brought against Kuhnian notions of radical paradigm-incommensurability, ideas that have left their deepest imprint on the 'strong'-sociological and 'science-studies' literature.[8] Thus, for instance, a term such as 'mass' may have undergone radical changes of sense and imputed reference in the passage from Newtonian to post-Einsteinian conceptions of gravity and space-time physics. Yet there is reason to suppose – as against the idea of sharply discontinuous paradigm-shifts – that 'mass' now has a range of well-defined senses ('absolute mass', 'rest-mass', 'inertial mass', 'relativistic mass') and that the shift in question was one that involved a progressive rethinking of the relation between them rather than a total break with earlier (pre-relativist) conceptions.[9] This basically semantic version of the case leads on to the more substantive claim that we can justify talk of scientific progress and challenge the sceptical meta-induction by adducing other instances – such as 'molecule', 'atom' and 'electron' – where the range of descriptive or identifying criteria has likewise been subject to large-scale revision but where these terms can nonetheless be taken as referring to the self-same entities. It is this kind of detailed engagement with particular issues in the history and philosophy of science that provides the best starting-point for discussion, rather than high-level abstract debates about the 'problem of knowledge' or the 'existence of an external world'. For the former approach has the great advantage of focusing squarely on concrete examples – such as those mentioned above – and obliging the sceptic to defend his position despite all the detailed evidence adduced in support of a convergent-realist account premised on inference to the best (most rational or truth-tracking) explanation.[10] Of course the sceptic may reject this whole approach as a species of circular argument, or one whose every term ('evidence', 'rational', 'truth', 'explanation') incorporates precisely those realist assumptions that he – the sceptic – is out to deny. If so, then the argument has shifted to a level where the sceptic will always have the last word, but only at the cost of renouncing any claim to provide an intelligible account of our everyday experience as well as our knowledge of the growth of scientific knowledge.

This dispute is within reach of the larger issue – one with an important ethical as well as epistemological dimension – as to whether such arguments may relativize truth to the point where it becomes nothing more than a product of communal acceptance within some particular (e.g., scientific) 'practice' or 'form of life'. On this Wittgensteinian view there is no appeal to values of truth, rationality or ethical and social justice beyond those that play a meaningful role in the language-game or life-form concerned.[11] Just as anti-realism of the Dummettian variety denies the existence of objective, recognition-transcendent truth-values for statements of the so-called 'disputed class', i.e., those for which we possess no means of ascertainment or decisive proof, so likewise in matters of ethical debate it is pointless to invoke culture-transcendent standards of objective moral good or natural justice. My point is that the widespread current retreat from realist conceptions of truth is one that leaves its advocates hard put to explain how the conditions of human existence might be changed for the better through certain kinds of responsible, ethically concerned and – above all – realistically achievable forms of applied scientific knowledge. Thus there is not much purpose in floating ideas about the good life if those ideas go along – as they do for a thinker like Rorty – with the kind of extreme descriptivist position according to which reality *just is* a product of our various language-games, metaphors or preferred 'final vocabularies'.[12] For this amounts to a vaguely utopian variant of the strong-constructivist claim, the idea that we are free to redescribe 'reality' in whatever way we choose since there is nothing in the nature of things – no source of extra-linguistic constraint – that would render some such descriptions true (or practically realizable) and others merely a result of wishful thinking. Indeed the very notion that by changing 'vocabularies' we can somehow bring about a change in the prospects for human physical and social flourishing is one that could only gain credence in a culture – that of Rorty's favoured 'North Atlantic postmodern bourgeois-liberal pragmatism' – which banks heavily on the no doubt attractive idea that wishing can make it so. However such thinking rather soon runs up against some harsh realities – among them the facts of incurable disease and looming environmental catastrophe – that place sharp limits on the scope for redescription except as a means of denying or evading those same recalcitrant facts. To be sure, there is a sense in which adopting some different range of descriptive or conceptual resources may open the way to new developments in medical science or fresh ways of thinking that might point beyond the present environmental crisis. Still they will need to be based on a realist assessment of what lies within the bounds of techno-scientific possibility, along with a well-developed grasp of the causal factors and the jointly enabling and limiting conditions that apply in any given case. For the Rortian descriptivist, conversely, all that is required is a switch to some alternative 'description' whereby the problems can be made to disappear (or the solutions to emerge) through a kind of verbal alchemy. What Rorty is thus proposing is a literalized version of Kuhn's arguably metaphoric claim that 'the world changes' with every major shift of scientific paradigms.[13] But where Kuhn allows for lengthy periods of 'normal', problem-solving science between episodes of drastic upheaval Rorty envisages a process of perpetual revolution, one in which the only constraint on our freedom to create a better world is the tendency to stick with old, habituated, routine habits of talk. For if realism is merely (as he argues) a secularized stand-in for outworn theological ways of thinking – if the idea that our statements should somehow 'match the facts' is just another version of the primitive belief that 'the gods can be placated by chanting the right words' – then indeed there is nothing to prevent us from changing the words and reinventing 'reality' in whichever way we choose.[14]

According to Rorty, 'the source of realist, antipragmatist philosophy of science is the attempt, characteristic of the Enlightenment, to make "Nature" do duty for God – the attempt to make natural science a way of conforming to the will of a power not ourselves, rather than a way of facilitating commerce with the things around us'.[15] It seems to me that this argument comes back like a boomerang and that in truth it is the Rortian 'strong'-descriptivist who invests language with a quasi-divine or miraculous power of transmuting the world. Such ideas no doubt possess a strong appeal for those who – understandably – view modern science and its technological applications with a high degree of mistrust, and who wish to see it directed in more humane, socially responsive, or ethically accountable ways. There is also, in the US cultural context, a prominent strain of mythic-utopian thinking that takes various forms, from literary genres 'high' and 'low' to the offerings of Hollywood romance, or from William James's pragmatist idea of psychological self-help through the 'will to believe' to Christian Science and faith-healing.[16] However, this confidence in the power of creative or imaginative thought to overcome bad realities can easily become something less attractive, as with the notion that people (individuals or cultures) have only themselves to blame if they can't muster the moral resources to believe what's good for them or to 'redescribe' their world in suitably uplifting terms. Thus – to put it plainly – there is something cruel about a self-help doctrine which informs the chronically or terminally ill patient that his or her condition must have resulted from a failure to think more positive, spirit-enhancing or suchlike salvific thoughts. And there is a similar objection, on ethical as well as scientific grounds, to the notion that 'redescribing' our various social, political and environmental ills can somehow *in itself* point a way beyond them, or allow us to break with the realist mind-set that would leave them firmly in place. Bertrand Russell put the case most forcefully in his rejoinder to James, namely that whatever its proclaimed spiritual or psychological benefits the 'will to believe' had absolutely no place in matters of knowledge or truth.[17]

This flipside aspect of utopian thinking comes most plainly out if one asks what follows from Rorty's idea that the whole scientifically recognized range of 'natural kinds' – atoms, molecules, elements, genes, biological species – are products, merely, of the language by which we describe them or our present, culture-relative schemes of classification. For the same would apply to malignant bacteria, flesh-eating viruses, cancer cells, or genetic mutation-inducing chemical substances, all of which – if they could only be brought under some alternative description – might exert nothing like so depressing an effect on our capacity for positive thought. My point, to repeat, is that the only hope for harnessing science more safely and securely to the prospects for human good is to keep a firm sense of what lies realistically within its power to achieve, a sense that can and should be fully responsive to ethical and socio-political values, but which doesn't take refuge in a wishful realm of untrammelled creative redescription. Besides, there is a danger – especially (again) in the present-day US context – that such thinking will lend itself to ideological agendas that would scarcely find favour with those, like Rorty, who count themselves on the liberal left. For the most powerful, politically effective anti-science lobbies are not composed chiefly – if at all – of philosophers and social thinkers who espouse a broadly progressivist conception of the communal good. Rather they comprise a strategic alliance of those on the Christian-fundamentalist, creationist, 'pro-life' (anti-abortion) and other such conservative fronts who can readily exploit the 'strong'-descriptivist line to their own persuasive purposes. In which case it may turn out to have some far from liberal implications, not least when applied to issues – like medical ethics or genetic research – where doctrinal adherence is apt to override the interests of reasoned, scientifically informed, democratic debate.

II

I have covered quite a range of topics in this book, from realism versus anti-realism in philosophy of language, science and mathematics to Donald Rumsfeld's ruminations on the nature of evidential reasoning and the question whether science can be thought of as socially responsive (or value-led) without giving way to extreme forms of cultural-relativist thinking. Where these topics converge is on the issue first raised in Plato's *Theaetetus*, that is to say, the relationship between truth, knowledge and belief.[18] While much of this discussion is highly specialized, i.e., intra-philosophical in character, it is still best viewed – as I have suggested here – in the wider context of debate in fields such as historiography, philosophy of science and ethics (where the realist/anti-realist controversy is a topic of central concern). Least of all can philosophers with a primary interest in epistemological matters afford to ignore the detailed evidence of scientific history to date or the kinds of challenge currently posed by versions of that history – like those put forward by the advocates of a 'strong'-sociological approach – that question the received or orthodox account.[19]

Moreover, this can be done in a way that presents both sides to each debate – and avoids the temptation of caricature – while not falling into the opposite trap of adopting a stance that is so even-handed (or studiously non-committal) as to let the whole argument go by default. For of course this approach would effectively amount to just a round-about endorsement of the relativist case, i.e., that any 'truth' in such matters can only be a matter of whatever fits in with our preconceptions or whatever is borne out by some existing consensus of widely accredited belief. I have made no attempt to disguise my conviction that realism is the only philosophic standpoint that offers an adequate account of these issues. All the same I would hope to have done so in a way that gives a fair hearing to dissident (e.g., sceptical, anti-realist or social-constructivist) views. In the current, sharply polarized context of debate this seems the best approach for anyone concerned to uphold the values of open-minded critical enquiry.

Besides, this issue – like all the central problems in philosophy – is one that has been batted around for so long and in such a range of alternative (more-or-less technical) idioms that any hope of coming up with a purely *philosophical* knock-down argument on either side is by now pretty remote. Thus the realist may be tempted (and I feel this temptation strongly myself) to carry on piling up examples of falsified truth-claims on the one hand and, on the other, claims borne out to the utmost of our rational-investigative powers with the aim of making the contrary position look downright absurd or perverse. Such (to repeat) is the basic case for convergent realism or – in a slightly different form – the 'no miracles' argument according to which the success of science in producing so many predictive, explanatory and applied technological advances would indeed be miraculous if not on the assumption that most of its theories were true and that most of its referring (e.g., natural-kind) terms picked out real-world objects, structures and properties thereof.[20] Of course the anti-realist can again come back with some version of the sceptical meta-induction from past scientific error. This is the argument that since so many items of erstwhile accepted or orthodox scientific 'knowledge' have since turned out to be false – or (like those of Galileo and Newton) to apply only within a certain restricted spatio-temporal domain – therefore we can scarcely be justified in taking our present best theories or range of candidate realia to possess any stronger claim to truth. However the realist can then point out that this thesis is plainly self-refuting in so far as it assumes the validity of just those cardinal distinctions – i.e., between truth and falsehood or scientifically justified and unjustified belief – which the sceptic is out to deny. Thus the argument from error is *ipso facto* one that not only brings truth-values into play but treats them as always in principle transcending any given (whether past, present or future) state of belief, no matter how expert or well-informed by the standards of its own time and place. So the case for realism is one that gains support both on metaphysical (or logico-semantic) and on epistemological grounds, that is to say, as best providing both a generalized account of the relationship between truth, knowledge and belief and a means of explaining just how that relationship is exemplified by various well-documented episodes of scientific theory-change.

One result of the so-called science wars – the recent much-publicized exchange of hostilities between scientists and sections of the 'cultural left' – has been to create a climate of reciprocal mistrust that tends to discourage free and open debate on these matters.[21] Many will feel the need to strike a balance between encouraging respect for the real achievements of the natural sciences – the fact that they have *discovered* (not 'constructed' or 'invented') a great many truths about the physical world – and, on the other hand, offering a sense of the historical or socio-cultural contexts in which scientific work actually gets done. At any rate it is clear that epistemologists – including those of a realist persuasion – have much to learn from the kinds of approach adopted by some sociologists of knowledge and cultural historians of science. After all, these researchers have produced some highly informative case studies concerning the everyday details of 'laboratory life', the role of ideological factors in provoking or settling scientific disputes, and the various motivating interests (political, religious, professional, etc.) that have affected the way scientists work and think.[22] However these findings can be taken on board without drawing the further cultural-relativist conclusion, that is to say, the 'strong'-sociological claim that scientific knowledge amounts to *no more* than a product of those same motivating interests. For if the argument is pushed that far then it does science (as well as philosophy and every other discipline of thought) a definite disservice by promoting an outlook of generalized scepticism, a facile presumption that truth *just is* whatever counts as such according to this or that consensus view.[23]

Old-style logical empiricism is deeply unfashionable nowadays but it did provide some useful arguments for distinguishing between 'context of discovery' and 'context of justification'.[24] The former had to do with various non-scientific (for instance, psychological or socio-historical) factors that may have influenced the conduct of research, while the latter had to do with those processes of evidential reasoning, replication of empirical results, hypothesis construction, theory-testing and so forth which made up the history of scientific thought, properly so called. However this distinction has pretty much gone by the board in a good deal of recent work under the 'science-studies' or 'strong'-sociological rubric. In its place there is the notion of 'parity of esteem', taken to require that we treat *all* theories – whether those that still enjoy some measure of acceptance among scientific experts or those that are standardly counted wrong in some decisive regard – as products of socio-cultural class-interest or some clearly marked ideological *parti pris*.[25] This is why writers like Shapin and Schaffer, in their brilliant but (I think) conceptually misguided book *Leviathan and the Air-Pump*, urge us not to jump to the orthodox conclusion that Thomas Hobbes was plain wrong – in the grip of an ideological prejudice – when he denied the existence of vacuum phenomena, and Robert Boyle demonstrably right (or on the right track) when he conducted his famous air-pump experiments and thereby showed himself a good, empirically minded physicist rather than an old-style dogmatic metaphysician with a political axe to grind.[26] Rather we should see that Boyle was just as much subject to class-based interests and pressures, although his methodology just happened to suit the emergent (bourgeois-liberal) social consensus, whereas Hobbes harked back to an older, residual set of beliefs about the need for a physical and a social ontology that excluded any empty space – any 'vacuum' – where conflicts of interest and allegiance might always arise and precipitate another crisis like that of the English Civil War. So the good sociologist should suspend all judgements of valid scientific method and operate on a strict principle of parity as concerns the truth-content – or rational warrant – of conflicting scientific theories.

I think there are two things principally wrong with this approach. One is that it fails to explain why so much of modern science – including its technological applications – should have turned out to vindicate the truth of Boyle's theory and to make no sense on the Hobbesian account. This is the idea of inference to the best, most adequate or rational explanation, an approach that is mostly rejected or ignored by the 'strong' sociologists but which has a fair claim to account most convincingly (i.e., with least need of miracles or 'cosmic coincidence') for our knowledge of the growth of scientific knowledge.[27] The other main problem with Shapin and Schaffer's methodology is that it tends to work on a kind of reverse-prejudice principle, one that purports to adopt a strictly even-handed approach as between 'successful' and 'unsuccessful' theories (or mainstream and 'deviant' historiography of science), but which in fact swings the balance very heavily against the dominant – scientifically 'respectable' – view. Thus Shapin and Schaffer side with Hobbes to this extent at least: that they share his proto-Foucauldian conception of knowledge as produced in and through the operations of social power, or of scientific truth-claims as always subject to the shaping pressures of one or another hegemonic discourse.[28] So there is an inbuilt bias which leads them to favour the Hobbesian theory as a clear-eyed recognition of this basic fact about the socio-political agenda of science and the fallacy of thinking that scientific 'truth' might somehow transcend its context of historical production. It is the same bias that predisposes them against Boyle's 'bourgeois-liberal' belief that truth can be arrived at through the free and open dialogue of empirical observers just so long as they avoid fixed preconceptions, consult the widest range of experimental evidence and so far as possible seek to exclude such distorting factors.

In other words the issue played out between Hobbes and Boyle can be seen as a rehearsal of the issue played out between present-day Foucauldians and 'strong' sociologists, on the one hand, and on the other hand thinkers like Jürgen Habermas who seek to conserve those 'enlightenment' values of uncoerced rational consensus.[29] Just as Habermas's talk of 'an ideal speech-situation' can be made to look hopelessly naive and self-deluding if viewed from a Foucauldian standpoint, so Boyle's idea of scientific progress as brought about by agreement amongst qualified observers over a range of empirical data can be made to appear nothing more than a product of unwitting ideological prejudice when treated from a standpoint with such markedly Hobbesian affinities. So there is something wrong – a kind of methodological sleight-of-hand – in this claim to be redressing the balance of justice through a 'principle of parity' which in fact works out as a covert endorsement of Hobbes's political and ideological views, if not as an endorsement of his fixed belief that nature abhors a vacuum. It seems to me that much recent work in the 'strong'-sociological mode makes this same mistake of pushing too far with the claim that knowledge is a social construct or that 'truth' is always and everywhere the product of ideological vested interests. Where it oversteps the mark is firstly in seeking to erase the distinction between true and false, valid and invalid, or scientifically productive and unproductive theories, and secondly – a direct consequence of this – in supposing that sociological explanations go 'all the way down', which leads straight on to an extreme form of cultural relativism.

Of course this idea has some prominent sources in current thinking across a range of fields and disciplines. Among them are Kuhnian paradigm-relativism, post-structuralist ideas about language and representation, Foucault's 'genealogies' of power/knowledge, and the postmodernist sceptical take on presumptively outmoded 'enlightenment' concepts like truth, progress and critique.[30] These in turn go along with the widespread (to some extent justified) public anxiety about just where science might be headed in fields such as nuclear research, biotechnology or genetic engineering. What results is the generalized – I think incoherent – notion that scientific 'truth' is always relative to a given cultural belief-system and the system determined by some given range of socio-political interests, values or power-knowledge differentials. However this creates real problems for anyone who wants to make rational sense of scientific discovery-procedures, even from a mainly cultural or socio-historical viewpoint. That is to say, it is hard to think to any purpose about the history of science without some grasp of what constitutes a genuine scientific *discovery* as opposed to a more-or-less random paradigm change, cultural mutation, or Foucauldian 'epistemological break'. For one will then be hard-put to explain why, for instance, Lavoisier was right about the role of oxygen in the process of combustion while Priestley was wrong about the role of 'phlogiston' or 'dephlogistated air'. Moreover the principle of parity, strictly applied, would suspend all criteria of scientific rationality and hence fail to explain what it was about the orthodox science of the day that made it perfectly possible for Priestley, an intelligent scientist-philosopher, to credit the existence of phlogiston. Yet such issues *can* be presented in a way that preserves the distinction between scientific truth and falsehood without subjecting one party – in this case Priestley – to what E.P. Thompson memorably called (in a different, though related, context) the 'massive condescension of posterity'.[31] Indeed there is more than a hint of this condescending attitude in the 'strong' sociologists' treatment of all theories – except (presumably) those of the social sciences – as possessing an equal claim to 'truth' by their own cultural lights.

So it should be possible to treat the history of science from a socially and culturally informed perspective while resisting the idea that scientific truths are *nothing more* than products of their socio-cultural background or conditions of emergence. The trouble with this latest round of 'science wars', like the old 'two cultures' debate, is that it has led to an attitude of deadlocked mutual hostility and a flat refusal, on both sides, to allow for any moderating approach that would seek to defuse the conflict between them.[32] This is why I have made reference to the terms of one such attempted *modus vivendi*, namely the logical-empiricist distinction between 'context of discovery' and 'context of justification'.[33] That is, one can raise all sorts of questions – psychological, historical, cultural, socio-political and so forth – concerning those various factors that have arguably influenced scientists in their choice of one hypothesis over another, or their conflicting interpretations of the evidence. All this has to do with the 'context of discovery', or the kinds of no doubt revealing circumstantial detail that help to explain why scientific controversies arose at some given historical juncture, or again, what it was that predisposed scientists toward one or another means of 'saving' the empirical data. However, this approach meets its limit at precisely that point – in the context of justification – where sociology and cultural history give way to science or philosophy of science. For it is then not a question of class interests, political pressures, ideological formations, etc., but a question of how hypotheses stand up to testing under certain specified conditions such as those of controlled experiment, detailed observation, replicability and consistency with the best (theoretical informed) evidence to hand.[34] In this context there is no warrant – disciplinary prejudice aside – for adducing various contingent facts about the social and cultural history of science. To do so is a sign that one has failed to grasp the most basic principles of scientific reasoning, principles that may be open to debate (as among inductivists, covering-law theorists, Popperian falsificationists and so forth), but which nonetheless embody a shared commitment to the idea of science as a truth-seeking enterprise with its own distinctive standards of rational accountability.

Now, of course, this argument will cut no ice with 'strong' sociologists of knowledge for whom it represents just another vain attempt, on the part of mainstream philosophers of science, to prop up the scientists' false self-image as purveyors of objective, disinterested truth. When judiciously applied such a sceptical outlook can offer genuine insights, even if it involves a curious tendency to accept the plain self-evidence of certain facts (i.e., those turned up by the social sciences) while in principle rejecting any claim to that status on behalf of the natural-scientific disciplines. In other words what the strong programme amounts to is a systematic inversion of the order of priorities which characterized the old 'unity of science' project with its notion of a hard-to-soft scale of descent from physics, chemistry and biology to psychology, sociology and the other humanistic disciplines, these latter conceived as laying some claim to scientific warrant just in so far as they espoused a properly empirical approach.[35] It is not hard to see why this doctrine has given way to various reactive movements of thought which challenge the predominance of a science-led conception of truth, knowledge and method. However the reaction goes too far when it places theorists in the awkward position of professing to doubt even the best-attested results of the physical sciences while staking their case on historical and sociological 'data' which surely lie open to a much wider range of plausible interpretations. Thus – to repeat – a work like *Leviathan and the Air-Pump* is one that undoubtedly has a great deal to teach us about the way that science actually gets done by certain members of certain (residual or emergent) social classes under certain specific historical and cultural conditions. But the 'science-studies' advocates are prone to overplay their hand when they make larger claims about the social construction of *all* scientific knowledge, or when they put the case for 'parity of esteem' as between theories that have held up under rigorous testing and theories that have failed by any such standard. On this view it is merely the wisdom of selective hindsight – or the Whiggish idea of scientific 'progress' – that leads us to single out some hypotheses as valid (or on the right track) and others as false or dead-end lines of enquiry.

No doubt this approach makes very good sense from a sociological viewpoint, since here the 'context of discovery' is all that counts, and practitioners clearly stand to gain by adopting a methodology that discounts any question of objective truth or falsehood. More than that: they can argue that the history of science affords some striking examples of the way that dominant opinion has worked to discredit or to marginalize theories that went against the orthodox grain.[36] However these examples tend to undermine the 'strong' sociologists' claim since they rely on the assumption that some past theories were true (or scientifically warranted) *despite* the weight of received opinion at the time. And their case looks even shakier if applied to the issue between Boyle and Hobbes as regards vacuum phenomena, or Galileo and the church authorities as regards celestial motion, or Lavoisier and Priestley as regards the process of combustion. In these instances 'parity of esteem' would entail so a drastic a suspension of belief with regard to the most basic tenets of current scientific thinking that its proponents would be forced back to an outlook of wholesale epistemological scepticism. For to *seriously doubt* that Boyle was justified (as against Hobbes) when he affirmed the possibility of a vacuum is to undercut the grounds for rational belief in a whole vast range of subsequent developments and causal-explanatory theories. Among them must be counted the entire science of modern aerodynamics and also subatomic particle physics, since the latter received its first impetus from the observation of cathode-ray (electron) emission in a vacuum tube. That is to say, such claims must be open to the same rejoinder that critics have brought against Kuhnian talk of radical paradigm-change; namely, that the thesis collapses into manifest incoherence when required to offer evidence on its own behalf.[37]

Besides, as I have said, there is a problem for the 'strong' sociologists in so far as they are prone to adduce just the kinds of historical, social and cultural 'evidence' that fare less well under sceptical pressure than the truth-claims of the natural sciences. Of course their whole approach is intended to challenge this idea that the natural sciences (physics in particular) should be thought of as possessing superior cognitive, epistemic or truth-telling warrant. Yet there is – to put it bluntly – something rather shifty and evasive about a programme that places such unquestioning trust in the methods and procedures of sociological enquiry while adopting an outlook of blanket scepticism (or principled disbelief) with respect to whatever falls outside its own disciplinary remit. Thus Shapin and Schaffer may profess to maintain an attitude of strict neutrality as between Boyle's (on the orthodox account) properly 'scientific' investigations of vacuum-related phenomena and Hobbes's (again on the orthodox account) metaphysically loaded and politically motivated denial that such phenomena could possibly occur. However, their approach will appear less even-handed if one considers how far it leans toward a Hobbesian (or Nietzschean-Foucauldian) view of scientific 'truth' as nothing more than a product of power-knowledge differentials, or scientific 'progress' as a purely ideological construct, or history as always a 'history of the present' that retroactively projects its favoured forms of narrative emplotment.[38] The sociologists purport to avoid this bias by building in a principle of 'reflexivity', which treats their own claims as equally subject to socio-cultural analysis.[39] However there is a fairly obvious sense in which the principle works out as a strong endorsement of their preferred methodology and one that pre-emptively excludes or discredits any other (e.g., realist or causal-explanatory) account. At which point the scientific realist may reasonably argue that anyone who takes such a line is adopting a curiously skewed perspective on the relative likelihood that methods adopted in the natural or the social sciences provide our best, most reliable sources of information.

This is not to deny that the old-style 'Whiggish' account of scientific knowledge as an onward and upward progress toward truth at the preordained end of enquiry is one that stood in need of significant revision. That revisionist approach has gained momentum over the past few decades, to the point where few philosophers or historians of science – even those who come out firmly against the 'strong'-sociological programme – would wish to defend an unqualified version of the Whiggish account. Still there is a need to present these issues in a way that doesn't overemphasize the problems with 'hard-line' scientific realism, and then – in consequence – swing right across to an equally hard-line social-constructivist position. However – as I have argued above – any attempt at complete even-handedness as between these opposing views would amount to no more than a philosophic cop-out or evasion of the central issue. Thus one may often want to take a definite stand, as for instance by remarking that a self-professed 'epistemological anarchist' like Paul Feyerabend is on dubious moral as well as scientific ground when he counsels an attitude of 'anything goes' in matters of scientific truth.[40] All the more so when, in an open letter, he advises the arbiters of present-day Catholic doctrine – lineal descendents of those who persecuted Galileo – to resist the conformist pressures of secular orthodoxy and not recant their original position that his (Galileo's) was merely one hypothesis that happened to 'save' the empirical appearances.[41] This is no doubt an extreme case – maybe (on the most charitable reading) a provocative *jeu d'esprit* – and would scarcely gain credence amongst most sociologists of knowledge, let alone amongst anti-realists of a more philosophical mind. Nevertheless their arguments are best engaged through a critical approach that gives due weight to the conceptual problems involved – problems such as those concerning the objectivity of mathematical truth or the underdetermination of physical theories by empirical evidence – while maintaining a vigorously principled commitment to standards of valid scientific method.

This is also to say (academic self-interest aside) that epistemology and philosophy of science have a useful role in science education. For there is clearly a sense in which issues like these link up with wider public concerns about the extent to which scientists can or should be held socially and morally accountable for the outcome of their various research projects. Since many people are likely to have encountered positions on both sides of the debate – arguments for the value-neutrality of science and arguments for its social responsibility – philosophers can usefully build on this background to point out some of the misconceptions that have led to the current, somewhat unedifying round of public hostilities. Thus, for instance, a relativist approach of the full-fledged Feyerabend kind may appear socially and ethically benign in so far as it encourages acceptance of the widest possible range of beliefs, from alchemy to post-Daltonian chemistry, or from voodoo magic to mainstream medical science, or from raindance rituals to modern meteorology. However such tolerance tends to be highly selective, involving as it does – like the 'strong'-sociological approach – a marked bias against any 'orthodox' conception that would distinguish between science and pseudo-science, or better and worse ways of reasoning on the evidence. In this book I have put the case for a robust conception of epistemology as the discipline whose range of normative, explanatory and critical resources render it best equipped to address these issues.

36580

NOTES

1: STAYING FOR AN ANSWER: TRUTH, KNOWLEDGE AND THE RUMSFELD CREED

1 For more on this press briefing and the debate it stirred up, try a Google search under 'Rumsfeld + known unknowns'.
2 See website at www.plainenglish.co.uk.
3 Mark Steyn, 'Rumsfeld Talks Sense, Not Gobbledegook', *Daily Telegraph*, 12 September 2003.
4 See Paul Boghossian and Christopher Peacocke (eds), *New Essays on the A Priori*, Oxford: Clarendon Press, 2000; Albert Casullo (ed.), *A Priori Knowledge*, Aldershot: Ashgate, 1999; J. Alberto Coffa, *The Semantic Tradition from Kant to Carnap: to the Vienna Station*, Cambridge: Cambridge University Press, 1991; Hans Reichenbach, *The Theory of Relativity and A Priori Knowledge*, trans. Maria Reichenbach, Berkeley and Los Angeles: University of California Press, 1965.
5 Hilary Putnam, 'There Is at Least One *A Priori* Truth', in *Realism and Reason*, Cambridge: Cambridge University Press, 1983, pp. 98–114.
6 See for instance J. Aronson, R. Harré and E. Way, *Realism Rescued: how scientific progress is possible*, London: Duckworth, 1994; Michael Devitt, *Realism and Truth*, 2nd edn, Oxford: Blackwell, 1986; Jarrett Leplin (ed.), *Scientific Realism*, Berkeley and Los Angeles: University of California Press, 1984; Stathis Psillos, *Scientific Realism: how science tracks truth*, London: Routledge, 1999.
7 Bertrand Russell, 'William James's Conception of Truth', in Simon Blackburn and Keith Simmons (eds), *Truth*, Oxford: Oxford University Press, 1999, pp. 69–82; William James, *Pragmatism: a new name for some old ways of thinking*, New York: Longmans, 1907. James's response to Russell may be found in his *The Meaning of Truth*, Longmans, 1909.
8 For further discussion, see Christopher Norris, *Truth Matters: realism, anti-realism and response-dependence*, Edinburgh: Edinburgh University Press, 2000 and *Philosophy of Language and the Challenge to Scientific Realism*, London: Routledge, 2004.

9 See especially Richard Rorty, *Objectivity, Relativism, and Truth*, Cambridge: Cambridge University Press, 1999 and *Truth and Progress*, Cambridge: Cambridge University Press, 1998.

10 See Note 7, above.

11 See especially Michael Dummett, *Truth and Other Enigmas*, London: Duckworth, 1978; also Dummett, *The Logical Basis of Metaphysics*, London: Duckworth, 1991 and *The Seas of Language*, Oxford: Clarendon Press, 1993; Michael Luntley, *Language, Logic and Experience: the case for anti-realism*, London: Duckworth, 1988; Neil Tennant, *Anti-Realism and Logic*, Oxford: Clarendon Press, 1987 and *The Taming of the True*, Oxford: Oxford University Press, 1997.

12 See for instance David Miller (ed.), *Tell Me Lies: propaganda and media distortion in the attack on Iraq*, London: Pluto Press, 2004.

13 See Note 11, above; also John Haldane and Crispin Wright (eds), *Realism, Representation and Projection*, Oxford: Oxford University Press, 1993; Norris, *Truth Matters*; Crispin Wright, *Realism, Meaning and Truth*, 2nd edn, Oxford: Blackwell, 1993 and *Truth and Objectivity*, Cambridge, MA: Harvard University Press, 1992.

14 See Notes 11 and 13, above.

15 See for instance William P. Alston, *A Realist Theory of Truth*, Ithaca, NY: Cornell University Press, 1996; Devitt, *Realism and Truth*; Jerrold J. Katz, *Realistic Rationalism*, Cambridge, MA: MIT Press, 1998; Scott Soames, *Understanding Truth*, Oxford: Oxford University Press, 1999.

16 Dummett, *Truth and Other Enigmas*.

17 See A.J. Ayer (ed.), *Logical Positivism*, New York: Free Press, 1959 and Nicholas Rescher (ed.), *The Heritage of Logical Positivism*, Lanham: University Press of America, 1985; also C.J. Misak, *Verificationism: its history and prospects*, London: Routledge, 1995.

18 See Dummett, *The Logical Basis of Metaphysics* and *The Seas of Language* (Note 11, above).

19 See especially Devitt, *Realism and Truth* and Norris, *Philosophy of Language and the Challenge to Scientific Realism* (Notes 6 and 8, above).

20 For discussion of these issues from the standpoint of historiography, see Joyce Appleby, Lynn Hunt and Margaret Jacob, *Telling the Truth About History*, New York: Norton, 1994; Richard Campbell, *Truth and Historicity*, Oxford: Oxford University Press, 1992; Richard Evans, *In Defence of History*, London: Granta Books, 1997; Christopher Norris, *Truth and the Ethics of Criticism*, Manchester: Manchester University Press, 1994; Paul Ricoeur, *History and Truth*, trans. Charles A. Kelbley, Evanston, IL: Northwestern University Press, 1965.

21 I take this example from Soames, *Understanding Truth* (Note 15, above).

22 Dummett *Truth and Other Enigmas*.

23 Dummett, *The Logical Basis of Metaphysics*, p. 7.

24 Dummett, *The Logical Basis of Metaphysics*, p. 7.

25 See Dummett, 'Can an Effect Precede its Cause?', 'Bringing About the Past' and 'The Reality of the Past', in *Truth and Other Enigmas*, pp. 319–32, 333–50 and 358–74.

26 Dummett, 'Bringing About the Past'.

27 See Note 25, above; also Norris, *Truth Matters* and – for some highly relevant discussion – Bernhard Weiss, *Michael Dummett*, Chesham: Acumen, 2002.

28 Dummett, *The Logical Basis of Metaphysics*, p. 7.

29 See Notes 12 and 20, above; also Norris, *New Idols of the Cave: on the limits of anti-realism*, Manchester: Manchester University Press, 1997 and *Resources of Realism: prospects for 'post-analytic' philosophy*, London: Macmillan, 1997; Gerald Vision, *Modern Anti-Realism and Manufactured Truth*, London: Routledge, 1988.

30 On this topic see especially Michael Williams, *Unnatural Doubts: epistemological realism and the basis of scepticism*, Princeton, NJ: Princeton University Press, 1997; also Barry Stroud, *The Significance of Philosophical Scepticism*, Oxford: Clarendon Press, 1984.

31 See especially Paul Benacerraf, 'What Numbers Could Not Be', in Benacerraf and Hilary Putnam (eds), *The Philosophy of Mathematics: selected essays*, 2nd edn, Cambridge: Cambridge University Press, 1983, pp. 272–94; also Putnam, *Mathematics, Matter and Method*, Cambridge: Cambridge University Press, 1975.

32 Michael Dummett, *Elements of Intuitionism*, Oxford: Oxford University Press, 1977.

33 Norris, *Truth Matters*.

34 See especially Kurt Gödel, 'What is Cantor's Continuum Problem?', in Benacerraf and Putnam (eds), *The Philosophy of Mathematics*, pp. 470–85; also Gödel, *On Formally Undecidable Propositions of Principia Mathematica and Related Systems*, trans. B. Meltzer, New York: Basic Books, 1962; Katz, *Realistic Rationalism*; Ernest Nagel and James Newman, *Gödel's Proof*, London: Routledge, 1971; Roger Penrose, *Shadows of the Mind: a search for the missing science of consciousness*, London: Vintage, 1995; and S.G. Shanker (ed.), *Gödel's Theorem in Focus*, London: Routledge, 1987.

35 See for instance Michael Detlefson (ed.), *Proof and Knowledge in Mathematics*, London: Routledge, 1992; W.D. Hart (ed.), *The Philosophy of Mathematics*, Oxford: Oxford University Press, 1996.

36 Thomas Reid, *Inquiry and Essays*, Indianapolis: Hackett, 1983; also Nicholas Wolterstorff, *Thomas Reid and the Story of Epistemology*, Cambridge: Cambridge University Press, 2001.

37 See especially C.A.J. Coady, *Testimony: a philosophical study*, Oxford: Clarendon Press, 1992.

38 See Note 17, above.

39 J.S. Mill, *A System of Logic*, 2 vols, ed. J.M. Robson, London: Routledge and Kegan Paul, 1974.

40 See Dummett, *Elements of Intuitionism*.

2: REALISM, REFERENCE AND POSSIBLE WORLDS

1 Saul A. Kripke, *Naming and Necessity*, Oxford: Blackwell, 1980; also Gottlob Frege, 'On Sense and Reference', in Peter Geach and Max Black

(eds), *Translations from the Philosophical Writings of Gottlob Frege*, Oxford: Blackwell, 1952, pp. 56–78 and Bertrand Russell, 'On Denoting', *Mind*, vol. 14 (1905), pp. 479–93.

2 Kripke, *Naming and Necessity*.

3 See Leonard Linsky (ed.), *Reference and Modality*, Oxford: Oxford University Press, 1971; Stephen Schwartz (ed.), *Naming, Necessity, and Natural Kinds*, Ithaca, NY: Cornell University Press, 1977; David Wiggins, *Sameness and Substance*, Oxford: Blackwell, 1980.

4 See especially Hilary Putnam, 'Is Semantics Possible?', 'The Meaning of "Meaning"' and 'Language and Reality', in *Mind, Language and Reality*, Cambridge: Cambridge University Press, 1975, pp. 139–52, 215–71 and 272–90.

5 See also Gregory McCulloch, *The Mind and Its World*, London: Routledge, 1995.

6 Thomas S. Kuhn, *The Structure of Scientific Revolutions*, 2nd edn, Chicago: University of Chicago Press, 1970; W.V. Quine, 'Two Dogmas of Empiricism', in *From a Logical Point of View*, 2nd edn, Cambridge, MA: Harvard University Press, 1961, pp. 20–46; also W.V. Quine, *Ontological Relativity and Other Essays*, New York: Columbia University Press, 1969.

7 See Frege, 'On Sense and Reference'; also Michael Dummett, *Truth and Other Enigmas*, London: Duckworth, 1978.

8 For further discussion, see Larry Laudan, *Progress and Its Problems*, Berkeley and Los Angeles: University of California Press, 1977; Peter Lipton, *Inference to the Best Explanation*, London: Routledge, 1993; Nicholas Rescher, *Scientific Progress*, Oxford: Blackwell, 1979.

9 See Note 6, above; also Sandra Harding, *Can Theories Be Refuted? essays on the Duhem-Quine thesis*, Dordrecht: Reidel, 1976.

10 See Quine, 'Two Dogmas of Empiricism'; also Peter Gibbins, *Particles and Paradoxes: the limits of quantum logic*, Cambridge: Cambridge University Press, 1987: Susan Haack, *Deviant Logic: some philosophical issues*, Cambridge: Cambridge University Press, 1974; Christopher Norris, *Quantum Theory and the Flight from Realism: philosophical responses to quantum mechanics*, London: Routledge, 2000.

11 For further argument to this effect, see entries for Gibbins and Norris under Note 10, above.

12 See especially Hilary Putnam, *Meaning and the Moral Sciences*, London: Routledge and Kegan Paul, 1978.

13 Cf. Niels Bohr, *Atomic Physics and the Description of Nature*, Cambridge: Cambridge University Press, 1934 and *Atomic Physics and Human Knowledge*, New York: Wiley, 1958.

14 See Christopher Norris, 'The Expert, The Neophyte, and the X-Ray Tube', in *Philosophy of Language and the Challenge to Scientific Realism*, London: Routledge, 2004, pp. 27–49.

15 See M. Gardner, 'Realism and Instrumentalism in Nineteenth-Century Atomism', *Philosophy of Science*, vol. 46 (1979), pp. 1–34; J. Perrin, *Atoms*, trans. D.L. Hammick, New York: Van Nostrand, 1923; Mary Jo Nye, *Molecular Reality*, London: MacDonald, 1972; also Ian Hacking,

Representing and Intervening: introductory topics in the philosophy of natural science, Cambridge: Cambridge University Press, 1983 and 'Do We See through a Microscope?', *Pacific Philosophical Quarterly*, vol. 62 (1981), pp. 305–22.

16 Kuhn, *The Structure of Scientific Revolutions*.

17 See especially Stathis Psillos, *Scientific Realism: how science tracks truth*, London: Routledge, 1999; also J. Aronson, R. Harré and E. Way, *Realism Rescued: how scientific progress is possible*, London: Duckworth, 1994; Michael Devitt, *Realism and Truth*, 2nd edn, Oxford: Blackwell, 1986; Jarrett Leplin (ed.), *Scientific Realism*, Berkeley and Los Angeles: University of California Press, 1984.

18 I take this example from Psillos (*Scientific Realism*).

19 See for instance Gareth Evans, *The Varieties of Reference*, ed. John McDowell, Oxford: Clarendon Press, 1982 and Schwartz (ed.), *Naming, Necessity, and Natural Kinds*.

20 See Note 4, above; also Christopher Norris, *Hilary Putnam: realism, reason, and the uses of uncertainty*, Manchester: Manchester University Press, 2002.

21 Putnam, 'The Meaning of "Meaning"'.

22 Tyler Burge, 'Individualism and the Mental', in P.A. French, T.E. Uehling and H. Wettstein (eds), *Midwest Studies in Philosophy*, vol. 10 (1979), pp. 73–121.

23 See Note 4, above; also Putnam, *Meaning and the Moral Sciences*, pp. 22–6.

24 McCulloch, *The Mind and Its World*.

25 See Notes 1, 3 and 4, above; also Raymond Bradley and Norman Swartz, *Possible Worlds: an introduction to modal logic and its philosophy*, Oxford: Blackwell, 1979.

26 W.V. Quine, 'Reference and Modality' and 'Quantifiers and Propositional Attitudes', in Linsky (ed.), *Reference and Modality*, pp. 17–34 and 101–11.

27 David Lewis, *On the Plurality of Worlds*, Oxford: Blackwell, 1986; also *Counterfactuals*, Blackwell, 1979.

28 For further discussion see William P. Alston, *A Realist Conception of Truth*, Ithaca, NY: Cornell University Press, 1996; Bob Hale, *Abstract Objects*, Oxford: Blackwell, 1987; Jerrold J. Katz, *Realistic Rationalism*, Cambridge, MA: MIT Press, 1998; Scott Soames, *Understanding Truth*, Oxford: Oxford University Press, 1999.

29 See Norris, *Quantum Theory and the Flight from Realism*; also *Logic, Language and Epistemology: a modal-realist approach*, Manchester: Manchester University Press, 2004.

30 David Deutsch, *The Fabric of Reality*, Harmondsworth: Penguin, 1997; B. de Witt and N. Graham (eds), *The Many-Worlds Interpretation of Quantum Mechanics*, Princeton, NJ: Princeton University Press, 1973; G.W. Leibniz, *Monadology*, trans. E. Latta, Oxford: Oxford University Press, 1972 and *New Essays Concerning Human Understanding*, trans. A.G. Langley, La Salle, IL: Open Court, 1926; also Hidé Ishiguro, *Leibniz's Philosophy of Logic and Language*, London: Duckworth, 1972.

31 See for instance – from a range of disciplinary standpoints – Geoffrey Hawthorn, *Plausible Worlds: possibility and understanding in history and the social sciences*, Cambridge: Cambridge University Press, 1991; J.L. Mackie, *The Cement of the Universe*, Oxford: Clarendon Press, 1974; Wesley C. Salmon, *Scientific Explanation and the Causal Structure of the World*, Princeton, NJ: Princeton University Press, 1984.

32 See Note 6, above.

33 Quine, 'Reference and Modality', pp. 20–1.

34 See Norris, *Language, Logic and Epistemology*.

35 Bradley and Swartz, *Possible Worlds*, p. 219.

36 See especially Paul Benacerraf, 'What Numbers Could Not Be', in Benacerraf and Putnam (eds), *The Philosophy of Mathematics: selected essays*, 2nd edn, Cambridge: Cambridge University Press, 1983, pp. 272–94; also W.D. Hart (ed.), *The Philosophy of Mathematics*, Oxford: Oxford University Press, 1996; Michael Dummett, *Elements of Intuitionism*, 2nd edn, Oxford: Clarendon Press, 2000.

37 See Dummett, *Truth and Other Enigmas*; also *The Logical Basis of Metaphysics*, London: Duckworth, 1991 and *The Seas of Language*, Oxford: Clarendon Press, 1993; Michael Luntley, *Language, Logic and Experience: the case for anti-realism*, London: Duckworth, 1988; Neil Tennant, *Anti-Realism and Logic*, Oxford: Clarendon Press, 1987 and *The Taming of the True*, Oxford: Oxford University Press, 1997.

38 See Laudan, *Progress and its Problems*; also 'A Confutation of Convergent Realism', *Philosophy of Science*, vol. 48 (1981), pp. 19–49.

39 Rescher, *Scientific Progress*, p. 61.

40 See for instance J.L. Aronson, 'Testing for Convergent Realism', *British Journal for the Philosophy of Science*, vol. 40 (1989), pp. 255–60; Richard Boyd, 'The Current Status of Scientific Realism', in Leplin (ed.), *Scientific Realism*, pp. 41–82; Putnam, *Mind, Language and Reality*.

41 Putnam, *Mind, Language and Reality*, p. 290.

42 See especially Bas C. van Fraassen, *The Scientific Image*, Oxford: Clarendon Press, 1980; also – for a range of views on the topic of 'constructive empiricism' – C.J. Misak, *Verificationism: its history and prospects*, London: Routledge, 1995; P.M. Churchland and C.M. Hooker (eds), *Images of Science: essays on realism and empiricism, with a reply from Bas C. van Fraassen*, Chicago: University of Chicago Press, 1985; Christopher Norris, 'Anti-Realism and Constructive Empiricism: is there a (real) difference?' and 'Ontology According to van Fraassen: some problems with constructive empiricism', in *Against Relativism: philosophy of science, deconstruction and critical theory*, Oxford: Blackwell, 1997, pp. 167–95 and 196–217.

43 See Notes 4, 15, 17 and 40, above.

44 Eugene Wigner, 'The Unreasonable Effectiveness of Mathematics in the Physical Sciences', in *Symmetries and Reflections*, Cambridge, MA: MIT Press, 1960, pp. 222–37; p. 237.

45 See Note 36, above.

46 For further argument along these lines, see Philip Kitcher, *The Nature of Mathematical Knowledge*, Oxford: Oxford University Press, 1983 and

Penelope Maddy, *Realism in Mathematics*, Oxford: Oxford University Press, 1990.

47 Wigner, 'The Unreasonable Effectiveness of Mathematics', p. 223.

48 See Notes 1 and 4, above; also Hilary Putnam, *Mathematics, Matter and Method*, Cambridge: Cambridge University Press, 1975.

49 See Roy Bhaskar, *Scientific Realism and Human Emancipation*, London: Verso, 1986; *Reclaiming Reality: a critical introduction to contemporary philosophy*, London: Verso, 1989; *A Realist Theory of Science*, 3rd edn, London: Verso, 1997; also Margaret Archer, Roy Bhaskar, Andrew Collier et al (eds), *Critical Realism: essential writings*, London: Routledge, 1998; Andrew Collier, *Critical Realism: an introduction to the work of Roy Bhaskar*, London: Verso, 1994; Jonathan Joseph and John Michael Roberts (eds), *Realism, Discourse and Deconstruction*, London: Routledge, 2004; Christopher Norris, *Philosophy of Language and the Challenge to Scientific Realism*, London: Routledge, 2004; also – in a closely related vein – Rom Harré, *The Principles of Scientific Thinking*, Chicago: University of Chicago Press, 1970; Harré and E.H. Madden, *Causal Powers*, Oxford: Blackwell, 1975.

50 See especially Bhaskar, *Scientific Realism and Human Emancipation*.

51 See Roy Bhaskar, *Dialectic: the pulse of freedom*, London: Verso, 1993.

52 See for instance Hilary Putnam, *Reason, Truth and History*, Cambridge: Cambridge University Press, 1981.

53 Immanuel Kant, *Critique of Pure Reason*, trans. Norman Kemp Smith, London: Macmillan, 1964.

54 See Notes 49 and 51, above.

55 See Bhaskar, *Dialectic*.

56 For the logical-positivist/empiricist account of this 'two contexts' principle, see Hans Reichenbach, *Experience and Prediction*, Chicago: University of Chicago Press, 1938; also various essays in A.J. Ayer (ed.), *Logical Positivism*, New York: Free Press, 1959.

57 Quine, 'Two Dogmas of Empiricism'.

58 Kuhn, *The Structure of Scientific Revolutions*.

59 Quine, 'Two Dogmas'; also Hans Reichenbach, *Philosophic Foundations of Quantum Mechanics*, Berkeley and Los Angeles: University of California Press, 1944 and Hilary Putnam, 'How to Think Quantum-Logically', *Synthèse*, vol. 74 (1974), pp. 55–61. For dissenting views, see M. Gardner, 'Is Quantum Logic Really Logic?', *Philosophy of Science*, vol. 38 (1971), pp. 508–29; Peter Gibbins, *Particles and Paradoxes: the limits of quantum logic*, Cambridge: Cambridge University Press, 1987; Susan Haack, *Deviant Logic*.

60 Bhaskar, *Reclaiming Reality*.

61 See for instance Nancy Cartwright, *How the Laws of Nature Lie*, Oxford: Oxford University Press, 1983 and *Nature's Capacities and their Measurement*, Oxford: Clarendon Press, 1989; also van Fraassen, *The Scientific Image* and *Laws and Symmetries*, Oxford: Oxford University Press, 1989.

62 Crispin Wright, *Truth and Objectivity*, Cambridge, MA: Harvard University Press, 1992.

63 For further discussion, see Christopher Norris, *Truth Matters: realism, anti-realism and response-dependence*, Edinburgh: Edinburgh University Press, 2002.

64 See Notes 1, 3 and 4, above; also Jerome S. Bruner, *Actual Minds, Possible Worlds*, Cambridge, MA: Harvard University Press, 1986; Charles S. Chihara, *The Worlds of Possibility: modal realism and the semantics of modal logic*, Oxford: Clarendon Press, 2001; Rod Gierle, *Modal Logics and Philosophy*, Teddington: Acumen, 2000 and *Possible Worlds*, Teddington: Acumen, 2002; G. Hughes and M. Cresswell, *A New Introduction to Modal Logic*, London: Routledge, 1996; M. Loux (ed.), *The Possible and the Actual: readings in the metaphysics of modality*, Ithaca, NY: Cornell University Press, 1979.

65 See Note 31, above; also Ernest Sosa (ed.), *Causation and Conditionals*, Oxford: Oxford University Press, 1975 and M. Tooley, *Causation: a realist approach*, Oxford: Blackwell, 1988.

66 Lewis, *The Plurality of Worlds*; also – for further discussion of the 'realist' versus 'actualist' issue – see entries under Note 64, above.

67 This debate is taken up by various contributors to J. Lopez and G. Potter (eds), *After Postmodernism: an introduction to critical realism*, London: Athlone Press, 2001 and to Joseph and Roberts (eds), *Realism, Discourse and Deconstruction*.

68 Kripke, *Naming and Necessity*; also Michael Devitt and Kim Sterelny, *Language and Reality: an introduction to the philosophy of language*, Oxford: Blackwell, 1989.

69 See Notes 8, 17 and 40, above.

3: 'FOG OVER CHANNEL, CONTINENT ISOLATED': EPISTEMOLOGY IN THE 'TWO TRADITIONS'

1 See for instance A.J. Ayer (ed.), *Logical Positivism*, New York: Free Press, 1959; Rudolf Carnap, 'The Elimination of Metaphysics through Logical Analysis of Language', in *Logical Positivism*, pp. 60–81; Hans Reichenbach, *Experience and Prediction*, Chicago: University of Chicago Press, 1938; Ludwig Wittgenstein, *Philosophical Investigations*, trans. G.E.M. Anscombe, Oxford: Blackwell, 1952.

2 Carnap, 'The Elimination of Metaphysics'.

3 See especially Edmund Husserl, *Formal and Transcendental Logic*, trans. Dorion Cairns, The Hague: Martinus Nijhoff, 1969; *Logical Investigations*, 2 vols, trans. J.N. Findlay, New York: Humanities Press, 1970; *Ideas: general introduction to pure phenomenology*, trans. W.R. Boyce Gibson, London: Collier-Macmillan, 1975.

4 See especially Gilbert Ryle, 'Phenomenology' and 'Phenomenology versus *The Concept of Mind*', in Ryle, *Collected Papers*, vol. 1, London: Hutchinson, 1971, pp. 167–78 and 179–96; also Gottlob Frege, 'Review of Edmund Husserl's *Philosophie der Arithmetik*', trans. E.-H. W. Kluge, *Mind*, vol. 81 (1972), pp. 321–37; Michael Dummett, *The Origins of Analytic Philosophy*, London: Duckworth, 1993; Leila Haaparanta

(ed.), *Mind, Meaning, and Mathematics: essays on the philosophical views of Husserl and Frege*, Dordrecht and Boston: Kluwer, 1994.

5 See especially Husserl, *Formal and Transcendental Logic*.

6 For a wide-ranging account of these developments, see J. Alberto Coffa, *The Semantic Tradition from Kant to Carnap: to the Vienna Station*, Cambridge: Cambridge University Press, 1991.

7 W.V. Quine, 'Two Dogmas of Empiricism', in *From a Logical Point of View*, 2nd edn, Cambridge, MA: Harvard University Press, 1961, pp. 20–46.

8 W.V. Quine, *Ontological Relativity and Other Essays*, New York: Columbia University Press, 1969.

9 Wittgenstein, *Philosophical Investigations*; also Saul Kripke, *Wittgenstein on Rules and Private Language: an elementary exposition*, Oxford: Blackwell, 1982.

10 See Sandra G. Harding (ed.), *Can Theories Be Refuted? essays on the Duhem-Quine thesis*, Dordrecht: D. Reidel, 1976.

11 Stanley L. Jaki, *Uneasy Genius: the life and work of Pierre Duhem*, Dordrecht: Martinus Nijhoff, 1987.

12 Thomas S. Kuhn, *The Structure of Scientific Revolutions*, 2nd edn, Chicago: University of Chicago Press, 1970.

13 Pierre Duhem, *To Save the Phenomena: an essay on the idea of physical theory from Plato to Galileo*, trans. E. Dolan and C. Maschler, Chicago: University of Chicago Press, 1969.

14 See Notes 7 and 8, above.

15 See Harding (ed.), *Can Theories Be Refuted?*

16 Pierre Duhem, *German Science*, La Salle, IL: Open Court, 1991.

17 See Jaki, *Uneasy Genius*.

18 Paul K. Feyerabend, *Science in a Free Society*, London: New Left Books, 1978.

19 On the history of this doctrine ('constructive empiricism') from its adoption by the church authorities in Galileo's time to its latest, albeit more sophisticated guise in the work of philosophers like Bas van Fraassen, see C.J. Misak, *Verificationism: its history and prospects*, London: Routledge, 1995.

20 Jaki, *Uneasy Genius*.

21 Reichenbach, *Experience and Prediction*.

22 See for instance David Bloor, *Knowledge and Social Imagery*, London: Routledge and Kegan Paul, 1976; Steve Fuller, *Philosophy of Science and its Discontents*, Boulder, Col.: Westview Press, 1989; Bruno Latour and Steve Woolgar, *Laboratory Life: the social construction of scientific facts*, London: Sage, 1979; Steve Woolgar, *Science: the very idea*, London: Tavistock, 1988; Woolgar (ed.), *Knowledge and Reflexivity: new frontiers in the sociology of knowledge*, London: Sage, 1988.

23 Alexandre Koyré, *Galileo Studies*, trans. John Mepham, Atlantic Highlands, NJ: Humanities Press, 1978. Among the most informative secondary works are Thomas S. Kuhn, 'Alexandre Koyré and the History of Science', *Encounter*, 34 (1970), pp. 67–9; P. Redondi (ed.), 'Science: the Renaissance of a History' (Proceedings of the International Conference

Alexandre Koyré), *History and Technology*, vol. 4 (1987); H. Speilberg, *The Phenomenological Movement: a historical introduction*, 2 vols, The Hague: Martinus Nijhoff, 1960.

24 See especially Alexandre Koyré, *From the Closed World to the Infinite Universe*, Baltimore, MD: Johns Hopkins University Press, 1957; also *Metaphysics and Measurement: essays on the scientific revolution*, Cambridge, MA: Harvard University Press, 1968 and *The Astronomical Revolution*, London: Methuen, 1980.

25 See especially Michel Foucault, *The Order of Things: an archaeology of the human sciences*, trans. A. Sheridan-Smith, London: Tavistock, 1970 and *The Archaeology of Knowledge*, trans. Sheridan-Smith, Tavistock, 1973.

26 Kuhn, *The Structure of Scientific Revolutions*.

27 See Note 1, above.

28 See Notes 3 and 5, above.

29 Edmund Husserl, *The Crisis of European Sciences and Transcendental Phenomenology*, trans D. Carr, Evanston, IL: Northwestern University Press, 1970.

30 Alexandre Koyré, *Etudes d'histoire et de la pensée philosophique*, Paris: A. Colin, 1961.

31 Edmund Husserl, *Cartesian Meditations*, trans. Dorion Cairns, The Hague: Martinus Nijhoff, 1960.

32 See especially Alexandre Koyré, 'Galileo and Plato', *Journal of the History of Ideas*, vol. 4 (1943), pp. 400–28.

33 See for instance Paul R. Gross and Norman Levitt (eds), *The Flight from Reason and Science*, New York: Academy of Sciences, 1996; Noretta Koertge (ed.), *A House Built on Sand: exposing postmodernist myths about science*, Oxford: Oxford University Press, 1998; Alan Sokal and Jean Bricmont, *Intellectual Impostures: postmodern philosophers' abuse of science*, London: Profile Books, 1998.

34 Michael Friedman, *Reconsidering Logical Positivism*, Cambridge: Cambridge University Press, 1999.

35 Dummett, *The Origins of Analytic Philosophy*; also Christopher Norris, *Minding the Gap: epistemology and philosophy of science in the two traditions*, Amherst, MA: University of Massachusetts Press, 2000.

36 See especially Edmund Husserl, *Experience and Judgment: investigations in a genealogy of logic*, trans. J.S. Churchill and K. Ameriks, Evanston, IL: Northwestern University Press, 1973.

37 For a range of views on this topic, see Michael Dummett, *Truth and Other Enigmas*, London: Duckworth, 1978; Christopher Norris, *Truth Matters: realism, anti-realism and response-dependence*, Edinburgh: Edinburgh University Press, 2002; Crispin Wright, *Truth and Objectivity*, Cambridge, MA: Harvard University Press, 1992.

38 Paul Benacerraf, 'What Numbers Could Not Be', in Paul Benacerraf and Hilary Putnam (eds), *The Philosophy of Mathematics: selected essays*, 2nd edn, Cambridge: Cambridge University Press, 1983, pp. 271–94.

39 See especially Reichenbach, *Experience and Prediction*.

40 See for instance Peter Galison and David J. Stump (eds), *The Disunity of Science: boundaries, contexts, and power*, Stanford, CA: Stanford University Press, 1996.

41 See Note 25, above; also Michel Foucault, *Language, Counter-Memory, Practice*, ed. D.F. Bouchard and S. Weber, Oxford: Blackwell, 1977 and Joseph Rouse, *Knowledge and Power: toward a political philosophy of science*, Ithaca, NY: Cornell University Press, 1987.

42 Richard Rorty, *Contingency, Irony, and Solidarity*, Cambridge: Cambridge University Press, 1989; *Objectivity, Relativism, and Truth*, Cambridge: Cambridge University Press, 1991; *Essays on Heidegger and Others*, Cambridge: Cambridge University Press, 1991.

43 John McDowell, *Mind and World*, Cambridge, MA: Harvard University Press, 1994; also – for some critical reflections – Christopher Norris, 'McDowell on Kant: redrawing rhe bounds of sense' and 'The Limits of Naturalism: further thoughts on McDowell's *Mind and World*', in *Minding the Gap*, pp. 172–96 and 197–230.

44 Coffa, *The Semantic Tradition from Kant to Carnap*.

45 See for instance Hilary Putnam, *Realism and Reason*, Cambridge: Cambridge University Press, 1983.

46 See entries under Note 22, above.

47 Edmund Husserl, *The Crisis of European Sciences and Transcendental Phenomenology*.

48 These issues are engaged most directly by Jürgen Habermas in *Knowledge and Human Interests*, trans. Jeremy J. Shapiro, London: Heinemann, 1972; *Theory of Communicative Action*, 2 vols, trans. Thomas McCarthy, Boston: Beacon Press, 1984; *The Philosophical Discourse of Modernity: twelve lectures*, trans. Frederick Lawrence, Cambridge: Polity Press, 1987.

49 See especially Peter Winch, *The Idea of a Social Science and its Relation to Philosophy*, London: Routledge and Kegan Paul, 1958.

50 See Note 33, above.

51 Foucault, *Language, Counter-Memory, Practice*; Jean-François Lyotard, *The Postmodern Condition: a report on knowledge*, trans. Geoff Bennington and Brian Massumi, Manchester: Manchester University Press, 1984.

52 Martin Heidegger, *The Question Concerning Technology and Other Essays*, trans. William Lovitt, New York: Harper and Row, 1977.

53 Mark Okrent, *Heidegger's Pragmatism: understanding, being, and the critique of metaphysics*, Ithaca, NY: Cornell University Press, 1988 and Richard Rorty, *Essays on Heidegger and Others*.

54 See for instance Rouse, *Knowledge and Power*.

55 Gaston Bachelard, *Le rationalisme appliqué*, Paris: Presses Universitaires de France, 1949; *The Philosophy of No: a philosophy of the new scientific mind*, New York: Orion Press, 1968; *The New Scientific Spirit*, Boston: Beacon Press, 1984; Georges Canguilhem, *Etudes d'histoire et de philosophie des sciences*, Paris: Vrin, 1968; *Ideology and Rationality in the History of the Life Sciences*, trans. A. Goldhammer, Cambridge, MA: MIT Press, 1988; also Mary Tiles, *Bachelard: science and objectivity*, Cambridge: Cambridge University Press, 1984.

56 Friedrich Nietzsche, 'Of Truth and Falsehood in an Ultra-Moral Sense', in Walter Kaufmann (ed.), *The Portable Nietzsche*, New York: Viking, 1967, pp. 46–7.
57 Ilkka Niiniluoto, *Critical Scientific Realism*, Oxford: Oxford University Press, 1999; Stathis Psillos, *Scientific Realism: how science tracks truth*, London: Routledge, 1999.
58 I take these examples from Psillos, *Scientific Realism*.
59 Reichenbach, *Experience and Prediction*.
60 Kuhn, *The Structure of Scientific Revolutions*.
61 See Note 33, above.
62 For further discussion, see Christopher Norris, *Resources of Realism: prospects for 'post-analytic' philosophy*, London: Macmillan, 1997 and *New Idols of the Cave: on the limits of anti-realism*, Manchester: Manchester University Press, 1997.
63 Bachelard, *Le rationalisme appliqué*.
64 Jacques Derrida, *Speech and Phenomena and Other Essays on Husserl's Theory of Signs*, trans. David B. Allison, Evanston, IL: Northwestern University Press, 1973; *Edmund Husserl's 'Origin of Geometry': an introduction*, trans. John P. Leavey, Pittsburgh, PA: Duquesne University Press, 1987; '"Genesis and Structure" and Phenomenology', in *Writing and Difference*, trans. Alan Bass, London: Routledge and Kegan Paul, 1978, pp. 3–30; 'White Mythology: metaphor in the text of philosophy', in *Margins of Philosophy*, trans. Alan Bass, Brighton: Harvester, 1982, pp. 207–71; *Le Problème de la genèse dans la philosophie de Husserl*, Paris: Presses Universitaires de France, 1990.
65 See various entries under Note 64, above; also Kurt Gödel, *On Formally Undecidable Propositions of* Principia Mathematica *and Related Systems*, trans. B. Meltzer, New York: Basic Books, 1962.
66 Jacques Derrida, *Of Grammatology*, trans. G.C. Spivak, Baltimore: Johns Hopkins University Press, 1976; also Christopher Norris, 'Derrida on Rousseau: deconstruction as philosophy of logic', in Christopher Norris and David Roden (eds), *Jacques Derrida*, 4 vols, London: Sage, 2003, vol. 2, pp. 70–124.
67 See Ayer (ed.), *Logical Positivism*; also Nicholas Rescher (ed.), *The Heritage of Logical Positivism*, Lanham: University Press of America, 1980.
68 John McDowell, *Mind and World*.
69 Frederick C. Beiser, *The Fate of Reason: German philosophy from Kant to Fichte*, Cambridge, MA: Harvard University Press, 1987.
70 Robert Brandom, *Making it Explicit: reasoning, representing, and discursive commitment*, Cambridge, MA: Harvard University Press, 1994.
71 See for instance Leonard Lawlor, *Derrida and Husserl: the basic problem of phenomenology*, Bloomington, IN: Indiana University Press, 2002 and various contributors to Norris and Roden (eds), *Jacques Derrida*.
72 See Note 64, above.
73 See Benacerraf and Putnam (eds), *The Philosophy of Mathematics*.
74 See Frege, 'Review of Edmund Husserl's *Philosophie der Arithmetik*'; also Notes 3, 4 and 64, above.

75 Note 4, above.
76 Benacerraf, 'What Numbers Could Not Be'; also W.D. Hart (ed.), *The Philosophy of Mathematics*, Oxford: Oxford University Press, 1996; Christopher Norris, 'The Platonist Fix: why "nothing works" (according to Putnam) in philosophy of mathematics', in *Hilary Putnam: realism, reason, and the uses of uncertainty*, Manchester: Manchester University Press, 2002, pp. 218–45.
77 Hilary Putnam, 'There Is At Least One *A Priori* Truth', in *Realism and Reason*, Cambridge: Cambridge University Press, 1983, pp. 98–114; also Christopher Norris, 'Is Logic Revisable? Putnam, Quine, and "Contextual Apriority"', in *Hilary Putnam*, pp. 192–217.
78 See Note 43, above.
79 See especially Donald Davidson, 'On the Very Idea of a Conceptual Scheme', in *Inquiries Into Truth and Interpretation*, Oxford: Oxford University Press, 1984, pp. 183–98.
80 See Note 4, above

4: RESPONSE-DEPENDENCE: WHAT'S IN IT FOR THE REALIST?

1 See for instance Mark Johnston, 'Dispositional Theories of Value', *Proceedings of the Aristotelian Society*, vol. 63 (1989), pp. 139–74; 'How to Speak of the Colours', *Philosophical Studies*, vol. 68 (1992), pp. 221–63; and 'Objectivity Refigured', in J. Haldane and C. Wright (eds), *Realism, Representation and Projection*, Oxford: Oxford University Press, 1993, pp. 85–130; Christopher Norris, *Truth Matters: realism, anti-realism and response-dependence*, Edinburgh: Edinburgh University Press, 2002; Philip Pettit, 'Realism and Response Dependence', *Mind*, vol. 100 (1991), pp. 597–626; *The Common Mind: an essay on psychology, society, and politics*, Oxford: Oxford University Press, 1992; and 'Noumenalism and Response-Dependence', *The Monist*, vol. 81 (1998), pp. 112–32; Peter Railton, 'Red, Bittter, Good', *European Review of Philosophy*, vol. 3 (1998), pp. 67–84; Ralph Wedgwood, 'The Essence of Response-Dependence', *European Review of Philosophy*, vol. 3 (1998), pp. 31–54; Crispin Wright, 'Moral Values, Projection, and Secondary Qualities', *Proceedings of the Aristotelian Society*, supplementary vol. 62 (1988), pp. 1–26; 'Euthyphronism and the Physicality of Colour', *European Review of Philosophy*, vol. 3 (1998), pp. 15–30; and *Truth and Objectivity*, Cambridge, MA: Harvard University Press, 1992.
2 Ludwig Wittgenstein, *Philosophical Investigations*, trans. G.E.M. Anscombe, Oxford: Blackwell, 1958; *On Certainty*, ed. G.E.M. Anscombe and G.H. von Wright, Oxford: Blackwell, 1969; and *Lectures on the Foundations of Mathematics*, ed. Cora Diamond, Chicago: University of Chicago Press, 1976.
3 Saul Kripke, *Wittgenstein on Rules and Private Language*, Oxford: Blackwell, 1982.
4 Michael Dummett, *Elements of Intuitionism*, Oxford: Oxford University Press, 1977; *Truth and Other Enigmas*, London: Duckworth, 1978; and *The Logical Basis of Metaphysics*, London: Duckworth, 1991.

5 See entries under Note 1, above.

6 Michael Williams, *Unnatural Doubts: epistemological realism and the basis of sceptism*, Princeton, NJ: Princeton University Press, 1996, pp. 56 and 74.

7 See Johnston, 'How to Speak of the Colours', and other entries under Note 1, above.

8 See Notes 2 and 3, above.

9 Wright, *Truth and Objectivity*.

10 Crispin Wright, *Wittgenstein on the Foundations of Mathematics*, Cambridge, MA: Harvard University Press, 1980.

11 John Divers and Alexander Miller, 'Arithmetical Platonism: reliability and judgement-dependence', *Philosophical Studies*, vol. 95 (1999), pp. 277–310.

12 Plato, *Euthyphro*, in *The Dialogues of Plato*, vol. 1, trans. R.E. Allen, New Haven: Yale University Press, 1984.

13 Wright, *Truth and Objectivity*, p. 80.

14 Wright, *Truth and Objectivity*, p. 80.

15 See entries for Dummett under Note 4, above; also Michael Luntley, *Language, Logic and Experience: the case for anti-realism*, London: Duckworth, 1988; Neil Tennant, *Anti-Realism and Logic*, Oxford: Clarendon, 1987; Crispin Wright, *Realism, Meaning and Truth*, Oxford: Blackwell, 1987.

16 Wright, *Truth and Objectivity*, p. 80.

17 See especially Scott Soames, *Understanding Truth*, Oxford: Oxford University Press, 1999.

18 See for instance Railton, 'Red, Bitter, Good' and Wedgwood, 'The Essence of Response-Dependence', Note 1, above.

19 Wedgwood, 'The Essence of Response-Dependence', p. 34.

20 Wright, *Truth and Objectivity*, p. 106.

21 Wright, *Truth and Objectivity*, p. 228.

22 Wright, *Truth and Objectivity*, p. 228.

23 See for instance Paul Benacerraf, 'What Numbers Could Not Be', in Paul Benacerraf and Hilary Putnam (eds), *The Philosophy of Mathematics: selected essays*, 2nd edn, Cambridge: Cambridge University Press, 1983, pp. 272–94.

24 See Kurt Gödel, 'What Is Cantor's Continuum Problem?', in Benacerraf and Putnam (eds), *The Philosophy of Mathematics*, pp. 470–85; also Roger Penrose, *Shadows of the Mind: a search for the missing science of consciousness*, London: Vintage, 1995.

25 Mark Johnston, 'Are Manifest Qualities Response-Dependent?', *The Monist*, vol. 81 (1998), pp. 3–43.

26 Alex Miller, 'The Missing-Explanation Argument Revisited', *Analysis*, vol. 61 (2001), pp. 76–86: p. 77; also Alex Miller, 'More Responses to the Missing-Explanation Argument', *Philosophia*, vol. 25 (1997), pp. 331–49; Duncan McFarland, 'Mark Johnston's Substitution Principle: a new counterexample?', *Philosophy and Phenomenological Research*, vol. 59 (1999), pp. 683–9; Peter Menzies and Philip Pettit, 'Found: the missing explanation', *Analysis*, vol. 53 (1993), pp. 100–9.

27 Miller, 'The Missing-Explanation Argument Revisited', p. 77.
28 Johnston, 'Are Manifest Qualities Response-Dependent?', p. 15.
29 Miller, 'The Missing-Explanation Argument Revisited', p. 85.
30 Maurice Merleau-Ponty, *The Phenomenology of Perception*, trans. Colin Smith, London: Routledge and Kegan Paul, 1962.
31 John McDowell, *Mind and World*, Cambridge, MA: Harvard University Press, 1994.
32 Immanuel Kant, *Critique of Pure Reason*, trans. Norman Kemp Smith, London: Macmillan, 1964.
33 Kant, *Critique of Pure Reason*, p. 112.
34 Johann Gottlieb Fichte, *The Science of Knowledge with the First and Second Introductions*, trans. and ed. Peter Heath and John Lachs, Cambridge: Cambridge University Press, 1980. See also Frederick C. Beiser, *The Fate of Reason: German philosophy from Kant to Fichte*, Cambridge, MA: Harvard University Press, 1987.
35 See also Note 31, above.
36 See P.F. Strawson, *The Bounds of Sense: an essay on Kant's Critique of Pure Reason*, London: Methuen, 1966; also *Individuals: an essay in descriptive metaphysics*, London: Methuen, 1959.
37 Wilfrid Sellars, *Empiricism and the Philosophy of Mind*, Cambridge, MA: Harvard University Press, 1997; also *Science, Perception and Reality*, London: Routledge and Kegan Paul, 1963.
38 For further discussion, see Israel Scheffler, 'Epistemology of Objectivity', in Peter J. McCormick (ed.), *Starmaking: realism, anti-realism, and irrealism*, Cambridge, MA: MIT Press, 1996, pp. 29–59.
39 Immanuel Kant, *Critique of Practical Reason*, trans. Lewis White Beck, Indianapolis, IN: Bobbs-Merrill, 1975.
40 McDowell, *Mind and World*, p. 41.
41 See entries under Note 1, above; also Alex Miller, 'Rule-Following, Response-Dependence, and McDowell's Debate with Anti-Realism', *The European Review of Philosophy*, vol. 3 (1998), pp. 175–97.
42 McDowell, *Mind and World*, p. 41.
43 McDowell, *Mind and World*, p. 154.
44 See especially Richard Rorty, *Philosophy and the Mirror of Nature*, Oxford: Blackwell, 1980.
45 See Notes 4, 15 and 23, above.
46 See Notes 17 and 24, above; also Jerrold Katz, *Realistic Rationalism*, Cambridge, MA: MIT Press, 1988.
47 See for instance David M. Armstrong, *Universals and Scientific Realism*, 2 vols, Cambridge: Cambridge University Press, 1978; Michael Devitt, *Realism and Truth*, 2nd edn, Oxford: Blackwell, 1986; Jarrett Leplin (ed.), *Scientific Realism*, Berkeley and Los Angeles: University of California Press, 1984; Stathis Psillos, *Scientifc Realism: how science tracks truth,* London: Routledge, 1999.
48 Wright, *Objectivity and Truth*.
49 Wright, *Objectivity and Truth*, p. 80.
50 Wright, *Objectivity and Truth*, p. 81.
51 Rorty, *Philosophy and the Mirror of Nature*; also Richard Rorty,

Objectivity, Relativism, and Truth, Cambridge: Cambridge University Press, 1991.

52 Kripke, *Wittgenstein on Rules and Private Language*; also Bob Hale and Crispin Wright (eds), *A Companion to the Philosophy of Language*, Oxford: Blackwell, 1997; Alex Miller and Crispin Wright (eds), *Meaning and Rule-Following*, Chesham: Acumen, 2002; Wright, *Wittgenstein on the Foundations of Mathematics*.

53 See Note 23, above.

54 See Note 4, above.

55 See especially Roy Bhaskar, *Reclaiming Reality: a critical introduction to contemporary philosophy*, London: Verso, 1989; also Andrew Collier, *Critical Realism: an introduction to Roy Bhaskar's philosophy*, London: Verso, 1994.

56 Roy Bhaskar, *Scientific Realism and Human Emancipation*, London: Verso, 1986, p. 283.

57 For a range of critical-realist arguments from various philosophical and disciplinary perspectives, see Bhaskar et al (eds), *Critical Realism: essential readings*, London: Routledge, 1998; Berth Danermark et al, *Explaining Society: critical realism in the social sciences*, London: Routledge, 2002; José Lopez and Garry Potter (eds), *After Postmodernism: an introduction to critical realism*, London: Athlone, 2001.

58 Bhaskar, *Scientific Realism and Human Emancipation*; also Margaret Archer, *Being Human: the problem of agency*, Cambridge: Cambridge University Press, 2000 and William Outhewaite, *New Philosophies of Social Science: realism, hermeneutics and critical theory*, Basingstoke: Macmillan 1987.

59 Bhaskar, *Scientific Realism and Human Emancipation*, p. 49.

60 Pettit, *The Common Mind: an essay on psychology, society, and politics* (see Note 1).

61 See especially Roy Bhaskar, *The Possibility of Naturalism: a philosophical critique of the contemporary human sciences*, Hassocks: Harvester Press, 1979.

62 Roy Bhaskar, *Dialectic: the pulse of freedom*, London: Verso 1993.

63 Rorty, *Objectivity, Relativism, and Truth*; also – for a full-scale critique of Rorty's arguments – Roy Bhaskar, *Philosophy and the Idea of Freedom*, Oxford: Blackwell, 1991.

64 See Note 26, above.

5: MAKING FOR TRUTH: SOME PROBLEMS WITH VIRTUE-BASED EPISTEMOLOGY

1 Aristotle, *The Nicomachean Ethics*, trans. J.A.K. Thomson, Harmondsworth: Penguin, 1976.

2 See for instance G. Axtell (ed.), *Knowledge, Belief and Character*, Lanham, MD: Rowman and Littlefield, 2000; Lorraine Code, *Epistemic Responsibility*, Hanover, NH: University Press of New England, 1987

and *What Can She Know? feminist theory and the construction of knowledge*, Ithaca, NY: Cornell University Press, 1991; M. DePaul and L. Zagzebski (eds), *Intellectual Virtue: perspectives from ethics and epistemology*, Oxford: Oxford University Press, 2002; A. Fairweather and L. Zagzebski (eds), *Virtue Epistemology: essays on epistemic virtue and responsibility*, Oxford: Oxford University Press, 2001; J. Kvanvig, *The Intellectual Virtues and the Life of the Mind: on the place of virtues in epistemology*, Lanham, MD: Rowman and Littlefield, 1992; J. Montmarquet, *Epistemic Virtue and Doxastic Responsibility*, Lanham, MD: Rowman and Littlefield, 1993; Ernest Sosa, 'Knowledge and Intellectual Virtue', *The Monist*, vol. 68 (1985), pp. 226–45 and *Knowledge in Perspective: selected essays in epistemology*, Cambridge: Cambridge University Press, 1991; M. Steup (ed.), *Knowledge, Truth, and Duty: essays on epistemic justification, responsibility, and virtue*, Oxford: Oxford University Press, 2002; L. Zagzebski, *Virtues of the Mind: an inquiry into the nature of virtue and the ethical foundations of knowledge*, Cambridge: Cambridge University Press, 1996.

3 W.V. Quine, 'Two Dogmas of Empiricism', in *From a Logical Point of View*, 2nd edn, Cambridge, MA: Harvard University Press, 1961, pp. 20–46.

4 W.V. Quine, *Ontological Relativity and Other Essays*, New York: Columbia University Press, 1969; cited in Christopher Hookway, 'Affective States and Epistemic Immediacy', *Metaphilosophy*, vol. 34, nos 1–2 (2003), pp. 78–96.

5 Hookway, 'Affective States and Epistemic Immediacy', p. 85.

6 Hookway, 'Affective States and Epistemic Immediacy', p. 91.

7 Hookway, 'Affective States and Epistemic Immediacy', p. 91.

8 David Hume, *Enquiries Concerning Human Understanding and Concerning the Principles of Morals*, ed. L.A. Selby-Bigge, Oxford: Clarendon Press, 1975.

9 Hookway, 'Affective States and Epistemic Immediacy', p. 95.

10 Quine, 'Two Dogmas of Empiricism'; also Sandra G. Harding, *Can Theories Be Refuted? essays on the Duhem-Quine thesis*, Dordrecht: D. Reidel, 1976.

11 See for instance William P. Alston, *A Realist Theory of Truth*, Ithaca, NY: Cornell University Press, 1996; Michael Devitt, *Realism and Truth*, 2nd edn, Oxford: Blackwell, 1986; Scott Soames, *Understanding Truth*, Oxford: Oxford University Press, 1999.

12 See Michael Dummett, *Truth and Other Enigmas*, London: Duckworth, 1978 and *The Logical Basis of Metaphysics*, London: Duckworth, 1991; Edmund Gettier, 'Is Justified True Belief Knowledge?', *Analysis*, vol. 23 (1963), pp. 121–3; Thomas S. Kuhn, *The Structure of Scientific Revolutions*, 2nd edn, Chicago: University of Chicago Press, 1970; Hilary Putnam, *Reason, Truth and History*, Cambridge: Cambridge University Press, 1981; Robert Shope, *The Analysis of Knowledge*, Princeton, NJ: Princeton University Press, 1983.

13 Ludwig Wittgenstein, *Philosophical Investigations*, trans. G.E.M. Anscombe, Oxford: Blackwell, 1953; Saul A. Kripke, *Wittgenstein on*

Rules and Private Language: an elementary exposition, Oxford: Blackwell, 1982.

14 For further discussion, see Dummett, *Truth and Other Enigmas*; also Christopher Norris, *Truth Matters: realism, anti-realism and response-dependence*, Edinburgh: Edinburgh University Press, 2002 and *Hilary Putnam: realism, reason, and the uses of uncertainty*, Manchester: Manchester University Press, 2002; Michael Williams, *Unnatural Doubts: epistemological realism and the basis of scepticism*, Princeton, NJ: Princeton University Press, 1996; Crispin Wright, *Realism, Meaning and Truth*, Oxford: Blackwell, 1987 and *Truth and Objectivity*, Cambridge, MA: Harvard University Press, 1992.

15 See especially Hans Reichenbach, *Experience and Prediction*, Chicago: University of Chicago Press, 1938.

16 Immanuel Kant, *Critique of Pure Reason*, trans. N. Kemp Smith, London: Macmillan, 1964, p. 112.

17 Immanuel Kant, *Critique of Practical Reason*, trans. Lewis White Beck, Indianapolis, IN: Bobbs-Merrill, 1977.

18 For a highly informative discussion of these post-Kantian developments, see Frederick C. Beiser, *The Fate of Reason: German philosophy from Kant to Fichte*, Cambridge, MA: Harvard University Press, 1987 and *Enlightenment, Revolution, and Romanticism: the genesis of modern German political thought*, Cambridge, MA: Harvard University Press, 1992; also Christopher Norris, *Minding the Gap: epistemology and philosophy of science in the two traditions*, Amherst, MA: University of Massachusetts Press, 2000.

19 John McDowell, *Mind and World*, Cambridge, MA: Harvard University Press, 1994.

20 J.G. Fichte, *The Science of Knowledge,* trans. and ed. P. Heath and J. Lachs, Cambridge: Cambridge University Press, 1980.

21 McDowell, *Mind and World*, p. 8, n. 7.

22 McDowell, *Mind and World*, p. 34.

23 McDowell, *Mind and World*, p. 34.

24 See especially Rudolf Carnap, *Meaning and Necessity*, Chicago: University of Chicago Press, 1956 and *The Logical Structure of the World and Pseudoproblems in Philosophy*, trans. R. George, Berkeley and Los Angeles: University of California Press, 1969; C.G. Hempel, *Fundamentals of Concept Formation in Physical Science*, Chicago: University of Chicago Press, 1972; Reichenbach, *Experience and Prediction*.

25 Quine, *Ontological Relativity and other Essays*, pp. 82–3.

26 Donald Davidson, 'On the Very Idea of a Conceptual Scheme', in *Inquiries Into Truth and Interpretation*, Oxford: Clarendon Press, 1984, pp. 183–98.

27 Davidson, 'On the Very Idea of a Conceptual Scheme', p. 198.

28 Richard Rorty, *Objectivity, Relativism, and Truth*, Cambridge: Cambridge University Press, 1991, p. 81.

29 Jaegwon Kim, *Supervenience and Mind*, Cambridge: Cambridge University Press, 1993, p. 232.

30 McDowell, *Mind and World*, p. 13.
31 McDowell, *Mind and World*, p. 41.
32 McDowell, *Mind and World*, p. 41.
33 Gettier, 'Is Justified True Belief Knowledge?'; also F. Feldman, 'An Alleged Defect in Gettier Counter-Examples', *Australasian Journal of Philosophy*, vol. 52 (1974), pp. 68–9; Dan O'Brien, 'Shakespeare and the Analysis of Knowledge', *Discourse*, vol. 4, no. 1 (2004–5), pp. 57–70; C. Radford, 'Knowledge – By Examples', *Analysis*, vol. 27 (1966), pp. 1–11; Shope, *The Analysis of Knowledge*; Timothy Williamson, *Knowledge and its Limits*, Oxford: Oxford University Press, 2000.
34 Plato, *Theaetetus*, trans. Robin Waterfield, Harmondsworth: Penguin, 1987.
35 See for instance R.M. Chisholm, *Theory of Knowledge*, Englewood Cliffs, NJ: Prentice Hall, 1966; Fred Dretske, *Knowledge and the Flow of Information*, Cambridge, MA: MIT Press, 1981 and Alvin Goldman, *Epistemology and Cognition*, Cambridge, MA: Harvard University Press, 1986.
36 Alvin Goldman, 'Discrimination and Perceptual Knowledge', *The Journal of Philosophy*, vol. 73 (1976), pp. 771–91.
37 Robert C. Brandom, *Articulating Reasons: an introduction to inferentialism*, Cambridge, MA: Harvard University Press, 2000.
38 See Note 2, above.
39 Kant, *Critique of Pure Reason*.
40 Kant, *Critique of Judgement*, trans. J.C. Meredith, Oxford: Clarendon Press, 1978.
41 Kant, *Critique of Practical Reason*; also – for some highly illuminating commentary – Onora O'Neill, *Constructions of Reason: explorations of Kant's practical philosophy*, Cambridge: Cambridge University Press, 1989.
42 Alasdair MacIntyre, *After Virtue: a study in moral theory*, London: Duckworth, 1981; Michael Sandel, *Liberalism and the Limits of Justice*, Cambridge: Cambridge University Press, 1982; Michael Walzer, *Spheres of Justice: a defence of pluralism and equality*, Oxford: Blackwell, 1983; Bernard Williams, *Ethics and the Limits of Philosophy*, London: Fontana, 1985.
43 See Alasdair MacIntyre, *Against the Self-Images of the Age*, London: Duckworth, 1971 and *After Virtue*.
44 Walzer, *Spheres of Justice*; also *Interpretation and Social Criticism*, Cambridge, MA: Harvard University Press, 1987.
45 See Williams, *Ethics and the Limits of Philosophy* and Peter Winch, *The Idea of a Social Science and its Relation to Philosophy*, London: Routledge and Kegan Paul, 1958.
46 McDowell, *Mind and World*.
47 Wittgenstein, *Philosophical Investigations*.
48 Kripke, *Wittgenstein on Rules and Private Language*.
49 See Notes 35 and 36, above.
50 See Note 33, above; also Goldman, *Epistemology and Cognition*.
51 Quine, 'Two Dogmas of Empiricism'.

52 See especially Goldman, *Liaisons: philosophy meets the cognitive and social sciences*, Cambridge, MA: MIT Press, 1992 and *Knowledge in a Social World*, Oxford: Clarendon Press, 1999.

53 McDowell, *Mind and World*, p. 43.

54 McDowell, *Mind and World*, p. 43.

55 Ernest Sosa, 'The Raft and the Pyramid: coherence versus foundations in the theory of knowledge', *Midwest Studies in Philosophy*, vol. 5, Notre Dame, IN: University of Notre Dame Press, 1980, pp. 3–26.

56 Sosa, *Knowledge in Perspective* (see Note 2, above.).

57 McDowell, *Mind and World*, p. 85.

58 McDowell, *Mind and World*, p. 65.

59 McDowell, *Mind and World*, p. 64.

60 See Note 2, above.

61 See for instance R.L. Arrington, *Rationalism, Realism and Relativism: perspectives in contemporary moral epistemology*, Ithaca, NY: Cornell University Press, 1989; David Brink, *Moral Realism and the Foundations of Ethics*, Cambridge: Cambridge University Press, 1989; G. Sayre-McCord (ed.), *Essays on Moral Realism*, Ithaca, NY: Cornell University Press, 1988.

62 See Alex Miller and Crispin Wright (eds), *Rule-Following and Meaning*, Aldershot: Acumen, 2002.

63 Sosa, 'Knowledge and Intellectual Virtue'.

64 Compare Jerry Fodor, *The Modularity of Mind*, Cambridge, MA: MIT Press, 1983 and *The Mind Doesn't Work that Way: the scope and limits of computational psychology*, Cambridge, MA: MIT Press, 2000.

65 See for instance R. Llinas and P. Churchland, *The Mind-Brain Continuum: sensory processes*, Cambridge, MA: MIT Press, 1996; A.D. Milner and M.A. Goodale, *The Visual Brain in Action*, Oxford: Oxford University Press, 1995; D. Rose and V.G. Dobson (eds), *Models of the Visual Cortex*, Chichester: Wiley, 1985; J.Z. Young, *Philosophy and the Brain*, Oxford: Oxford University Press, 1987.

66 Quine, *Ontological Relativity and Other Essays*, pp. 82–3.

67 Norwood Russell Hanson, *Patterns of Discovery: an enquiry into the perceptual foundations of science*, Cambridge: Cambridge University Press, 1958; also – for an exposition and critique of Hanson's argument – Christopher Norris, 'The Expert, the Neophyte, and the X-Ray Tube', in *Philosophy of Language and the Challenge to Scientific Realism*, London: Routledge, 2004, pp. 27–49.

68 Fodor, *The Mind Doesn't Work that Way*, p. 78.

69 Gilbert Harman, 'Inference to the Best Explanation', *Philosophical Review*, vol. 74 (1965), pp. 88–95; Peter Lipton, *Inference to the Best Explanation*, London: Routledge, 1993; Wesley C. Salmon, *The Foundations of Scientific Inference*, Pittsburgh, PA: University of Pittsburgh Press, 1967.

70 Sosa, *Knowledge in Perspective*.

71 John Greco, 'Internalism and Epistemically Responsible Belief', *Synthèse*, vol. 85 (1990), pp. 245–77 and 'Virtues and Vices of Virtue Epistemology', *Canadian Journal of Philosophy*, vol. 23 (1993), pp. 413–32.

72 Wright, *Truth and Objectivity*.
73 Marie McGinn, 'Reply to Hookway', *Metaphilosophy*, vol. 34, nos 1–2 (2003), pp. 97–105: pp. 101–2.
74 Hookway, 'Affective States and Epistemic Immediacy'.
75 See Reichenbach, *Experience and Prediction*.
76 See Wright, *Truth and Objectivity*; also 'Moral Values, Projection, and Secondary Qualities', *Proceedings of the Aristotelian Society*, supplementary vol. 62 (1988), pp. 1–26 and 'Euthyphronism and the Physicality of Colour', *European Review of Philosophy*, vol. 62 (1998), pp. 15–30.
77 See Notes 2, 55 and 71, above.
78 For further discussion see E.F. Paul, F.D. Miller and J. Paul (eds), *The Communitarian Challenge to Liberalism*, Cambridge: Cambridge University Press, 1996; David Rasmussen (ed.), *Universalism versus Communitarianism: contemporary debates in ethics*, Cambridge, MA: MIT Press, 1990; also – for the bearing of this debate on epistemological issues – M. Kusch, *Knowledge by Agreement: the programme of communitarian epistemology*, Oxford: Clarendon Press, 2002.
79 See especially MacIntyre, *After Virtue*.
80 Code, *Epistemic Responsibility*.
81 Code, *What Can She Know?*
82 For further discussion, see David Bloor, *Knowledge and Social Imagery*, London: Routledge and Kegan Paul, 1976; Augustine Brannigan, *The Social Basis of Scientific Discoveries*, Cambridge: Cambridge University Press, 1981; Steve Fuller, *Philosophy of Science and its Discontents*, Boulder, CO: Westview Press, 1989; Sandra Harding, *The Science Question in Feminism*, Ithaca, NY: Cornell University Press, 1986; Bruno Latour and Steve Woolgar, *Laboratory Life: the social construction of scientific facts*, London: Sage, 1979; Steve Woolgar (ed.), *Knowledge and Reflexivity: new frontiers in the sociology of knowledge*, London: Sage, 1988.
83 See Note 82, above; also Steven Shapin and Simon Schaffer, *Leviathan and the Air-Pump: Hobbes, Boyle, and the experimental life*, Princeton, NJ: Princeton University Press, 1985 and Christopher Norris, 'Why Strong Sociologists Abhor a Vacuum: Shapin and Schaffer on the Hobbes/Boyle controversy', in *Against Relativism: philosophy of science, deconstruction and critical theory*, Oxford: Blackwell, 1997, pp. 265–94.

CONCLUDING SCIENTIFIC-REALIST POSTSCRIPT

1 G.E. Moore, 'Proof of an External World', in *G.E. Moore: selected writings*, ed. Thomas Baldwin, London: Routledge, 1993, pp. 147–70.
2 Ludwig Wittgenstein, *Philosophical Investigations*, trans. G.E.M. Anscombe, Oxford: Blackwell, 1953.
3 See for instance J.L. Aronson, 'Testing for Convergent Realism', *British Journal for the Philosophy of Science*, vol. 40 (1989), pp. 255–60; Gilbert Harman, 'Inference to the Best Explanation', *Philosophical Review*, vol.

74 (1965), pp. 88–95; Peter Lipton, *Inference to the Best Explanation*, London: Routledge, 1993.

4 See for instance Larry Laudan, 'A Confutation of Convergent Realism', *Philosophy of Science*, vol. 48 (1981), pp. 19–49.

5 I take this example from Stathis Psillos, *Scientific Realism: how science tracks truth*, London: Routledge, 1999. See also Michael Devitt, *Realism and Truth*, 2nd edn, Oxford: Blackwell, 1986; J. Aronson, R. Harré and E. Way, *Realism Rescued: how scientific progress is possible*, London: Duckworth, 1994; Jarrett Leplin (ed.), *Scientific Realism*, Berkeley and Los Angeles: University of California Press, 1984; Wesley C. Salmon, *Scientific Explanation and the Causal Structure of the World*, Princeton, NJ: Princeton University Press, 1984; Peter J. Smith, *Realism and the Progress of Science*, Cambridge: Cambridge University Press, 1981.

6 Psillos, *Scientific Realism*.

7 Hilary Putnam, *Pragmatism: an open question*, Oxford: Blackwell, 1995.

8 Thomas S. Kuhn, *The Structure of Scientific Revolutions*, 2nd edn, Chicago: University of Chicago Press, 1970; also K. Knorr-Cetina and M. Mulkay (eds), *Science Observed*, London: Sage, 1983; Bruno Latour, *Science in Action: how to follow scientists and engineers through society*, Milton Keynes: Open University Press, 1987; Bruno Latour and Steve Woolgar, *Laboratory Life*, London: Sage, 1979; Andrew Pickering, *The Mangle of Practice*, Chicago: University of Chicago Press, 1995.

9 Hartry Field, 'Theory Change and the Indeterminacy of Reference', *Journal of Philosophy*, vol. 70 (1973), pp. 462–81 and 'Quine and the Correspondence Theory', *Philosophical Review*, vol. 83 (1974), pp. 200–28.

10 See Notes 3 and 5, above.

11 This Wittgensteinian case has been argued most influentially by Peter Winch in his book *The Idea of a Social Science and Its Relation to Philosophy*, London: Routledge and Kegan Paul, 1958.

12 See for instance Richard Rorty, *Contingency, Irony, and Solidarity*, Cambridge: Cambridge University Press, 1989 and *Objectivity, Relativism, and Truth*, Cambridge: Cambridge University Press, 1991.

13 See Note 8, above; also Paul Horwich (ed.), *World Changes: Thomas Kuhn and the nature of science*, Cambridge, MA: MIT Press, 1993.

14 Rorty, *Objectivity, Relativism, and Truth*, p. 80.

15 Rorty, *Objectivity, Relativism, and Truth*, p. 87

16 See for instance William James, *Pragmatism: a new name for some old ways of knowing*, New York: Longmans, 1907.

17 Bertrand Russell, 'James's Conception of Truth', in Simon Blackburn and Keith Simmons (eds), *Truth*, Oxford: Oxford University Press, 1999, pp. 69–82. See also James's response to Russell in *The Meaning of Truth*, New York: Longmans, 1909.

18 Plato, *Theaetetus*, trans. Robin Waterfield, Harmondsworth: Penguin, 1987.

19 Note 8, above.

20 See Note 5, above; also Hilary Putnam, *Mind, Language and Reality*, Cambridge: Cambridge University Press, 1975 and Richard Boyd, 'The

Current Status of Scientific Realism', in Jarrett Leplin (ed.), *Scientific Realism*, pp. 41–82.

21 See Alan Sokal and Jean Bricmont, *Intellectual Impostures: postmodern philosophers' abuse of science*, London: Profile Books, 1998; also Paul R. Gross and Norman Levitt, *Higher Superstition: the academic left and its quarrels with science*, Baltimore: Johns Hopkins University Press, 1994; Paul R. Gross, Norman Levitt and Martin W. Lewis (eds), *The Flight from Science and Reason*, New York: The New York Academy of Sciences, 1996; Noretta Koertge, *A House Built on Sand: exposing postmodernist myths about science*, Oxford: Oxford University Press, 1998.

22 Note 8, above.

23 See especially David Bloor, *Knowledge and Social Imagery*, London: Routledge and Kegan Paul, 1976; Barry Barnes, *Scientific Knowledge and Sociological Theory*, London: Routledge and Kegan Paul, 1974; Steve Fuller, *Social Epistemology*, Bloomington, IND: Indiana University Press, 1988; Steve Woolgar, *Science: the very idea*, London: Tavistock, 1988. For some critical perspectives, see Martin Hollis and Steven Lukes (eds), *Rationality and Relativism*, Oxford: Blackwell, 1982; W.H. Newton-Smith, *The Rationality of Science*, London: Routledge, 1981; R. Nola (ed.), *Relativism and Realism in Science*, Dordrecht: Kluwer, 1988; Christopher Norris, *Against Relativism: philosophy of science, deconstruction and critical theory*, Oxford: Blackwell, 1997.

24 Hans Reichenbach, *Experience and Prediction*, Chicago: University of Chicago Press, 1938 and *The Rise of Scientific Philosophy*, Berkeley and Los Angeles: University of California Press, 1951.

25 See Bloor, *Knowledge and Social Imagery*, and other entries under Notes 8 and 23, above.

26 Steven Shapin and Simon Shaffer, *Leviathan and the Air-Pump: Hobbes, Boyle and the experimental life*, Princeton, NJ: Princeton University Press, 1985.

27 See Notes 3 and 5, above.

28 This Hobbesian as well as Nietzschean aspect of Foucault's thought is most evident in the volume *Power/Knowledge: selected interviews and other writings*, ed. D.F. Gordon, Brighton: Harvester, 1980.

29 See Jürgen Habermas, *Theory of Communicative Action*, 2 vols, trans. Thomas McCarthy, London: Heinemann, 1979 and *The Philosophical Discourse of Modernity: twelve lectures*, trans. Frederick Lawrence, Cambridge: Polity Press, 1987.

30 See for instance Kuhn, *The Structure of Scientific Revolutions*; Foucault, *Language, Counter-Memory, Practice*, trans. D.F. Bouchard and S. Simon, Oxford: Blackwell, 1977; Jean-François Lyotard, *The Postmodern Condition: a report on knowledge*, Manchester: Manchester University Press, 1984.

31 E.P. Thompson, *The Making of the English Working Classes*, Harmondsworth: Penguin, 1972.

32 See especially C.P. Snow, *The Two Cultures, and a second look*, Cambridge: Cambridge University Press, 1963.

33 Note 24, above.

34 For a sustained argument against this position from the 'strong'-sociological quarter, see Harry Collins, *Changing Order: replication and induction in scientific practice*, Chicago: University of Chicago Press, 1985.
35 For other, more nuanced criticisms of the 'unity of science' programme, see Nancy Cartwright, *How the Laws of Physics Lie*, Oxford: Oxford University Press, 1983; John Dupré, *The Disorder of Things: metaphysical foundations of the disunity of science*, Cambridge, MA: Harvard University Press; Peter Gallison and David J. Stump (eds), *The Disunity of Science; boundaries, contexts and power*, Stanford, CA: Stanford University Press, 1996.
36 See Notes 8 and 23, above.
37 For a useful conspectus, see Paul Horwich (ed.), *World Changes*.
38 See Notes 28 and 30, above.
39 See especially Bloor, *Knowledge and Social Imagery*.
40 Paul K. Feyerabend, *Against Method*, London: New Left Books, 1975.
41 Paul K. Feyerabend, *Science in a Free Society*, London: New Left Books, 1978.

INDEX

36580